A Woman Like

A Woman Like Me

A Woman Like Me

A Memoir

DIANE ABBOTT

PENGUIN
VIKING

VIKING

UK | USA | Canada | Ireland | Australia
India | New Zealand | South Africa

Viking is part of the Penguin Random House group of companies
whose addresses can be found at global.penguinrandomhouse.com

Penguin
Random House
UK

First published 2024
001

Set in 12/14.75pt Bembo Book MT Pro
Typeset by Jouve (UK), Milton Keynes
Printed and bound in Great Britain by Clays Ltd, Elcograf S.p.A.

The authorized representative in the EEA is Penguin Random House Ireland,
Morrison Chambers, 32 Nassau Street, Dublin D02 YH68

A CIP catalogue record for this book is available from the British Library

ISBN: 978-0-241-53641-4

www.greenpenguin.co.uk

To my mother, Julia Adassa Abbott. Born and brought up in rural Jamaica, she left school at fourteen, came to Britain an intrepid young woman and lived to see her daughter elected as Britain's first Black female member of Parliament.

Contents

At my brother's christening ready to take on the world at just one year of age. Here with my parents, Reginald Nathaniel Abbott and Julia Adassa Abbott, and my baby brother Hugh Abbott, outside St Peter's Church in Paddington in 1954.

1.   The Early Years

One of the first photographs of me was taken by a professional photographer at my younger brother Hugh's christening, which took place in 1954, almost a year after my own. My mother always swore that she had named me after a singer in the church choir, but I was sure my name had more to do with her own mother, to whom she was very attached. Dinah Dale, my maternal grandmother, was known to everyone as Miss Di. Although she never left the Jamaican countryside, Miss Di made her impact felt: she was a charismatic woman, an adored parent and was hugely respected in her community.

My brother's christening service took place in St Peter's Church on the junction of Elgin Avenue and Chippenham Road in the London borough of Paddington, so the official photographs were taken in front of St Peter's. The streets around it made up one of the hubs of London's Caribbean community, en route to Notting Hill. In the photo my mother, Julia Adassa Abbott, is wearing a smart suit, the kind of ankle-strap shoes favoured by movie starlets of the time and an elegant hat with veiling. Cradling my newly christened baby brother Hugh in her arms, she looks shy, almost wary. Only she knew what it was about her life that caused that wariness. My father, Reginald Nathaniel Abbott, is equally smartly dressed and appears far more confident, a cigarette dangling from the fingers of one hand. But nobody in that photograph looks more self-assured than the smiling Diane Abbott, not yet two years old. She is wearing a stylish trouser suit with a princess jacket and matching bonnet. She stands slightly ahead of the family group, her feet apart as she takes a step forward, with her forefinger raised in a commanding manner. In adulthood, my brother always remarks on how this photo shows that, even at such a young age, I wanted to boss everyone about.

Family has always been the backdrop to my life, even when I thought, as a teenager, that I was moving beyond them. And Jamaica was always the backdrop to family.

My parents were among the earliest post-war migrants from Jamaica to Britain. They had been born and raised in the same place – a village called Smithville nestled in the Jamaican hills – and they were young when they first caught each other's eyes. Long before the advent of television and online entertainment, there was not much for young people in those communities to do in the evenings but flirt.

By 1950 Julia and Reginald had decided, independently of each other but at about the same time, to migrate from Jamaica to seek a better life in Britain. Migration was in the air all around the Caribbean. As was conventional, my mother travelled by boat – not on the now-legendary *Empire Windrush* that had sailed two years earlier, reaching Tilbury, near London, on 22 June 1948, but on the SS *Ariguani*, which was operated by the importers Elders & Fyffes. They mostly shipped bananas, but on this ship they also carried a hundred passengers. When, on 12 September 1950, the *Ariguani* docked at the port of Avonmouth near Bristol, my mother was one of those passengers.

Returning to that self-assured little girl at her brother's christening: where did her confidence come from? Though I was born in England, both my parents had been born in Jamaica, and it was that heritage that shaped me from my earliest days. On the one hand, post-war Caribbean migrants, including Jamaicans, were very proud of being British; they kept their British citizenship until they gained independence, which for Jamaica came in 1962. On the other hand, they also remained strongly attached to their Jamaican culture and identity. My parents and their friends saw no contradiction between loving Jamaica passionately and being proudly British.

My parents did not teach me about Jamaica in a didactic way. They did not have to: I grew up surrounded by Jamaican family and friends and absorbed a sense of the culture almost through my pores. Some things I understood the significance of only many years later; for instance, I grew up hearing my parents' friends and our family members referring to the other islands in the Caribbean, with the merest hint of superiority, as 'small islands'. The people who lived on these islands were known as 'small islanders', or even 'smallies'. Because I heard these descriptors so often while growing up, in my imagination Jamaica was at least the size of Australia, with countries such as Trinidad just specks offshore. Of course a glance at an atlas would have put me right; but this showed how attached Jamaicans were to the idea of their superiority.

The year of my birth, 1953, was also the year that Queen Elizabeth II was crowned. I have no memory of it, but no group of British people was more excited about it than Britain's West Indian migrants. Whatever challenges they faced in Britain itself, West Indians were passionate monarchists. My parents, like most of their friends and family in Britain, had a picture of the Queen in pride of place on the wall in the front room. West Indians were the largest group of Commonwealth migrants in London, and Jamaicans formed by far the majority of West Indians. It was a tight-knit community, which settled mainly in two areas of the capital: Brixton in south London, and Paddington and North Kensington in west London. Jamaican identity was important to my parents and their family and friends, and consequently it became important to me. They talked about Jamaica all the time and loved their Jamaican food, from yam and sweet potato to green banana and ackee. Back on the island, much of this was grown in the fields around one's home, which made it both nostalgic and difficult for Jamaican migrants to find in 1950s Britain. At home my father would eat nothing but Jamaican cuisine, savouring his particular favourites – red-pea soup, rice and peas, ackee and saltfish.

Nowadays, although I eat and enjoy all types of food, Jamaican cuisine remains my comfort food.

This was not the only thing that animated those early years; Jamaican music was hugely popular at the time, especially sung by Harry Belafonte. I can still sing his folk songs and the calypsos that my mother loved, including 'Scarlet Ribbons', which was particularly evocative because it reminded me of the freshly washed and ironed ribbons that my mother would plait my hair with daily as a child. When I eventually visited Jamaica as a young university student, it felt to me like a place that I had known all my life. And, in a way, I had.

Smithville, the small Jamaican village in which my mother and father were both brought up, lay in the hills in the parish of Clarendon. As I was growing up, the place names within that parish – Chapelton, May Pen and Frankfield – were as familiar to me as London's Portobello Road and Shepherd's Bush. Smithville is not the typical tourists' Jamaica, being many miles from a beach, but it is the Jamaica that I fell in love with. Most of Clarendon's towns and villages are green, pretty and agricultural, and Clarendon is a big producer of bauxite, the raw material for aluminium. The families living there survive mainly on subsistence agriculture and remittances that flow back to them from Jamaican migrants overseas.

Jamaica is about more than sun, sea and sand. It is an island with a history of rebellion and insurrection. In the early 1930s the entire British West Indies erupted in a series of riots and disturbances. Jamaicans – alongside the rest of the West Indians – protested against unemployment, poverty and British neglect, and nowhere in the region were the insurrections fiercer. Jamaicans were determined to challenge the might of the British Empire, and if necessary they were prepared to set the sugar-cane fields alight, from one end of the island to the other, to protest against injustice. The Jamaicans who came to Britain in the 1950s brought with them that same willingness to challenge authority.

My mother's journey from Jamaica to Britain was part of a wave of migration after the Second World War, building on the small presence of West Indian ex-servicemen. She was brave to migrate alone, at a time when most Caribbean migrants were single men. But Jamaicans have long seen migration as a means of escape from an economy ossified by the legacy of slavery. My mother's father, Basil McLymont, was one of thousands of Jamaican workers who travelled to Central America to help with the visionary infrastructure project of the early twentieth century: building the Panama Canal. At an early stage of the project, out of 12,875 labourers on the payroll, 9,005 were Jamaican. Itinerant workers experienced bad living conditions and a high death rate from diseases such as malaria and yellow fever, but wages were higher than in Jamaica, and my grandfather returned home with money in his pocket and a smattering of Spanish. My mother used to repeat his Spanish patois to me as a child.

Of my mother's seven siblings, some stayed at home in Jamaica, while others migrated all over North America in the years after the war. Among them were Aunt Julia who migrated to New York, Aunt Hermine who moved to Toronto to train as a nurse, Uncle Paul who migrated to Chicago and became an insurance agent, and my Uncle Dale who moved to Ottawa. Uncle Dale was the youngest of the siblings and later became Jamaica's ambassador to Canada. All the siblings showed a fearlessness that was typical of Jamaican migrants of the time.

Uncle Charles was particularly outgoing and ebullient, and his trajectory mirrored that of many of his demographic: often starting off doing menial work, they ultimately progressed to comfortable lifestyles, in which they were able to cultivate their interests in politics and society. For Uncle Charlie, this began with his move to Florida in the 1950s as a farm worker. He used to tell me the story of how, after his first week's work, he saw that the white workers were allowed to queue inside the farm office for their wages, while the Black workers were expected to queue outside. The Black American workers took this system for granted, but Uncle Charlie and his fellow Jamaicans refused to accept a second-class payment system and muscled their way inside the office for their money. Maybe because Jamaican labour was particularly needed that season, the farm labourers' supervisors reluctantly allowed the Jamaicans parity of esteem when it came to the system of payment. In taking that defiant action, the Jamaican workers had shown emphatically that they had not rioted against injustice in pre-war Jamaica only to accept second-class citizenship in Florida. Charlie spent the following decades as a stalwart of the US civil-rights organization Congress of Racial Equality (CORE), and moved on from farm work to a well-paid unionized job on the docks.

My mother was small, round and shy, but she was also motivated to make a success of her life. In common with many of her generation, she did not allow her aspirations to be dampened by the possibility of some white people seeing her as inferior. She was powered by determination, a trait proven by her resolve to sail thousands of miles on her own to Britain to seek a better life.

In Jamaica she had worked as a pupil teacher – a student who taught younger children in the same school. Later in life I met elderly men who fondly remembered being taught by her, recalling her whacking them around the head with a ruler if they misbehaved and reminiscing about how clever she was. When her ship from Jamaica docked that Tuesday in September 1950 at Avonmouth, the young Julia McLymont confidently told the British immigration authorities that she wanted to teach. Working as a pupil teacher might ordinarily have been one route to becoming a fully qualified teacher, but in fifties Britain it was more difficult for a Black woman to get a teaching job than my mother realized.

Unable to get into the education system, she took up a profession that was very popular with Black women migrants of that time: nursing. The National Health Service had been set up under the post-war Labour government two years earlier and was facing a shortage of nursing staff; many wards were not yet open as there weren't enough nurses to staff them. The government therefore eagerly welcomed thousands of would-be nurses from overseas, including from Ireland and the Commonwealth. Becoming a nurse was not easy for my mother's generation. She had to travel to the hospital where she was training on a coach, where nobody would ever sit next to her. Some patients whom she tried her best to nurse did not want a Black woman touching them. Black nurses often found that a glass ceiling stopped their progress; instead of being trained as State Registered Nurses – however great their aptitude – they were steered towards the State Enrolled Nurse grade, a lower level with fewer promotion opportunities. With limited choices, they sometimes ended up in less popular special-ities, such as geriatrics or mental health. Nevertheless nursing still held status for the hard-working Black woman. Throughout her life Mummy was intensely proud of being a nurse.

Like my mother, Daddy was aspirational and daring all his life. His father, John Abbott, had spent his life as a farmer in Smithville. Unusually, Daddy travelled to Britain by aeroplane, which was much more expensive than going by sea; I still have no idea how he raised the money for the air fare. It was a move that revealed his impetuous nature. Daddy was forceful, with something of a swag-ger, and he naturally took charge of any situation in which he found himself. Unlike my mother, he had no qualifications at all, and in 1950s Britain a white-collar job was virtually out of reach for a Black man with no paper qualifications. However, he did not find it difficult to get a job using his craft skills and his willingness to work. His first job was as a machine operator at an electric light-bulb factory, and later he became a sheet-metal worker. There was no chance of him climbing the ladder into management, but he was a well-respected worker and eventually had his own apprentices.

Because my parents had been brought up in the same small vil-lage in Jamaica, it was only a matter of time before their paths crossed again in the extremely close-knit Jamaican community in London. The connection was made when a neighbour from Smithville bumped into my father in the street in Paddington and yelled, 'Guess who is in London?' before adding, 'Little Lucille!' Though my mother's given name was Julia, everyone who knew her from Jamaica called her 'Little Lucille'.

My father was delighted to meet an old girlfriend from Jamaica. In the early 1950s, when most Caribbean migrants to Britain were unmarried men, Daddy no longer wanted to live that single life. Their getting together again coincided with my mother's need for a partner and a settled domestic situation, and so it was that on Saturday, 4 August 1951 my mother and father were married at Paddington Register Office.

In the tight-knit Caribbean community in Paddington, people relied on one another for all kinds of support. The West Indian community in London was just beginning to establish itself, and the racism it faced was crude and sometimes even violent. Going from a rural society in the Caribbean to the smoke, noise and clamour of London, one of the largest capital cities and industrial hubs in the world, West Indians quickly realized that not all the white people they encountered in Britain looked on them entirely favourably. Despite that, they never doubted that they were British. As children, they had been brought up singing the British national anthem and revering their monarch, King George VI, and that reverence for monarchy lasted their whole lives. They even contributed their pennies to pay for Spitfires in the Second World War. In their minds, by migrating to Britain they had come to the 'mother country'.

Houses in North Paddington and Notting Hill are now among the most expensive in London, but when my mother and father came to the capital, the large, white stucco terrace buildings were often in multiple occupation, shabby and verging on slum housing. Many were controlled by landlords such as the notorious Peter Rachman, who operated 144 properties in the area and made his money by exploiting desperate Black tenants, who did not have the benefit of protected tenancies and rent controls.

West Indian migrants mostly became home-owners through force of circumstance. There might be no alternative if they did not want to be exploited by the likes of Rachman. Councils in the 1950s, including Labour councils, were often reluctant to let accommodation to Black people and had various rules to keep them out, such as the 'sons and daughters' rule that prioritized the children of existing (white) council tenants. Residency rules also put recent migrants at a disadvantage by stipulating that those seeking a home had to have lived in an area for at least three years before being considered for council housing. Private landlords at this time, however, had a freedom to exploit that was almost absolute. They could demand a bigger deposit or could refuse point-blank to give accommodation to Black people. This was completely legal until the introduction of the 1968 Race Relations Act, when it became against the law in Britain to refuse housing, employment or public services to someone on the grounds of colour, ethnicity or national origin.

My parents' generation no doubt strove to become home-owners partly because, with their rural background, owning land mattered to them. An even more important driving factor was the blanket institutional racism they faced in the rental market, both private-sector and local-authority. Raising the money to buy property was a challenge, because they were usually in low-paid work: for the families that we knew, factories and London Transport were the main employers for men, and nursing was the most common occupation for women. Public-sector jobs might have been unionized and secure, but they were not well paid. People worked hard to increase their income through overtime, but however much they toiled and however hard they saved, funding a house purchase was still a struggle. Some high-street banks would not even allow Black people to open accounts, claiming that was due to their lack of credit history in the UK.

The arrangement that enabled many West Indian migrants to buy their own houses, in defiance of the obstacles, was the 'pardner hand' system. This was a form of community savings that was common in the West Indies, so new migrants brought the system with them to Britain. Everything was done in cash. A group would come together and each week everybody would agree to put the same sum of money into the pot, and each week it would be someone's turn to take the entire pot. This was known as 'throwing your pardner'. With enough people involved, quite substantial sums of money could be raised on a weekly basis. It was a vital way of saving money for that early wave of migrants, who did not have access to banks or building societies. For the system to work, people had to be part of a close-knit community and show total trust in one another; there was little recourse if someone were to abuse that trust.

Before I was even born, my father made a decision that would shape my entire life. At the time it was not uncommon for families to send newborn children 'home', thousands of miles away, to family in the Caribbean to be raised. From a certain perspective this may seem drastic or even heartless, but if the entire extended family had still been living in the Caribbean, it would have been unremarkable for a grandmother or an aunt to play a major role in bringing up the new baby. In London, migrant families often lived in overcrowded accommodation and there might be a pressing need for the mother to go out to work. This meant that sending a baby home to grandmother was a purely practical option.

In order to continue her career as a nurse, my mother planned to send me to Smithville in Jamaica, for her mother, Miss Di, to raise. Some of her brothers and sisters had done the same with their children, as I realized when I first went to Jamaica in my early twenties and met my family there. They included a whole set of cousins that I had never seen before, who had been brought up by my grandmother. My father, though, put his foot down. I was his first child. He wanted us to stay together as a family unit, and he wanted his wife to stop working and be a full-time housewife and mother. It was about his status as a man as much as anything: being in control was all the more critical because, as a Black man, he was in control of very little outside the four walls of his home. So he insisted that his eldest child was not going anywhere: not only would I be born in Britain, but I would also stay and be raised there.

My mother gave in on the matter of sending me back to Jamaica. Like most married women of the time, she usually acceded to her husband's demands.

I was born in Paddington Hospital in Harrow Road and, as my father expressly wished, I was brought up in Britain. Being a former workhouse, the hospital was hardly posh; I was one of the first Black babies born there, which was an event of sorts for the hospital. My mother loved to recall how, after I was born and was snuggled in my cot in her room, doctors and nurses would come in to surreptitiously lift my cot blankets and take a peek. In the end she felt obliged to say, 'She hasn't got a tail, you know!'

In 1951 my father bought a house at 33 Edbrooke Road in North Paddington, having raised the money for the deposit through the 'pardner hand' system. Although my parents may have felt they had no choice but to do this, they could not possibly afford to live in the whole property on their own. It was a three-storey house with a basement flat; we lived in one room and there were tenants on each floor, with communal cookers on the landings. Renting the basement was an Irish family who had been there long before my father bought the house, and who would continue to live there for years after he sold it. As 'sitting tenants', they had the right to stay and could not be evicted so long as they paid their rent. The head of the family was a man I always knew as 'Uncle' Jimmy. My parents got on well with Uncle Jimmy, and he doted on me as a baby. Each morning my mother would give me breakfast, and each morning Uncle Jimmy would come and scoop me up to take me downstairs to his basement flat and feed me a second breakfast, accompanied by much cooing from him and gurgling from me.

Not everyone in Paddington had Uncle Jimmy's freedom from prejudice. There was already hostility towards Black people in the area, which worsened in response to the wave of Black migration of the time. The 1950s were the heyday of blatantly racist organizations such as the Union Movement (known before the war as the British Union of Fascists), led by Oswald Mosley, and the White Defence League, headed by Colin Jordan. Both groups had 'Keep Britain White' as their predominant ideology. In addition, the youth subculture that reigned at the time was that of the 'Teddy boys'. They combined a dress style based on Edwardian dandies, a passion for rock and roll and a propensity for violent attacks on Black people. In some clashes they would be armed with iron bars, butchers' knives and weighted leather belts. They would come together in gangs, sometimes hundreds strong, and look for Black people to beat up. This culminated in the notorious 1958 Notting Hill race riots, when Teds were implicated in attacks on the West Indian community.

Mummy would sometimes tell me of one particular night when Teddy boys roamed the streets of North Paddington on a 'nigger hunt'. They went from house to house on our road, knocking on each door to see who owned the house, and if a Black man answered, he would get abused and assaulted. One night my mother and father were in their house listening fearfully as the racist hooligans went up and down Edbrooke Road looking for Black people. Uncle Jimmy heard the marauding racists, too. Coming up from his basement flat, he said firmly to my parents, 'They are not getting our Diane.' When the hooligans banged on our door, it was Uncle Jimmy who went to open it. Assuming that this burly white man was the home-owner, they went on their way.

In 1958, when I was five, my father decided to move us all from Paddington and take us to live in Harrow, Middlesex. Our little family left our house on Edbrooke Road in Paddington, which we had shared with tenants and with Uncle Jimmy and his family, and went off to Harrow, where we lived in a house all on our own. It was almost as big a step as migrating from Jamaica to Britain in the first place. My father's family and friends were incredulous that he had moved somewhere that was virtually all white: 95 per cent of those living in Harrow had been born in Britain – which at the time definitely meant white; of the remaining 5 per cent, the vast majority who had been born overseas were Irish. When I started going to school, if I saw another Black person in the street I would rush home to tell my mother.

Even the architecture in Harrow differed hugely from the streetscape we had known. Paddington was all three-storey stucco terraces and, probably because everyone was living in cramped flats or even one overcrowded room, life was largely lived on the street. People would make a point of greeting those they knew and would often stand around chatting. By contrast, Harrow was made up of neat semi-detached houses, with the Tudor architectural touches that are typical of suburbia, and nearly always there were privet hedges. Life was lived behind those hedges and behind firmly closed front doors. Where Paddington was rackety, Harrow was relatively quiet and intensely respectable. Our neighbours included a teacher, an electrical engineer, a driver for the Gas Board, clerical assistants and a photographer based at Unilever's local research lab. Meanwhile, my father was still a factory worker. Around the time that we moved to Harrow he changed jobs and became a sheet-metal worker in a small local factory. On any given day, the most exciting thing in the part of Harrow where we lived was the sound of an enormous hooter at the huge local Kodak manufacturing plant, which went off every day at 7 a.m. sharp, summoning to work their 6,000 workers who lived nearby. My father, too, would get up early every weekday to go to work, and on a Friday when he brought home his wage packet he would dole out the housekeeping allowance to my mother and pocket money to my brother and me.

Though my mother had to give up nursing once she had me, she did not let marriage and the lack of a full-time job crush her spirit, instead generating a small income either by making clothes for friends on her beloved Singer sewing machine or by selling Avon cosmetics door-to-door to other housewives. Her background as a pupil teacher in Jamaica came in handy for her keenest pupil: her daughter. Before I started school, she taught me to read. We used to sit in the glass conservatory at the back of our house in Harrow, with the sun shining through the roof, and Mummy would painstakingly teach me to read with a set of large, brightly coloured plastic letters that clipped together. My parents did not read books – the main volume in the living room of our house was a huge set of the *Encyclopaedia Britannica*, which was a form of interior decoration as much as anything else – but my mother absolutely understood the importance of reading, and she took me to join the local library when I was still at primary school. Books became my passion, and libraries are still very special to me. Unlike other youngsters of my age, I did not go through an Enid Blyton phase, which might have limited me to the usual contemporary favourites. Some of the first items I spent my pocket money on were children's books from a general shop round the corner from our house, and it was a thrill to buy my own books. Because it was a general store, though, there was just one shelf allocated to children's titles, so it was a lack of choice that accounted for my earliest reading material being 'classics' from a previous era, from Louisa May Alcott's *Little Women* to Susan Coolidge's *What Katy Did*.

The public lending library offered me a much wider selection of books. I read a great deal of historical fiction, and the Regency romances of Georgette Heyer were a favourite. I was there so often that I began to believe the librarian was a personal friend. One day I was in the library at the same time as a friend from school and I proudly introduced them to one another. I was mortified when the librarian gave me a chilly look. That was when I realized that, whatever I thought, the librarian did not view me as her friend.

Back in Paddington, as far as everyone we knew was concerned, we might as well have moved to the far side of the moon. 'Reggie,' they would say to my father, 'why have you gone to live in the bush!'

Harrow is now a London suburb, but when we moved there it was always termed 'Harrow, Middlesex' and was considered truly remote from the capital. That we should have left the tight-knit West Indian community in west London to go and live in lily-white Harrow continued to amaze our family friends. Objectively, the transition from Black London to white suburbia was about moving to a new house; subjectively, it was an aspirational move, about transitioning to a different way of life. At the time I was not sure exactly why my father made the move – he was not necessarily hankering after gentility, but he sometimes claimed that we made the move because the schools in Harrow were better, and education was key to moving up in the world.

In addition, although he did not mention it to me then, we relocated at a time when marauding groups of violent white racists – whether it was Colin Jordan followers or Teddy boys – were all around Paddington and Notting Hill. It was in 1959, after we had moved out of west London, that the West Indian migrant Kelso Cochrane was stabbed to death in Notting Hill by a gang of white youths. This sparked a surge of racial tension, and 1,200 people attended his funeral. It could have been true, therefore, that Daddy felt we would be safer living out in suburbia. He did not consult my mother about the decision, just as he never consulted her about anything. His move to white suburbia was done in the same spirit as he migrated to Britain by plane: striking out for pastures new.

Bold as my father was, he was also very careful and organized with money. Instead of selling the house in Paddington, he let it out to tenants, including Uncle Jimmy, and used the income to help pay the mortgage on our more expensive semi-detached house in Harrow.

Despite the move, there was no question whatsoever of cutting our ties to Paddington and family and friends in the West Indian community in west London. For years, every Saturday without fail, Daddy would pack us all into the car and drive us back to Paddington. For starters, he needed to check on the Edbrooke Road property and collect his rent.

Almost as important was my mother's need to shop for the Caribbean staples that she could not find in Harrow. We might have been living in suburbia, but we were still eating Jamaican food, and there was no finding yams, green banana or ackee out in the suburbs of London. So on our Saturdays in Paddington I would traipse after my mother to the specialist greengrocer who stocked Caribbean fruit, vegetables and general provisions and buy spices and other essentials from the 'continental' shop. I can still recall its delicious aromas – partly spices such as peppers, garlic and pimento, and partly the scent of the vegetables.

Our weekly trips kept us in touch with our community in that part of London, as if an umbilical cord bound us to them. Although my father was the first to make the daring move to suburbia, quite soon many of our relatives and friends were living in areas such as Harlesden, Kilburn and Willesden, where they too bought their own houses. My family became regular attendees at weddings and christenings in west London, and because my father was popular and well known in the Jamaican community, I would often be enlisted as a bridesmaid, resplendent in an elaborate frock with a mass of petticoats, ribbons in my hair and a matching bonnet. More than a few mantelpieces in west London's Jamaican households featured a photograph of me attending on a bride and groom in all my bridesmaid's finery. Typically, after the wedding reception, the day ended with a dance. Wedding-goers feasted on curry goat and rice (in Jamaica goats were slaughtered specially for the occasion, though in London the curry was usually made from mutton). Strong drinks were a staple of these wedding dances, and if we children were lucky, we might sometimes snaffle a Babycham.

If there was not a wedding, then my family's days out in our former west London stomping ground often ended in the kitchen or living room of someone's house. The living room was always called 'the front room', even if it was at the back of the house. The adults would spend the entire evening reminiscing about Jamaica. In wintertime all those homes often smelled the same, too, since the heating of choice was the paraffin heater, the cheapest form of heating in a Britain that was cold and damp for most of the year; central heating was not common in 1950s working-class homes. The strong smell of paraffin penetrated our clothes easily, and for me it became the smell of poverty. But the real problem with paraffin heaters was how easily they could tip over and cause a fire. Apart from the destruction of property they caused, many children suffered terrible burns from those paraffin-heater fires.

The decor of the rooms where we were entertained was always the same. There was no such thing as tasteful neutral colours: Caribbean front rooms had brightly coloured carpets, wallpaper and upholstery. There would usually be a three-piece suite covered in velvet-like Dralon; some families deliberately kept the three-piece suite in the plastic covers in which it had arrived from the furniture showroom, all the better to preserve its velvety magnificence. Rooms also invariably had a glass-fronted cabinet full of china ornaments and vases of flamboyant plastic flowers, and without exception there would be a radiogram, a massive wooden instrument for listening to the radio and playing music. The top brand of radiogram then favoured by the community was Blue Spot. We often listened to calypso music, and to country-and-western singers such as Jim Reeves, a particular favourite of my mother. There was nearly always a cocktail cabinet, too; it did not occur to me to wonder why most people I knew had a cocktail cabinet, yet I never actually saw anyone making a cocktail. The height of sophistication was a drink such as Babycham or Cherry B, which was meant for women. Cocktail cabinets usually had a section at the bottom for bottles of special alcohol – including Stone's Ginger Wine and Emva Cream sherry – but they were rarely touched. For a real drink, men drank rum. There would be another section, normally mirror-lined, at the top of the cocktail cabinet for glasses. When the proud owner pulled down the lid of this section, those glasses would glitter magnificently. One of the most impressive cocktail cabinets I ever saw had its splendour enhanced by a glass ballerina in a tutu, who would emerge when the glasses section was opened and would twirl round and round to tinkling music coming from the cabinet.

Then there were the elaborate crocheted doilies that adorned every available surface in the front room, including tables, cupboards and the backs of chairs. These doilies were a testament to the needlework skills of my mother's generation, brought up in rural Jamaica. They had all learned to crochet as girls and lovingly created doilies with lacy patterns and elaborate frills, which were starched so that the frills stuck upwards. Special ornaments all had their own doily, too, and one of my weekly chores as a child was to lift each doily and dust underneath it. One of my relatives bought an electric mixer in the days when they were a rare symbol of conspicuous consumption. I never saw her use it for any actual mixing, which she continued to do by hand in the way she had been taught as a girl, but her mixer was too high-status an object to leave in its box; instead she exhibited it with great pride on its own particularly fancy doily on the mantelpiece in her front room.

Every Black family that I knew, while growing up in the 1950s and 1960s, had a front room of this type, and they rarely differed in their colour schemes, furniture and ornaments. They were seemingly modelled on the Victorian parlour of the Caribbean colonial elite. The godfather of Black British photography, Vanley Burke, captured these 'front rooms' beautifully, challenging the stereotypical images of Black people in the mainstream media as thugs or criminals. Their lasting inspiration is also seen in the work of playwright and artist Michael McMillan, whose parents were migrants from St Vincent and the Grenadines. I saw his first play, titled *The School Leaver*, at the Royal Court Theatre in 1978, which premiered when he was just sixteen years old. Michael has continued to write plays, as well as some amazing multimedia work, including in 2005–6 an installation called *The West Indian Front Room* at the Museum of the Home, which garnered such an overwhelmingly positive response (including from people my age who remember those exact same front rooms) that it is now a permanent exhibit.

Although listening to these conversations was an early driver for making Jamaica part of my identity, the talk on these Saturday nights was rarely about Jamaica as a nation. Rather it would usually concern Clarendon, the rural parish in which my parents, their family and friends had been born and brought up. They would speak of the people, places and incidents they remembered from what they called 'home'. Many of those with whom my family spent time when I was a child went on to stay in Britain for the rest of their lives. Yet in their minds Jamaica was home and they were going back there (in reality, there was little to no chance of returning even for a holiday, because international travel was so expensive).

Life in the suburbs was probably most difficult and isolating for my mother, who was in our house all day on her own. She was not going out to work, she did not drive and there were no easy public-transport routes to the parts of west London that she was familiar with, so she was as good as stranded in Harrow. Nor was there anyone to teach her the unwritten rules of white suburbia. Once, when I wanted to contribute to a school fete, my mother decided that I should bring something for the bottle stall. When the day of the fete came, she produced some carefully washed out and completely empty jam jars for us to take. I queried whether this was really what the fete organizers had in mind for a bottle stall. My mother was firm: white people valued empty jam jars, she said emphatically. They would pay money for them, she added, so that they could have something to put preserves in. 'Wrong but strong' might have been her motto. In the end, nobody had the heart to tell either her or me that a bottle stall at a fete was not at all about empty bottles.

Another time she decided to throw me a birthday party. I was thrilled – I had never had one before. Mummy baked me a beautiful cake and carefully iced it in white and pink. The day of my birthday dawned and I hurried home from school full of anticipation, excited at the prospect of my party. But when I got back to the house, there were no guests there at all. My mother and I looked at one another, both wondering what could have gone wrong. After waiting a while, we worked out what the problem was: nobody had been invited. My mother knew nothing of the ritual of printed invitations and the precise details necessary to organize a successful children's birthday party in British suburbia. It did not help that I was hardly ever invited to white children's parties, so I knew no more than she did about the correct arrangements. In rural Jamaica such a celebration was usually put together by word of mouth. Instead my mother and I endured the unforgettable humiliation of an empty house and a non-existent birthday gathering.

My parents had just two children: me and my younger brother Hugh. There are photographs of us siblings together as toddlers, where we almost look like twins. In some ways we had a very stable nuclear family; my mother was always at home when my brother and I returned from school, and my father came back from work at the same time every evening. We did most things as a family. While the four of us did not go away on what might be termed holidays – that was not something working-class West Indians did in the 1950s – we did go on day-trips by coach. Sometimes it would be to resorts such as Brighton on the south coast, or as a particular treat we would drive all the way to Blackpool in the

North-West to see the famous illuminations. This was a spectacular display of lights switched on every autumn along the promenade, and a visit there was a popular outing for many working-class families. To make sure that we would not want for nourishment, my mother would pack home-made food – West Indian chicken and rice and peas – in a large Thermos flask.

One of the biggest differences between my brother and me, from a very young age, was his passion for anything on wheels. When we were toddlers, our parents gave us both children's bikes with training wheels. My brother threw off the training wheels in no time at all and was soon cycling happily up and down the streets of Harrow. By contrast, I never got beyond the training-wheels stage, and sixty years later still cannot ride a bicycle. My brother is fiercely intelligent, and more scientifically minded and practical than me. He is also sportier, whereas my lack of sporting ability was the despair of my teachers at school. They seemed to be of the fixed opinion that, as a Black girl, I should be naturally good at games. One PE teacher took to lecturing me about how good Jamaican girls normally were at netball, but I was unmoved. There were many aspects of my Jamaican heritage that were important to me; netball was not one of them.

Most West Indian parents of the time were fervent believers in the maxim of 'spare the rod and spoil the child', and mine were no different, although Mummy rarely gave either my brother or me more than the occasional sharp slap. Her preferred way of imposing discipline was to say meaningfully, 'Wait until your father gets home.' My brother and I knew what that meant: Daddy always kept a leather belt hanging behind the parental bedroom door. When he got home from work on the day of whatever wrong-doing we had committed, Mummy would explain portentously to him, having saved it up all day, what one or other of us children had done wrong. I do not remember ever being asked to tell my side of the story. My parents were definitely not ones for Socratic debate. Instead my father would say sternly, 'Go and get the belt.'

The truly remarkable thing was that my brother and I would always obediently trot upstairs to fetch it, knowing full well that we were going to get beaten with it. My parents were not unusual among the families and community that we knew in seeing physical punishment as a legitimate parenting tool, though they rarely actually had to smack us. The fact that my brother and I knew they *might* do so had the desired effect. Now, of course, I do not believe in smacking and corporal punishment, but I also do not think Mummy and Daddy were particularly cruel. They simply thought they were doing the right thing.

While my brother was out on his bicycle, I was often found reading. I fell in love with the written word the first time my mother took me to join the local public library and it became the one undying romance of my life. I adored books, bookshops, libraries, the smell and feel of books. My mother would often try to send me up the road on errands, and since I was not prepared to interrupt my reading, it was not unusual for me to trot off on an errand with whatever book I was reading clasped in my hands as I walked, my arms stuck out in front of me.

My love of books was legendary in my family. One of my mother's favourite brothers in Britain was Uncle Mackie, a long-serving porter at Euston station. If he ever found a book that had been left behind by a passenger and not claimed, he would proudly hand it to me the next time our families met, never really considering whether it was a subject that I was interested in or by an author I enjoyed. The fact that it was a book and he knew that I liked books was enough, and he was certainly correct in that belief. I loved just the physical reality of books, and the fact that I could leave the real world behind and be absorbed into another world. Nothing could be further from suburban Harrow in the 1970s than the historical romances of Georgette Heyer. As I grew older, I devoured the books and poetry of Black American women such as Toni Morrison and Maya Angelou, who represented a different world that I could still identify with emotionally.

In our household, as with most working-class families, broadcast media was the most important. When I was a child the highlight of my family's viewing week was a variety show called *Sunday Night at the London Palladium*. We would gather around the television to watch the show, which was compèred by the popular entertainer Bruce Forsyth. One segment featured the game show *Beat the Clock* and famous singing stars. It always ended with Forsyth, the showgirls and the week's acts standing on a revolving stage that turned round and round as the orchestra played. I was as enthralled as anyone in my family by this simple entertainment, and in its heyday it was ITV's most-watched programme. I had left university before I discovered that broadcast media could be more sophisticated than that.

My mother and father were loyal Labour voters and though we never talked about politics as a family, there were some family habits that indirectly contributed to my interest in politics. Mummy was a devoted listener to the BBC Home Service, later known as Radio 4. When I was at primary school, every morning she would stand me in front of her dressing-table mirror, comb out my mass of frizzy hair, plait it and put in fresh, carefully ironed ribbons. All the while we would both be listening to the eight o'clock news on the Home Service. I listened with particularly rapt attention. Mummy never discussed what we heard; it was merely part of our morning routine, but it cultivated an early fascination with news and current affairs, which shaped my internationalist outlook. Events such as the Vietnam War and the first man landing on the moon made a strong impression on me. The radio news made me aware that there was a whole wide world outside suburban Harrow and I would think to myself, *If I were prime minister, I would do . . . this*, or, *If I were Secretary-General of the UN, I would do . . . the other*. It did not cross my mind that, as a Black girl, I had virtually no chance of doing any of these things. From those earliest years I saw myself as a political actor – someone who not only had plenty of ideas about what I would do in politics, but who actually did them.

My father brought the *Daily Mirror* newspaper home from work every day and I would consume it more avidly than anyone else in the house. In the 1960s the *Mirror* was in its heyday as a Labour-supporting tabloid, reaching a huge readership, particularly among the working class. It painted for me, in suburban Harrow, a vision of the world where all things were possible and in which young people should reach for the stars. The 1964 general election saw the triumph of the Labour Party led by Harold Wilson, and although I was too young to understand much about it, I had the clear impression that it was a hopeful thing for ordinary people after the long years of post-war Tory rule.

As I grew older, books and magazines became ever more essential in introducing me to politics. Books broadened my horizons; writers such as Betty Friedan, author of *The Feminine Mystique*, and magazines such as *Spare Rib*, founded in 1972 by Marsha Rowe and Rosie Boycott, helped to teach me about feminism in an era when the women's movement had moved into second-wave feminism, debating issues such as sexuality, family, domesticity, the workplace and reproductive rights. My late teens saw me consuming path-breaking feminist books such as Germaine Greer's *The Female Eunuch* and Kate Millett's *Sexual Politics*.

Inspired by my feminist reading, I decided to join a women's group. This was the main organizational way of learning about feminism and offering mutual support to other women at the time. By studying the pages of *Spare Rib*, I found a group near me. As a Black teenager in a room full of older white women I was a little uncomfortable at first, but I kept attending faithfully. Then, in one meeting where we were discussing a fund-raiser, one woman, giggling, suggested they get a Black male stripper. I realized that this was not the group for me and I never went back.

My discovery of Black writers and books on issues of specific interest to Black people was a more positive experience. My local library did not have any titles about Black politics and, needless to say, my school did not put them on the curriculum, if my teachers even knew that they existed. So in my late teens I was thrilled to discover the Black-bookshop movement that had sprung up, which went on to have a profound impact on the community from the 1970s onwards. The one I frequented most was New Beacon Books in Finsbury Park, but I also favoured the Walter Rodney Bookshop in West Ealing, Grassroots in Ladbroke Grove and Headstart in Seven Sisters. These were not just shops where books were sold; they were informal meeting places, hubs for community organization and sources of information about political activity. It was all a far cry from *Little Women* and *Good Wives*, my childhood reading. Bookshops such as New Beacon helped me identify some of the gaps in my formal education. Among the authors I discovered were Alice Walker, C. L. R. James, Walter Rodney, Andrew Salkey and James Baldwin.

Reading helped with my education from the outset. It meant that throughout my school career I had a bigger vocabulary than other children of my age, and reading novels voraciously made me comfortable with textbooks. Though my parents were not readers themselves, they took school and reading very seriously. Every afternoon when my brother and I came home from school it was expected that we change into our 'house clothes' and do our homework. Mummy and Daddy never went to our school sports days because they did not understand what they were about, but they religiously attended our parents' evenings. On these evenings my father would change out of his work overalls and wear his suit and tie, and he always took a shiny brown briefcase that he never carried anywhere else or used in any other situation. It had a highly distinctive smell of new leather, and it was always completely empty. As a child I was puzzled that he would take such care to carry this empty case. I put it down to one of those strange adult rituals that I did not understand. It baffled me for more than thirty years, until I realized that my bold and intrepid father was frightened of those meetings, frightened of the middle-class parents at the grammar school where I was the only Black girl, frightened of the teachers and the words he might not understand and, above all, frightened that they would look down on a working-class Black man who worked with his hands. The briefcase was his talisman, an object that made him as good as the white teachers he was talking to, and one that would cause them to take him seriously.

My family life was stable, calm and organized for much of my childhood. Daddy was certainly difficult and authoritarian by temperament, but he was not a frequenter of pubs. He had a steady income, supplementing his wages with rental income from his properties. In his own eyes, he was an exemplary husband and father. But there were underlying tensions that I did not really understand. If Mummy had still been living in Jamaica, or even in Paddington among the West Indian community, she would have had friends on her doorstep. Instead she was marooned in London suburbia. Although there might not have been Teddy boys patrolling the streets of Harrow, my mother knew that the world outside her front door was not entirely welcoming. Some days she might have no one at all to talk to until my brother and I came home from school.

Although Daddy at least had people to converse with, since he was going out to work every day, he was still a Black man in a white world, in those earliest years of significant Caribbean migration to Britain. He was obliged to absorb any number of racial microaggressions and unadulterated racism, and he could never answer back. In those days there was no legislation to temper bigoted or racist behaviour. A Black employee who was considered the slightest bit 'uppity' could be thrown out of the door before they had time to draw breath. So my father had to suck it all up and laugh along with the 'jokes' being told at his expense. No doubt one reason he was at home with his family every evening was that he would not necessarily have been welcome in the pubs and working men's clubs that his white colleagues went to. Because Daddy could not vent his anger and pain about the racial indignities he had to put up with in his workplace or in the outside world, he brought that rage home. At the time I thought he was a baffling and inexplicable tyrant; with hindsight, I believe that it was the rage he was bottling up, because of his treatment in the outside world, that accounted for his habitual shouting and dictatorial manner towards my mother, my brother and me.

Growing up, I thought Daddy was unfair and unreasonable. Nevertheless you could not say that he was indifferent to my mother, my brother and me, or that he did not care about us or failed to take his family responsibilities seriously. Aside from us, Daddy was a dependable rock for his other relatives. He had been one of the first members of his family to come to Britain at the start of the 1950s. Then, year after year, as his nieces, nephews and cousins migrated, he was their first port of call. Sometimes they lived with us, either in the Paddington house or in Harrow, while they found their feet. Even for those who did not stay with us, my father was a mentor, advisor and guide. Years later his younger relations in Britain regarded him with the greatest respect.

The trickiest aspect of family life was the tension between my parents. For years my mother never challenged my father about anything, but gradually the marriage began to crumble.

Once my brother and I had begun attending secondary school in the mid-1960s, Mummy managed to get a job in the local Sainsbury's, slicing meat in a space behind the shop counters out of sight of the customers. At the time it seemed that Sainsbury's did not want a Black woman worker visible and serving their patrons. But Mummy was out of the house at last and earning her own money. My father, however, did not seem to want her to work at all. He was the head of the household, a conscientious parent, working hard to support his family and to be a good provider; but there is no denying that he could also be difficult, shouty and controlling. When Mummy got her job at Sainsbury's he was not supportive, instead deriding her about it. His insistence on micromanaging my mother was difficult for her. He wanted to decide which of her relatives she visited and when.

His behaviour became coercive, and the shouting became more frequent.

Matters came to a head when my brother and I were teenagers. My mother defied my father by going to a relative's wedding that he had expressly banned her from attending. Although she did not come back home particularly late, Daddy was beside himself with rage. His method of 'punishing' her was to refuse to let her sit with the rest of us in the living room to watch television in the evening. She had to remain in the kitchen on her own. There she had nothing to do except knit by herself. It was a ridiculous way to treat a grown woman, but I did not challenge him. I would creep out of the living room occasionally, to sit with her and keep her company.

It must have been her banishment to the kitchen in the evenings to sit on her own that made my mother snap. She took her courage in both hands and moved out of the family home in 1968, when I was fifteen. I was shocked and upset, even outraged, by her leaving home, but as a schoolgirl there was nothing I could do. Mummy quickly left London altogether, putting the greatest possible distance between herself and her husband. She went to live in Huddersfield in West Yorkshire, hours away from London. At the time Huddersfield had a small but growing Caribbean community, most of whom had moved there to work in the mills. In Huddersfield Mummy was able to take up her beloved nursing again. It was wonderful for her to be free and have a proper job. But Huddersfield in the late 1960s was a little less welcoming to non-white people than London was, and there was a degree of unspoken segregation. My mother worked in Storthes Hall Hospital, a mental institution in Kirkburton, not far from Huddersfield. Many nurses there were Black, but when my mother had to go into hospital herself in the Huddersfield Royal Infirmary there was not a Black nurse to be seen.

I remained living with Daddy and my brother in Harrow, although my father was determined to move onwards and upwards.

For months he and my brother drove around the area looking for a house that Daddy liked the look of, but every time they contacted an estate agent about a property, they were told it was sold. Finally he bought a house in Edgware whose owner sold it to him directly, without using an estate agent. A few days after we moved in, Daddy was outside mowing the extensive lawns. One of our neighbours walked past and asked if my father would come and mow his lawn, having assumed that Daddy was the gardener. A little later I learned that the man who had sold the house to my father hated Jewish people and, as he had a number of Jewish neighbours, he sold to Daddy to spite them.

The decision that I should remain with Daddy and my brother was a tough and challenging one, but in the end I decided that I wanted to stay at my grammar school, where I was about to start in the sixth form studying for my Advanced Level exams, the school-leaving qualification that was a stepping stone towards further education. It did not seem practical to have to find a new school somewhere else, where Mummy would not necessarily have a place for me to live.

Mummy leaving home came as a shock to all of us, not least my father. He could not believe that his quietly obedient wife had defied him in the most decisive way, by walking out from under his roof. He was enraged by her defiance. If he had shouted while she lived at home, he shouted even more now that she was gone, ranting and raving for months about what had happened. There could not have been a more complete affront to his authority.

I was very frightened by his threats, worried that he might actually find Mummy and do her physical harm. One of the worst times came when he found a photograph of my mother, slashed it with a knife, scribbled on it with a red pen and pinned it over the cooker in the kitchen, where I had to look at it every time I prepared a meal for the family. The unchallenged expectation was that I would be the one to do this after my mother left; while studying for my exams, I took on the traditional day-to-day female household tasks of cooking and cleaning (despite the fact that my brother was far more practical). Though I struggled with the role, and the stress that the situation caused me, I did not resist it.

My parents had a toxic divorce. The acrimony between them meant that, for years afterwards, they did not even speak. Although I only saw Mummy every few months, I kept in close touch with her by letter and telephone and, once I left school, I went to live with her up in Huddersfield during university holidays. My brother felt she had abandoned him, although I understood why she felt she had no choice but to leave. Hugh and I took different sides in our parents' divorce and did not speak for years afterwards.

In the 1970s Bob Marley and reggae took off in Britain. This was a long way from the mellifluous, unchallenging calypsos of Harry Belafonte that I had grown up listening to. Reggae music had a thumping rhythm track designed to get you up and on the dance floor. But it also posed a challenge to the established order, talking about rebellion, Black empowerment and the culture of the Jamaican ghetto. Bob Marley, with his dreadlocks, became a cultural icon, and reggae went on to shape the soundtrack of the rest of my life.

I was in my early twenties before I eventually visited Jamaica for the first time with Mummy. She and her brothers there masterminded the trip. Although she had kept in touch with her relatives via the blue airmail letters they all exchanged, she had not been back to the island since migrating to Britain in 1950. Going home after so long was a huge event for her, and she packed a large number of gifts to take back for family there, particularly for her mother. Mummy had made the long journey from Huddersfield to London and was staying with friends for a few days. Given the amount of luggage she had with her, getting to the airport would be a challenge, so I plucked up the courage to ask my father to give Mummy, me and our bags a lift in his car. I was not sure what he would say, because of all the bad blood between them, but to my surprise he agreed to drive us there.

When we arrived at Heathrow, my father and I walked through the busy airport steering the luggage trolley on which the bags were piled high. My mother was a little bit behind us, struggling to keep up since her legs were somewhat shorter than Daddy's, and I had matched my stride to his. After a little while my father paused. He turned to look at my mother trotting along as quickly as she could manage. Given everything that had gone on between them, especially the terrible collapse of their marriage, I assumed that he was about to say something cross and impatient. Instead his gaze softened. It was as if he was seeing in his mind's eye the young girl he had known when they were both growing up in Smithville, Jamaica.

'She did always . . .' he said reflectively, in his strong Jamaican accent, 'walk slow.'

It was only one sentence. But I realized then, amid the noise and bustle of Heathrow airport, something I had never understood before. I grasped in that moment that, despite all the terrible things he had done and said in the past, my father loved my mother. Not only that, but he had loved her from the first moment he saw her as a schoolgirl in Jamaica. And he loved her still.

I nearly pulled out of this first trip to Jamaica at the last minute, for I rather truculently thought that holidaying with my mother would be tedious. Then she revealed to me that her brothers in Jamaica had clubbed together to pay my air fare. I was an undergraduate by this point and my maternal uncles were determined to meet this young academic superstar, as they evidently thought me to be.

I spent the early part of that initial visit to Jamaica meeting my mother's siblings in the capital city of Kingston. It was a city nothing like London – instead it was warm, green and sunny. Downtown were the notorious ghettos, though I had no reason to see them, since none of my family lived there. Uptown were hotels such as the Jamaica Pegasus, in buildings several storeys high, surrounded by tropical gardens and intended for tourists and visiting businessmen. Middle-class Kingston residents lived in one-storey bungalows, usually painted white, with carefully tended gardens.

We went to stay with Uncle Len, another of Mummy's brothers. He was a lovely man who had been close to my mother since they were children in Jamaica. From the moment of our first meeting, we clicked. Uncle Len had not migrated across the ocean, like most of his brothers and sisters, but instead had got a job at Cable & Wireless, a telegraph, radio and telecommunications company that had operated in Jamaica since the 1930s. Working for them was an extremely respectable job for a Black man in 1950s Jamaica. With his savings, Uncle Len was able to buy a big piece of land on a picturesque hillside called Stony Hill in the suburbs of Kingston. It was a little above and beyond the city. There he built a large house for himself, complete with a swimming pool, and constructed other houses tucked away among the greenery. One was for his sister Inez, another was for his brother Fred. The others were let to tenants, to help supplement his income. He could not have been a more benevolent landlord. Although Uncle Len was unmarried and did not have any children, the fact that his sister and brother lived a stone's throw from his own house gave the Stony Hill property the feel of an extended family setting.

I loved spending time with Uncle Len, and we often passed our days just chatting to each other. From the first time I set foot in his home, I was enchanted by it. The rooms were airy and beautifully furnished. There was a houseman called Fred, who was around to make food and help whenever necessary. It was very different from my relatives' houses in London, where nobody I knew would have had the faintest notion of employing household help. Uncle Len's house in Jamaica became my home away from home, not only on that initial visit, but for many years afterwards. Whenever I rang him to ask if it was okay to visit, before I could even get the words out of my mouth he would invariably say warmly, 'Just come!' When he died in 2008 I was bereft.

After a week or so in Kingston with my uncle, Mummy and I travelled out to Smithville, the country village where she and my father had been born, and where her mother Miss Di still lived. We travelled there on a country bus, which was an adventure in itself. A Jamaican country bus carried not only human beings, but livestock such as chickens. And one of the best aspects of the bus ride for me was that you got a wonderful view of the hillsides, riverbeds and scenery of rural Jamaica.

I liked Smithville straight away. All I had known was an urban upbringing – even the suburbs of London are not particularly green. But Smithville was peaceful, lush and surrounded by woodland. Everyone seemed to know everybody else, if not be related to them. I had heard people talking about this Jamaican village all my life, and it was amazing to be there finally for real.

My grandmother was always called 'Miss Di', although the 'Miss' was not a clue to her marital status. It was the normal honorific for any older woman in the Jamaican countryside. As it happens, Miss Di had had seven children by five different men and never did marry. She was a pillar of the local church, and in truth had the utmost respect for the institution of marriage. However, precisely because rural Jamaicans regarded marriage with great seriousness, it was common for them to give birth to quite a few children before getting round to the display of conspicuous consumption that a 'proper' wedding demanded. This included: a marital home (which you or your family were likely to have constructed); a custom-tailored groom's suit (no such thing as 'off the peg'); a handmade long, elaborate wedding dress; and unlimited supplies of stewed chicken, curried goat and roast pork, as well as vast quantities of rum.

Despite the fact that Miss Di was not formally married, the close-knit nature of the tiny Jamaican village where she lived gave her children stability, security and an abundance of adult role models. She and other watchful grandmothers provided twenty-four-hour surveillance. Though she never officially married her

children's fathers, they never disputed their obligations and fulfilled them as best they could, with community disapproval as an
effective enforcer.

Miss Di loved all her children and grandchildren dearly,
although she was very conscious of, and even a little wistful about,
the fact that I was a grandchild whom she did not get to rear – the
one who got away. I met her for the first time on that visit to
Jamaica and we made a strong and favourable impression on each
other. Miss Di was lovely and elegant; in her younger years she
had been one of the belles of the community, and she was also
something of a career woman. She had moved to Smithville from
elsewhere in Clarendon, originally to be the postmistress, which
was one of the few professional jobs open to women in rural
Jamaica. She had a natural dignity, a striking personality and was
not in any way shy, retiring or meek. All her children adored her.

We spent a happy time with Miss Di in her countryside cottage
lit by oil lamps, with the sound of crickets outside at night. I mused
a great deal about what it might have been like to grow up with
her in Smithville, in the beautiful Jamaican countryside. It would
surely have been a happy childhood. I could tell that, from seeing
how content and cheerful my cousins who had been brought up
with Miss Di were, and how much they loved her. Yet, much as I
liked Smithville and was enchanted by my grandmother, I never
doubted that beyond rural Jamaica there were worlds for me to
conquer.

Miss Di, for her part, seemed entranced by me. One day I was
sitting on the steps in front of her house chatting to a cousin while
she listened to me and noticeably marvelled. 'Lord,' she said to
herself in her soft Jamaican accent, 'how refined she is! How can
she be so refined?'

In fact I wasn't refined at all, but my English accent enthralled
Miss Di. No other grandchild she knew spoke like that. My relatives in Britain were loving, but I had met no one who admired me
in such an unequivocal way.

When the time came for my mother and me to return to Kingston on the same country bus that had brought us to Smithville, Miss Di offered to help us with the luggage. I was taken by surprise to see her deftly scoop up all our suitcases and pile them, with practised ease, on top of her scarfed head, making light of their weight. Standing erect by the side of the road with my mother and me waiting for the bus, with our suitcases balanced on her head, my grandmother looked completely poised. You could see why she had turned men's heads when she first came to Smithville as a young woman, graceful, pretty and fancy-free.

So from that day on, whenever I was faced with doing something I was nervous about, such as delivering a big speech, I would think of Miss Di and try as best I could to emulate her dignity, grace and poise.

Top: Aged eight in my primary school uniform. My brother and I were the only Black students at Vaughan Road Primary in Harrow.

Bottom: Both my parents left school at fourteen but they lived to see me go up to Cambridge University where I read history at Newnham College. Here I am pictured outside King's College in 1976.

2. A Shock to the System

Shortly after my family moved to Harrow from Paddington in 1958, I started primary school aged five, at Vaughan Road Primary, a brick-built London County Council school. In my early years there, my father said something to me that stayed with me all my life: 'You should not just be as good as white people. You always have to be better.'

My brother and I were the only Black children at the school, apart from a mixed-race boy who was parented by an elderly white couple. I never knew whether he was related to them or fostered, and I was not concerned about it, either way. As I grew accustomed to this virtually all-white school in an all-white suburb, and as we continued our weekly visits to see friends and family in west London (who were nearly all Black), this marked the beginning of the Abbott family effectively living in two worlds. This segregation was not something I questioned at the time – it was simply how things were. Occasionally some teachers were unaccountably hostile to both me and my brother – like the one who got cross about the way I held my song book. She glared at me and said pointedly, 'Why do you always have to be different?' I had no idea what she meant.

My best friend was a girl called Marilyn Macey. We had coat pegs next to each other, and we would skip together in the playground and eventually became inseparable. Except for one thing: I was never invited to her house and, even more bafflingly, was never invited to her birthday parties, either. I was not resentful, and I certainly did not blame Marilyn. It was just one of life's mysteries. My brother had similar experiences with his school friends, but it was not something we spoke about at the time, not with each other and certainly not with our parents.

In my final year at primary school I sat the 'eleven-plus', an exam that pupils in the ten-to-eleven age group took to get into grammar school, as opposed to the less academic secondary modern school. In that era the eleven-plus was a significant rite of passage. It separated children into two groups. One group went on to grammar school, having proved their academic prowess, and before them stretched the road to university and success in life. The other group went on to secondary modern school, where the expectations were lower; pupils there were perceived by some as second-class citizens who were unlikely to go on to any type of further education, though many of these children went on to become very successful high-achievers. By dividing up children by academic ability, the eleven-plus exam effectively favoured those who had had better access to education earlier in life, and so in some ways entrenched existing class divisions.

Once I had waited nervously for some time after taking the exam, the letter finally arrived to tell me that I had passed. I had never been more excited than on that morning – even then I knew it was an important day. My father's daring move to suburbia, so that my brother and I could go to better schools, had paid off. I certainly did not know any other child of my parents' friends and family, living as they did in the inner city, who passed the exam; I imagine that it did not occur to any of their teachers that they might do so. I went on to one of the top selective secondary schools in the area, Harrow County Grammar School for Girls, which marked the beginning of my assimilation into the middle classes. Selective schooling and the eleven-plus exam were already becoming controversial then. My parents were loyal Labour voters all their lives, but they had no idea that good socialists were not supposed to send their children to selective schools. They were typically aspirational immigrants who valued education above all else as the means of ascent for their children, so they considered getting into grammar school an achievement to be proud of.

The palaver of buying the Harrow County Girls' uniform was the first clue that going to grammar school was not merely about the textbooks that I would read – it was also about finding myself on a certain social trajectory. It began with the journey to Oxford Street to seek out John Lewis department store, a very large and prestigious establishment. I had never shopped there before, nor had my mother. Normally she bought my clothes in Shepherd's Bush market, unless she had sewn them herself on her trusty Singer sewing machine. But the school had expressly directed that the uniform be bought at John Lewis.

As soon as my mother and I stepped into the store, I realized that we were in a temple of respectability. The genteel shop assistants were a far cry from the market-stall holders I was used to. We had been instructed to buy many items of uniform in navy-blue with pink detailing. It was a formal uniform and, even for the time, a little old-fashioned; there was a blazer and a variety of school-uniform accessories, including a navy felt hat for the winter and a navy straw boater for the summer. Those hats, into which I had to cram my Afro hair, were to become the bane of my life. The straw boater was always blowing off.

Togged out in my smart new uniform, I began my career at Harrow County Grammar School for Girls in the Queen Anne-style building it occupied. I was the only Black girl there, but it was not simply on account of my skin colour that I felt quite different from the other girls. Many of their parents were white-collar workers with office jobs, who wore bowler hats while dropping off their children at school. My father was a factory worker who went to work in overalls.

The school was at the bottom of Harrow Hill, and the famous Harrow public school for boys was, appropriately enough, at the top. On my first day in September 1964, I did not feel cripplingly shy, but I was nervous. There was a strict uniform code, high expectations of standards of behaviour and the prompt handing-in of homework, and 'order marks' were handed out for any infringements of the rules. If our teachers suspected that our skirts were shorter than the rules allowed, they thought nothing of making us kneel down so that they could measure exactly how far the hem of the skirt was above the ground. Humiliatingly, they would even do this in public. At the time the miniskirt was just becoming fashionable, not only as an item of clothing, but as a symbol of the 'Swinging Sixties'; in London suburbia, however, none of us girls dreamed of wearing an actual miniskirt to school, even if we did dream of what it represented. As teenagers, we felt that this was our time – a whirlwind of social change, pop music and permissiveness, of the Beatles and Mary Quant, and of young people parading along the King's Road in Chelsea.

At primary school I had been something of a star when it came to English composition. My completed essays were often pinned up on the classroom wall as examples of excellence for other children to admire. So when, at my very first English lesson at Harrow County, the teacher gave out an essay assignment, I happily handed in my completed work the following week. Up to that point I had never written an essay that had not received a positive response from teachers. I would normally have expected an A-grade or even an 'Excellent' mark for my diligent efforts.

At the next lesson the English teacher, Miss Platt, read out to the assembled class the grades she had awarded each pupil, together with their names. She began with the highest, and I waited expectantly. She read out the names of the girls who had been given an A, then those who had received an A-minus. By the time she reached B-plus and I had not heard my name, I was a little surprised. As she went through all the grades down to D and still did not read my name out at all, I became baffled. After she had finished reading out the grades for the essay assignment, from top to bottom, she briskly began the lesson.

I put up my hand. 'Please, Miss, you haven't read out my grade . . .' I said in a puzzled voice.

She looked at me and her lip curled. 'Come and see me after class,' she replied brusquely.

The class ended and I went up to the front of the room, not knowing what to expect. Her desk was on a small platform that allowed her to look down on me. She picked up my essay disdainfully between her thumb and forefinger and glared at me.

'Where did you copy this from?' she asked bluntly.

I was shocked. She did not even bother to ask *whether* I had copied the essay. That teacher thought she knew, without a shadow of a doubt, that this chubby, bespectacled Black girl looking up at her could not possibly have written anything of that standard. I was stunned by what I was hearing and somewhat unnerved by her aggression; whatever troubles I may have had at primary school, my prowess at writing stories had never been in doubt. I had no answer for that accusatory teacher. I slunk away from her desk, my mind a whirlwind of hurt.

I did not talk to my parents about what had happened, realizing early on in life that I could not expect them to decipher the white world for me. It did not actually occur to me that my new English teacher's assumption of me being a cheat was in fact about her own racism. I thought that perhaps she had taken a dislike to me for some reason. When you are only eleven years old, adults seem to do all manner of random things, and this was merely another such inexplicable, if upsetting, act. What I did know was that I never again wanted to feel that burning humiliation.

For the rest of the school year, while I was in that woman's class, I deliberately did not write as well as I was able to. I was careful not to use the wide vocabulary I possessed, for fear that the teacher would question how I knew all those words. Around the same time my brother was also told by one of his teachers that he would never make a scientist (even though he went on to be a highly successful civil engineer). Fortunately, neither of us was thrown off-course educationally as badly as we might have been – for me, no doubt, because I continued to read incessantly – but it was a horrible experience.

The next year in my English lessons, matters took a turn for the better. We had a new teacher, an iconoclastic little Welsh woman called Mrs Landry. I was relieved to find she had no problem believing that I could write my own essays. English was generally my best subject, but I did well at several others, too, despite my habit of sometimes sitting at the back of the class and chatting to a friend when I was bored. I was not the most organized schoolgirl, which did not endear me to my teachers.

At the age of sixteen, children in Britain had to do a set of exams called the General Certificate of Education, or GCE Ordinary Level (known simply as O-levels). Passing that got you into the 'sixth form', which meant two further years in school from sixteen to eighteen; but if you failed, that was the end of your school career. I did seven GCEs in all. The term before the actual exams we prepared for them by taking the 'mock' GCEs. When my mocks came round, I – like everyone else in my class – was given a timetable in advance. In my usual chaotic fashion, I promptly lost the piece of paper. I was not unduly worried at first, because I thought I would be able to rely on my memory to recall which exam came on what day; and, indeed, everything nearly went off without a hitch. However, I had one exam with the title 'Physics and Chemistry'; although it counted as one O-level, it involved two separate papers. When I turned up at school ready to do the physics exam, I was horrified to find that I had transposed the two papers in my mind and that morning was in fact scheduled for the chemistry paper.

I panicked. I was the queen of last-minute revision and had done no chemistry revision whatsoever, intending – as was my habit – to leave it to the night before. I had no choice but to confess everything to the teacher invigilating the exam. She was in no way sympathetic, scarcely bothering to hide the look of disgust on her face. At length, she agreed with some reluctance that, in order to give me some time to revise, she would delay the start of the exam by exactly an hour. It was one of the worst hours of my life. I stared glumly at my chemistry notes for sixty minutes, then fearfully took the exam. Despite all the drama, and based on virtually no revision, I managed to get an A-grade in physics and chemistry. I heard afterwards that my teachers were not best pleased, as they did not think I deserved it.

In fact my demonstrable cleverness was aggravating for some of my grammar-school teachers. They might have been happier had I been good at sports but poor at academic subjects, as Black girls were expected to be. But I attributed the antagonism of some teachers to the oddness of grown-ups in general and the strange nature of school teachers in particular. Although it was at times disconcerting, I did not let the hostility of some of these teachers fatally damage my confidence.

There were certain events relating to race at that time that made a definite impact on me. One was Enoch Powell's 'Rivers of Blood' speech, which he made on 20 April 1968. Among other things, he said, 'We must be mad, literally mad, as a nation to be permitting the annual inflow of some 50,000 dependants, who for the most part were the material of the future growth of the immigrant-descended population . . . As I look ahead, I am filled with foreboding. Like the Roman, I seem to see the River Tiber foaming with much blood . . .' I remember going to school the next day and everything seemed different. I felt a little scared, as if something had happened that carried a hint of menace towards me personally. It was the same year in which, at the Summer Olympics in Mexico, the African American sprinters John Carlos and Tommie Smith stood on the podium, fists raised and heads bowed in a Black Power salute as the American national anthem played, to protest at racism and injustice against African Americans.

Whenever there were challenges that I had to overcome, music was always guaranteed to lift my spirits and power me forward. As I blossomed into my late teens, I left behind the calypsos and Jim Reeves records of my childhood and discovered the Detroit-based Tamla Motown. The very first record I bought was 'Ain't Too Proud to Beg' by The Temptations, a top Motown singing group.

I loved the rhythm and soulfulness of Motown music, and I admired how glamorous and beautifully groomed artistes like Diana Ross & the Supremes were – a sophisticated image of Black people that you did not normally see in the public eye.

In the sixth form at my school we all studied for three Advanced Level exams (A-levels), which were designed to be more academic and in-depth than the O-levels we had taken two years earlier. I chose my three favourite subjects, English, history and religious education, and further annoyed my teachers by talking my way out of attending English lessons in favour of studying the set texts on my own, together with another girl who was also a 'smart alec'. We both scored A-grades in the final exams, and I can only imagine how irritated my teachers were by this success. As well as studying for the standard three A-levels, I also waged a war of wills with my teachers to be allowed to do a fourth A-level: art. They were opposed to it, claiming that it would be too difficult to timetable all four subjects, but I was stubborn and eventually got my way. Although it meant spending many lunch hours in the art-room in order to stay on top of the syllabus, I never regretted doing it. I have always loved painting, drawing and sculpture; it's a passion I was born with. At one time I seriously considered going to art school, but even I could not work out how that was a route to making a living.

Debating was another passion of mine at school. We took on Harrow County Boys, defeating them in debates on topics such as women's liberation. I genuinely loved debating, unlike some of the other girls, who I suspect may have joined the debating society solely in order to have something to put on their university application form. I was regarded as flamboyant – good at speaking up and speaking out. It was a very traditional girls' grammar school and we were not encouraged to discuss matters openly, nor did we do much public speaking. The existing debating society was quite poorly attended, but I was so keen on it that I volunteered to use the time I saved by not attending English lessons to run a debating club for younger girls at the school. I enjoyed working with and encouraging them, and seeing them grow in confidence. As the only Black girl in the school, I stood out no matter what I did, so I was not afraid to put my head above the parapet. That did not necessarily go down well with the teachers, though I was by no means unpopular with every one. My history teacher in the sixth form, Anne West, later recalled that our lessons were never dull because we were always willing to get into discussion and debate – she noted that I was particularly good at that! I was always willing to question a perspective, to disagree sometimes and to offer a different critical opinion, but never in a way that she could object to.

The year after I passed my eleven-plus exam, my brother also passed his and went to Harrow County Grammar School for Boys. Both our schools were, figuratively and literally, in the shadow of the imposing Harrow School, one of the top public schools in the country (although I did not know this at the time). We had absolutely nothing to do with each other. Initially the main reason that I knew the public school was up the road was because I had read about it in novels.

Harrow County Boys was consciously modelled on the public school: it had a head boy, for instance, who wore a gown on special occasions. And just as the boys' school modelled itself on the public school, so Harrow County Girls modelled itself on the boys' school. Their school was much bigger than ours, with a sixth form of 300 boys and eight science labs to our four. But my school took itself seriously. One year it even invited the Labour MP Merlyn Rees (who later became a Cabinet minister) to speak to our sixth-form society about Northern Ireland.

On sunny days a small group of friends and I used to walk out of school and up Harrow Hill in our lunch hour. Often we would go to a café on the high street for a soft drink. The public school was set in extensive grounds well back from the road, and we did not give it any thought. After taking this little expedition several times, my friends and I were nonplussed when one day the café proprietor came out to speak to us and asked us not to visit her café again. We puzzled about what the problem might be. Perhaps she thought we were there to lure Harrow boys into wrongdoing, although anything less alluring than us lumpy girls in our school uniform would be hard to imagine. Or maybe she thought that state-school children brought down the tone of her establishment. I never found out, but in my mind it reinforced a sense of social apartheid between state and private schools.

In the sixth form I started going out with boys from the grammar school. My first serious boyfriend, Peter, was from Harrow County Boys. Our social lives were mostly restricted to parties at our parents' houses or lying in the sun on the hillside opposite our schools, flirting discreetly. No clubbing, no live bands, no illicit substances, just casual get-togethers most weekends in our family homes. It may have been the 'Swinging Sixties', when teenagers were becoming more assertive, but that carefree attitude hadn't filtered through to suburbia yet. Peter was a gentle white boy; he was attracted to me straight away, after he first spotted a girlfriend and me arguing with another boy at Harrow County, but had been too shy to come up to me. He assumed at the time that we were from Heriots Wood, another girls' grammar school in Harrow that was a little less genteel than Harrow County. A year later I went to a party at Peter's house and our romance took off. He was allowed to drive his mother's car, a lime-green Mini called Tilia, and when we were together we would often take walks, go to pubs, visit art galleries and attend parties.

I also got to know some other boys at Harrow County Boys through the joint sixth-form drama society, which was called Convergence. Some of the girls from our school who got involved in Convergence might have been real drama aficionados, but I suspect there were others who simply wanted to meet members of the opposite sex in an officially sanctioned scenario. The club met regularly, and among the drama productions that I was involved in were Shakespeare's *Macbeth* and T. S. Eliot's *Murder in the Cathedral*. A number of boys whom I met in those years, usually through the drama society, went on to make their mark in the wider world. Among them were Geoffrey Perkins, who was to become head of comedy at the BBC; Clive Anderson, who became a barrister, comedy writer, television presenter and radio host; Nigel Sheinwald, who had a distinguished Foreign Office career and became Britain's ambassador to the United States; and Michael Portillo, who went on to be a Tory MP, Cabinet minister and contender for the leadership of his party, although when we were sixth formers he was apparently a Labour Party supporter. We were not so close then, but he claims to have given me my first screen test for the role of Lady Macduff in *Macbeth*.

In the upper sixth form I performed well in my A-levels and was one of two girls who came joint top of the year. I got distinctions in three of my four A-levels. Before I sat them, I had already made an important and unusually bold choice: I had decided to go to Cambridge University. Going to any university was extremely aspirational for a girl whose Jamaican immigrant parents had left school at the age of fourteen, and although Harrow County Girls did send some pupils on to further and higher education, unlike Harrow County Boys School the girls' school did not routinely send pupils to Oxford or Cambridge.

The ambition took hold of me when, in the sixth form, I went on a school-organized coach trip to Cambridge, some fifty-five miles north of London. Being more accustomed to coach trips with my family to seaside resorts, I did not know what to expect, but as soon as I arrived I thought Cambridge was nothing short of magical. On that unforgettable trip I saw King's Parade for the first time, a central street in the heart of Cambridge around which most of the oldest and most impressive colleges were grouped. These included Gonville & Caius, Peterhouse, Pembroke, St

Catharine's and King's College. The vista was dominated by King's College Chapel with its late-Gothic architecture. I had never seen a more beautiful building. I gazed from the windows of the coach at the students wafting around the city's wonderful buildings, with their striped college scarves floating behind them. They seemed completely at ease. It may well be true that many Cambridge students were as awkward and lacking in confidence as young people anywhere else, but to me they looked like princes and princesses.

Nobody in my immediate family had been to university, let alone Oxford or Cambridge. My parents believed devoutly in education and wanted what was best for me, but Oxford and Cambridge were entirely outside their field of vision. Attending Cambridge University was altogether my own idea, perhaps inspired by the novels I had consumed from a young age, in which the characters invariably attended one of those two universities – and the sensational architecture I saw on the day of that school trip clinched it for me.

Cambridge is an institution that is challenging enough for working-class children and Black children to get into today. Fifty years ago, when I decided that I wanted to give it a try, it was much more difficult, and being a girl made it even harder. Cambridge is a collegiate university, and at the beginning of the 1970s only six out of the thirty university colleges admitted women at all. Four of those were the all-female colleges: Girton, Newnham, New Hall and Lucy Cavendish. In the early 1970s only 17 per cent of Cambridge undergraduates were female and, to add insult to injury, an institutional bias favoured privately educated children, just as it does today. At that time only 7 per cent of British children went to private school, but 60 per cent of Cambridge undergraduates were privately educated; and Oxford University was no better.

The systemic problems that Black children from a state school would encounter in the process made trying to get into Oxford or

Cambridge seem unimaginable. Applications were not accepted on the basis of A-level results alone, and candidates had to sit a special Oxford or Cambridge entrance exam. To make this even more challenging, we were also required to sit a separate Latin exam. Cambridge designated subjects such as Classics, history, geography or any modern language as arts subjects, and the rule was that if you wanted to study any arts subject, then you had to sit the separate Latin exam. This eliminated a great many state-school children who had never studied Latin at all. Luckily I had at least a GCSE in Latin, but I had dropped the subject at A-level, so by the time I started thinking about Cambridge it was nearly two years since I had touched a Latin textbook.

Next came the Cambridge interview, which posed a challenge for state-school children, who did not necessarily have the confidence or the verbal fluency – not to mention the sense of entitlement – that characterized many privately educated children. Fee-paying schools tended to have plenty of experience in preparing for these hurdles and what was needed to surmount them. I, however, in common with most state-school children, had to come back to school after the end of the upper sixth and do another term to sit the Oxford and Cambridge entrance exam. Anyone who even considered applying needed support and extra tuition from their school, but unfortunately my teachers at Harrow County Girls were not very encouraging.

I went to see my history teacher, Miss Buckley, still starry-eyed from my Cambridge visit, and declared emphatically to her that I wanted to sit the entrance exam. She gave me a hard stare, paused and then said, 'I don't think that you are up to it.'

Returning her stare, I said firmly, 'But I *do* think I am up to it. And that is what matters, isn't it?'

Where I found the courage and determination to stand up to my teacher like that, I still do not know, but I got what I wanted. The reluctant teacher finally set about preparing me for the Cambridge entrance exam. There were just two of us applying from the school, me and a middle-class white girl named Penny. Without consulting us, the teachers put her application in for Girton College and mine in for Newnham College. They seemed to think that Newnham was less prestigious, perhaps because in the nineteenth century Girton was seen as a college for ladies while Newnham was seen as being for governesses. Of the two of us, my teachers unquestionably saw Penny as the lady.

One of the first questions my history teacher asked me, when she had resigned herself to coaching me for Cambridge entrance, was, 'What daily newspaper does your family read?'

I said brightly, 'The *Daily Mirror!*'

She looked pained. After that, every week she would bring into school for me a copy of a newspaper called *The Guardian Weekly*, a bumper version of the daily *Guardian* broadsheet that I found a little dull. I assume she brought it in to compensate for what she considered the cultural and intellectual wasteland of my family home.

For that whole extra term I laboured over the practice papers and plugged away at my Latin. I don't remember rehearsing for the interview, but fortunately the one thing I have always been able to do is talk – and all that reading meant I had plenty of ideas to draw on.

My headmistress had to write an evaluation of me to accompany my Cambridge application, in which she said that I had shown from a relatively young age the 'powers of penetrating insight, mature understanding and a capacity for abstract reasoning which have marked her out as a rare pupil. She has a quick mind and unusual independence of judgement though the tenacity of her personality, not to say stubbornness at times, occasionally has led her to persevere in somewhat idiosyncratic views which she nevertheless argues with great cogency . . . She is blessed with a sense of humour which makes her a witty and provocative conversationalist.'

The interview at Newnham College, which took place in

December 1972, went quite well, although as it was my first time actually being inside a Cambridge college, it was a somewhat intimidating experience for me. Founded in 1871, Newnham was not the university's oldest college, but everything about it was designed to awe you: the beautiful red-brick buildings in Queen Anne style, the lovely gardens, the paintings. One interviewer's study was lined with books and I was particularly impressed to see on the shelves one of her own books, with her name printed down the spine: it was the first time I had met a published author. With the other interviewer I gave a good account of myself, but I was so overcome with nerves that I spent the whole interview staring down at her shoes. I was looking at them so intently that they engraved themselves on my memory: navy, very smart, with bows on the front.

Both interviewers were positive afterwards. One noted, 'I thought this girl a definite possibility. Eager – a bit sprawling. But might come on quite well. Definitely interested in art history. Talked intelligently about it.' The second interviewer agreed with her colleague's positive assessment: 'Passionate enthusiasm, very good on the uses of religious knowledge to historians. Is stubborn – but determined. Worth having a go at.'

And so it was that, in 1972, Newnham College offered me a place to read history. As a fresh undergraduate walking through the gardens at Newnham, I spotted someone wearing a familiar pair of navy shoes. It was, of course, my second interviewer – those shoes had so deeply burned themselves into my consciousness that I recognized them even before I recognized her.

I learned later that I was only the third Black girl ever to be awarded a place at Newnham. A Nigerian called Adetoun Ogunsheye had studied there in the 1950s, and a Ghanaian woman called Akua Asabea Ayisi went there as a mature student, graduating in 1959. Had I known the odds against me being offered a place at Cambridge, I might have thought twice before putting in my application. The fact that my teachers were not keen might also have put off a less stubborn girl. But I did not know the scale of the task I had set myself, so I simply got on with it.

Once I had my place at Cambridge, preparing for life as an undergraduate was challenging. I was still dating Peter, my boyfriend from school, but he had left a year earlier for Bath University, where he was studying geophysics. Meanwhile his mother and mine masterminded most of the practicalities of my student life, though neither of them had been to university themselves or had any experience of the world into which I was being propelled. Ever the devoted mother, Mummy – who was still living and working as a nurse in Huddersfield at the time – scoured the market stalls of West Yorkshire for tasteful dresses, jumpers and cardigans. Peter's mother was a whizz with a sewing machine and bought bulk quantities of green and brown polyester, labouring away to make me a set of carefully coordinated outfits. I had two sets of polyester trousers, skirts, jerkins, jackets and capes, one set in green and the other in brown. It was a labour of love on the part of both women. The only problem was that university students in the mid-1970s did not wear coordinated polyester outfits, together with matching acrylic jumpers from street markets. Generally female students wore jeans and cheesecloth tops. I stood out at Cambridge primarily because you could count the Black students there on the fingers of one hand; but in my early weeks I also stood out like a green-polyester sore thumb.

Being an undergraduate at Newnham was a revelation. I soon learned that at Harrow County Girls' Grammar School I had merely dipped a toe into the world of the white middle class: Cambridge meant complete immersion. It was a whole new world in so many ways. In the first meeting with our college tutor, I met the other history students in my year, as we all sat cross-legged on the floor of her study. For so long I had been focused on getting into Cambridge for its own sake. Apart from knowing that I would be surrounded by lovely architecture, I had not given much thought to what it would be like when I finally got there.

Now, looking at my fellow students sitting on the floor around me, I felt a sinking realization for the first time that I had unwittingly propelled myself somewhere alien, full of posh white girls with whom I had little in common apart from a certain facility in taking exams. *What have you gone and done now?* I thought gloomily to myself.

I was also struck by the endless formality of everything. My first meeting with my college tutor, on my own, was at noon. I was taken aback to be offered a glass of wine. My parents did not drink wine at all. In the Abbott family household – apart from Christmas, high days and holidays – there would be one bottle of Emva Cream sherry stored in the cocktail cabinet, which often lasted several months. Formal college dinners at Newnham began with toasts to the Queen and the founders and benefactors of the college, and there was a strong sense of being part of British history. As the child of immigrants, I had mixed feelings about the emphasis on history. On the one hand, I was genuinely interested in it; after all, I was doing a degree in the subject. On the other hand, the more I was immersed in this history, both formally and informally, the more I began to wonder how much I personally identified with it. It did not escape my attention that the history I was being taught – the history that informed the college rituals – was not about people who looked anything like me. I never learned a single thing about the transatlantic slave trade, or Black people living in Britain or those in the former British Empire.

At these regular formal dinners the students and fellows wore academic gowns. The students themselves even put on sherry parties for one another. The occasional glass of Emva Cream sherry for visitors at home was one thing, but an actual sherry party was a social phenomenon I had not come across before. Some students had parties in the college where the men wore dinner jackets. I had never in my life been to a party where anyone wore a dinner jacket. Once, while dining in hall at Newnham, I was taken by surprise to hear a fellow undergraduate talk airily about her family's country cottage. My parents had held on to their house in Paddington, but it was split into flats for rental. No family that I knew had a country cottage.

In those first few weeks I met a fellow history student named Adam Low. We were both initially unhappy at Cambridge, which drew us together. He was riveted by me when he first met me, later remarking, 'I had never met anyone so green in my life.' I think he was referring to the colour of my polyester outfits, but he might well have meant my social understanding. He was far more used to academic life than me, since his father was vice-chancellor of the Australian National University. His doting mother used to fly regularly from Australia to see Adam. When on every visit I was the only girl that he introduced her to, she might have thought she was going to end up with a Black daughter-in-law. In fact Adam was gay, although he did not come out to his family until he was thirty-five.

Adam became a good friend and ally. He soon spotted that, however well read I was, nothing had prepared me for the social niceties of Cambridge. He lived in a small house on the edge of town that his parents had bought for him. As the university term rolled on, he would hold little dinner parties for me and his other friends. They were fun, informal affairs and I always had a great time. Every meal would feature some edible item that I had never seen before in my life. It was at one of Adam's dinner parties that I first came across artichokes. In the most casual way imaginable, he taught me how to eat the novel foodstuff, so while I was getting used to being the only Black person in the room, thanks to Adam at least I would never be the only person in the room who did not know how to tackle an artichoke.

Apart from this friendship, I often felt lonely in the early months at Cambridge. I realized that many of the other undergraduates already knew people there. This might have been because they were at school together, or maybe acquaintances from a school that they knew of. More generally, other under-graduates tended to come from the same social milieu as their fellow students and I was sometimes caught out by that. At one gathering I was ranting on about the new Labour Home Secretary, Roy Jenkins, calling him 'smoothie chops' and complaining about how slimy he was. It was only afterwards that someone pointed out to me that his son, Ed Jenkins, had been standing nearby, listening quietly.

Although I made friends at Cambridge, my social life was not particularly hectic. There was a continuing undercurrent of racism that often reared its head; at least once I was refused service in a shop because I was Black. My unease at being from a different social background than most of my peers did not fade easily, and I felt much more socially isolated than many of them did. Penny was the only other girl from my school studying at Cambridge when I was there, but she was at Girton College, quite a way out of the town centre. In any case we had not been friends at school, and we never spoke during the whole three years that we were at Cambridge.

Those early months were often spent sitting alone in my room in Peile Hall. My faithful boyfriend, Peter, thought that it was a large and lovely room compared to his university lodgings, but somehow I did not spend much time taking in its interior. Instead, one of my main recreations, when Peter was not visiting, was toasting bread in front of the gas fire. Sometimes consuming that toast was the highlight of my day. Thankfully I was able to see more of Mummy by then, having moved out of Daddy's house. I either stayed with friends of hers in London or visited her in Huddersfield.

Peter and I kept in close contact throughout my first term and I thought of him as a comforting presence, although this didn't necessarily make me feel less lonely from day to day. We telephoned each other regularly, wrote lots of letters to one another and took innumerable railway journeys between Bath and Cambridge. I would smuggle him into Cambridge libraries so that he could get on with his academic work, and Peter even accompanied me to some of the drinks parties given by the principal of Newnham College, Jean Floud. At the end of one of his visits to Cambridge, as we were on our way to the railway station for Peter's return train to Bath, something startling and upsetting happened that rather shattered our bubble of young love. We were walking past the Perse School, an elite private school in Cambridge, when a group of boys on an upstairs floor spotted us and promptly leaned out of the window and started making monkey noises at me as loudly as they could. Shocked, upset and furious, we wrote to the Perse complaining about the offensive behaviour by their pupils. The school and the ringleaders sent three separate very polite letters of apology back. But it was a reminder to me not to get too caught up in the lovely architecture and the aura of unreality surrounding me. Racism was as real at Cambridge as anywhere else.

The university itself was an extremely white world. There were only two other non-white undergraduates at Newnham when I was there: one was South Asian and the other was a mixed-race girl. Apart from that, in my three years studying at Cambridge I never met a Black British student except when I unexpectedly bumped into a male student while browsing the shelves of the university library. We were both so startled to see one another in such a monolithically white environment that neither of us could think what to say and we scuttled off in opposite directions.

After the first few miserable months at Newnham, during the Christmas break of 1973 I got a temporary office job and started talking with a friendly neighbour at the next desk. Eventually I confided in him that I was so overwhelmed by Cambridge, and felt so out of place, that I was thinking of leaving altogether. He was very firm in saying that I should do no such thing, insisting that I would overcome all my angst and should just get on with things. We never met again, but I didn't forget that conversation. During that Christmas break I gave myself a makeover. The coordinated green and brown polyester outfits were jettisoned in favour of denim and cheesecloth. I bought myself contact lenses and got a smart new hairstyle. Adam said later that I had come back as a different person.

When I had finally settled down to being a Cambridge undergraduate, I discovered that I loved spending hours in Heffers Bookshop on Trinity Street. Being surrounded by books was my idea of heaven, and stepping into Heffers was what I imagined it would be like to board an ocean liner. I relished walking along the streets of Cambridge and drinking in the beautiful architecture – not just King's Parade and all the picturesque colleges, but also the Sidgwick site, across the road from Newnham, which housed many of the arts faculties. These were all in modern buildings, and none was more spectacularly contemporary than the Seeley Library, which was named after the Victorian historian John Robert Seeley, a passionate defender of empire (though I did not know it at the time). For three years, when I was not in lectures, I spent most of my daylight hours there. It was so close to my college that I could virtually roll out of bed and get on with my studies. It was the Gothic architecture of King's that had attracted me to Cambridge in the first place, but I spent so much time at the Seeley that it engraved itself on my mind as the ultimate image of studying at Cambridge. The Seeley was as impressive as any Cambridge Gothic gem, but it could not have been more different from something like King's College Chapel. I was astonished by this uncompromising example of modern architecture, all red brick, elaborate glazing and spectacular glass roof. It was a high building with all kinds of precarious-looking outside steps and staircases. I later found out that the architect, James Stirling, had been a paratrooper, so it clearly did not occur to him that some people might have a fear of heights.

The academic rigour of Cambridge took some getting used to. At school, despite the hostility of some of my teachers, I had been conscious of being among the top girls academically. But at

Cambridge I was, rather depressingly, merely one of many clever students. I had always been taught in a classroom with as many as forty pupils, so the one-to-one tutorial system that was a distinctive feature of undergraduate study at Cambridge was a shock to the system. There is a world of difference between sitting in a lecture hall crammed with other students taking notes, and sitting in your lecturer's study, just you and him (and it usually was a 'him', apart from the female senior tutors at Newnham) once a week. For one thing, it is harder to mask the fact that you have not actually done the reading. What's more, the academic who is running the tutorial might well have written the textbook.

A memorable tutor of mine was Professor John Dunn of King's College, who had written what was, on its publication in 1972, the definitive book on the subject of modern revolutions. The book covered the Russian, Chinese, Vietnamese, Mexican, Turkish, Algerian and Cuban revolutions and ruminated on how close these uprisings were to their supposed Marxist origins. Tutorials with Professor Dunn took place in his study in the shadow of King's College Chapel, and there could not have been a more dramatic architectural expression of the British Church and state. It was remarkable to sit so close to that spectacular traditional edifice while discussing the key revolutionaries of the twentieth century, from Vladimir Lenin to Fidel Castro. If there was one book I studied at Cambridge that provided a backdrop to my political thinking for many a year, it would be John Dunn's *Modern Revolutions*. I had read nothing about revolutions in O-level or A-level history and it was exciting to read that political activity, shaped by Marxism, could overthrow a right-wing state and build a better world. Sadly, in years to come most of the revolutions that John Dunn wrote about did not build a better world at all, but as an undergraduate I was young and idealistic, and reading how committed individuals can contribute to positive change was a lasting inspiration. I am not sure that Professor Dunn was as impressed with me as I was with his work. In his final report on me he wrote, 'I shall remember her . . . as the only student who has ever stamped their foot at me (and managed to do it sitting down).'

Professor Edward Norman, another of my tutors, was less influential. He would never have written a book about revolutions. In fact, had he reflected on revolutions at all, it was doubtless with distaste. He was a high Tory and for seventeen years was dean of the famously right-wing Cambridge college, Peterhouse. Mrs Thatcher thought so highly of Norman that she invited him to Chequers, the sixteenth-century country manor house at the disposal of British prime ministers. He argued that Christianity and conservatism were natural allies based on the moral superiority of the free market. Unsurprisingly, he did not think much of me. He made that clear, if obliquely, to my director of studies at Newnham, though I was never sure whether it was the colour of my skin or my politics that he objected to.

Despite the challenges of studying under historians like Norman, I also benefited from the work of a whole gang of younger progressive historians, many of whose lectures I attended; of these, Professor Simon Schama was perhaps the best known. The mere existence of this group gave a particular energy to the Cambridge history faculty in the early 1970s, for they demonstrated that, while Cambridge University is one of the institutions most emblematic of the British establishment, it was possible to be at the heart of it and remain questioning.

The Cambridge academic who had the most influence on me, however, was Professor Jack Pole, who taught the special subject 'Race Relations in the United States 1863–96', which covered the period after the American Civil War. I took the paper because it was the only thing in the entire Cambridge history syllabus that enabled me to look at race. I had studied in Britain from the age of five until my early twenties and, in some ways, it was a very fine education. I was taught by excellent teachers at my grammar school and by some top academics at Cambridge. Yet there was never any mention, or notion, of there ever having been a Black presence in Britain, let alone recognition that people who looked like me had made any contribution whatsoever to British society. It was a sharp contrast to my childhood world, where outside school, everyone I knew was Black. Although none of them were politicians or white-collar professionals, I never doubted that they were making a solid contribution to British society.

Jack Pole was the first academic who showed me that Black people had played an active role in history. I learned much later on that he had a lifelong hatred of racial injustice and had campaigned for the rights of Commonwealth immigrants in the 1960s, which was perhaps why he took a particular interest in me. In his teaching, he humanized slaves in a way that I had never seen a mainstream historian do previously. In addition he explained how, even after the Civil War, the white majority in the United States was reluctant to give Black Americans anything approaching genuine equality; but he also taught us how the former slaves stood up for themselves and did their best to rebuild their lives. Not long after we met, he introduced me to two distinguished Americans, Professor Robert Fogel and his wife, Enid. Robert was a white American and his wife Enid was Black. It was the first time I had seen a mixed-race couple up close. Robert and Enid were devoted to each other. They had to be – as late as the 1960s interracial marriages were illegal in some American states.

Robert Fogel had begun his career as a Communist Party organizer and then went on to become an academic. He was a distinguished economic historian at Harvard University, and in 1974 he wrote an important book on slavery called *Time on the Cross*. When I met him, he was spending a year as the Pitt Professor of American History at Cambridge. The formidable Enid was an associate dean at the University of Chicago's business school, and she was the first Black woman I had seen in an undoubted position of authority, in an era when most Black women one saw in the public space were popular music singers. There were certainly no Black female academics at Cambridge.

The Fogels had a big influence on me, mainly because they were so different from other Cambridge academics. Most of the others I admired from a deferential distance, but the Fogels were warm, kind and definitely more radical than most of their Cambridge peers. We got to know each other well. They were keen for me to do postgraduate study in America, although I ultimately decided that the academic life was not for me. Through them, I came to realize that there was a whole wide radical world outside Cambridge.

In my second year at university I got engaged to my long-term boyfriend, Peter. By this point he had forgiven me for straightening my hair in the sixth form (in the 1970s it was a rite of Black womanhood to stop wearing your hair naturally and to straighten it, but Peter had grown accustomed to my hair in its natural state, so this annoyed him). He had supported me through the traumatic aftermath of my parents' break-up and had put up with my father being suspicious and hostile towards him. Travelling to see one another at our universities on opposite sides of the country should have weakened the relationship but, if anything, it strengthened it. Above all, Peter was funny and kind. I was delighted with the ring he bought me, a diamond with sapphires clustered around it – blue being one of my favourite colours.

I had done another term at school in order to take the Cambridge entrance exams, so I began university a year after Peter and accordingly he graduated a year before me. Still in the throes of love, I attended his graduation with his parents, all of us glowing with pride.

At university I was able to dip a toe into politics, which I had mostly only read about until then. In the early months I went to a women's group in Newnham a couple of times; after all, an all-women's college such as Newnham, with more than a century of women's academic achievement – a college in which I was surrounded by confident and clever female academics – was bound to have some feminism going on. I didn't feel entirely comfortable at this group, in no small part because the other girls were so middle-class, and because they seemed to have mastered the rhetoric of 1970s feminism in a way I had not. Nevertheless I persisted in going to the meetings.

One week the group leader told us proudly that she was going to get a 'woman from the town' to speak to us the following week. I was not quite sure what the significance of the phrase 'woman from the town' was, but I went along to the next meeting anyway. It was when I got there and saw an ordinary Cambridge woman being inspected by female undergraduates as if she were a speci-men under a microscope that I realized that 'woman from the town' was a euphemism for working class. I still considered myself a passionate feminist, but after this I gave up going to that women's group.

One of the most important arenas for anyone with even a flicker of interest in politics was the Cambridge Union debating society, founded in 1815. Many of the Cambridge Union's former presi-dents went on to successful political careers. During one of the earliest debates that I attended, I spoke from the audience to argue vigorously against the Vietnam War, which was at the time ongoing, lasting almost twenty years until the fall of Saigon on 30 April 1975. I had loved debating at school and did not think I was doing anything remarkable; but a Black woman speaking in such a traditionally white and predominantly male institution caused something of a flutter. Max Beloff, a Tory academic from Oxford who later became the first principal of the University College of Buckingham, spoke in the same debate and commented favourably on my speech. Rather than feeling flattered, I found the furore a little off-putting – it made me feel like a laboratory specimen. I only occasionally took part in the Cambridge Union debates after that; you had to have quite a strong stomach for it. The Union was full of young men and a few women with a massive sense of entitle-ment, who seemed to be preparing themselves to give speeches in the House of Commons and generally be more eminent than other people in the outside world. It seemed to me that the Union debates were all for show and were essentially detached from reality, and all that self-important preening did not appeal to me.

Perhaps on the basis of that maiden speech in the Cambridge Union, the principal of Newnham College later sent me a note to say that Max Beloff and another prominent academic, Noel Annan, the provost of University College London, had written to her to express an interest in my future career at Cambridge. There was no formal mentorship that followed this, but I felt my presence at Cambridge had been noted.

Although I kept away from Cambridge Union politics, I did get involved in a lower-status but more practical type of student activity. In 1974, after six years of protest and negotiation, Cambridge University agreed that three student representatives would be elected to the History Faculty Board. Much of their work was mundane: they approved lecture lists, granted funds to buy a new photocopier, noted reports from bodies such as the history faculty library and granted leave of absence to various lecturers. I decided to stand for election to the board, and in 1975, after a short campaign, I topped the poll and was elected the first student member of the History Faculty Board. It was my initial election victory. I was seen as strong and bold, ambitious and excited by interesting ideas, someone who had a sense of mission – and someone who was determined not to go quietly. I was aware of being in a minority, and I was vocal and even quite angry about the lack of representation of women of colour and the way that women generally could be put down. Above all, I was determined to change things.

The History Faculty Board was far less high-profile than the Cambridge Union was, but it gave me experience of politics, where I had none before. It taught me what it meant to sit on a committee, how a committee works, when the right moments are to intervene and how to talk over men.

In my final year I went to a series of Cambridge May Balls, by far the most glamorous form of social interaction at the university. Held in each college after exams, these balls were lavish, formal affairs for which tickets were suitably pricy. With relatively few girls studying at Cambridge, it was not hard to get a date, and in my final year I went to three such balls. One, at Selwyn College, was particularly memorable. Wearing a carefully chosen long evening dress, and made up to within an inch of my life, all in all I was quite pleased with my appearance. I entered the college through the Porter's Lodge, tottering slightly on my high heels.

I was scarcely inside when one of the student organizers of the ball rushed up. 'Oh, good!' he exclaimed. 'You must have come to do the washing up.'

It was completely jarring. He did not ask himself why anyone would wear an evening dress and diamanté to do the washing up. He saw only that I was a Black woman and therefore must belong in the kitchen. It was one of those moments – just as when the schoolboys from the posh Perse school made monkey noises at me in the street during my first term – that reminded me that I was a lone Black woman in an elite white institution and would be foolish to imagine I would ever really belong.

My final year at Cambridge was about more than simply May Balls. The more serious task ahead of me was giving consideration to what I would do after graduation. In my final year at Cambridge, my tutors submitted supervision reports that variously described me as 'an intelligent girl with a talent for challenging everyone and everything in sight', 'able and hard-working' and 'particularly interested in those larger issues which seem most relevant to contemporary social and political questions'. But, unlike some of my fellow students, I did not have family, or friends of family, to give me advice or to open doors towards careers. As a Cambridge graduate, I did not have to worry much about *whether* I would get a job; the issue was *what* exactly I would do.

Careers advice at Cambridge was rudimentary, particularly if you were a woman. I did, however, get two advice sessions. The first was courtesy of the university itself. It involved going to see the Cambridge Appointments Board. There I met a tall, rather grand lady. That grandeur is not what singled her out, however; most women academics and administrators at Cambridge, if they did not start out grand, became so. I remember her for the one thing she said to me. 'Whatever you do,' she advised portentously, 'do not learn to type. And if you do learn to type, do not tell anyone.'

It was not as silly a piece of advice as it might sound. She had seen too many women graduates, who happened to be able to type, going into ostensibly prestigious jobs in areas such as publishing and ending up as glorified secretaries. I followed her advice religiously, and to this day I cannot touch-type.

For my other session of career advice, courtesy of my college, Newnham, I went to see my hall tutor in her book-lined study. Hall tutors, although they were academics, were there to take a vaguely maternal interest in the young women in their halls. So in that final year, my hall tutor arranged to see me about my future career. She got straight to the point. 'What do you want to do?' she asked.

Without pausing for breath, I said firmly, 'I want to do good.'

She was undeterred by a response that managed to be both naive and grandiose. After a few seconds' reflection, she said, 'Ah . . . you want to be a civil servant.'

Though this seemed at first like a total non sequitur, women graduates' career options in the 1970s were so narrow that she might have suggested the civil service in response to any number of paths that I might have expressed an interest in.

My hall tutor reflected for a few more seconds before saying, 'The most powerful department is the Treasury.' Then she added, 'But you are not very numerate . . .' She concluded, 'The second most powerful department is the Home Office.'

And that was my Newnham College careers advice wrapped

up. I had no idea what the civil service did, let alone the Home Office. In particular I did not really know how the civil service operated at a senior level. However, I took my tutor's advice and I applied for the civil service via the administrative traineeship, a fast-track graduate entry scheme. The process was almost as elaborate as getting into Cambridge itself. First, we sat written exams. There were so many applicants from Cambridge that thirty of us took the exam in a hall at the university. We all went to some trouble to look quite elegant, even though it was an academic rather than a sartorial examination.

In the second stage applicants were divided into small groups. Then, under the gaze of an examiner, we had staged discussions and took decisions in a series of mock-up situations, to test our leadership qualities. If Cambridge taught me nothing else, it showed me how to assert myself in a group. So I sailed through this stage, and a few short months later found myself in Whitehall for the final selection board, which took place in London in a set of civil-service offices behind Admiralty Arch.

I rarely forget what I was wearing at the fateful moments of my life. That day I wore a blue smock in a floral print, embellished with frills. I had long strings of blue plastic beads around my neck, and my hair was styled in bobbly curls. It took so long to find the room where the final selection board was taking place that I began to think locating it must be part of the test. Eventually I did find it – a huge room with a very large round table, around which my interview panel waited, all white and male, except for the chair, the Oxford philosopher Mary Warnock, who was known for her writing on ethics and existentialism and who, incidentally, went on to be principal of Girton College. She was decidedly intimidating and, even then, one of the great and the good. What the panel must have thought when I bounced into the room, all frills and shiny curls, I dread to think. Anyone looking less like a top-flight civil servant was hard to imagine. To their credit, none of the five-person interview board flinched.

Mary Warnock fired the first question at me: 'Why do you want to be a civil servant?'

I looked her straight in the eyes and said confidently, 'Because I want power.'

Almost immediately I felt, rather than heard, a sharp intake of breath from the entire interview panel, with the sole exception of Mary Warnock herself.

But I did secure my job as a fast-track civil-service administrative trainee. Some months later I got to know James Warnock, who was one of Mary Warnock's sons. He was also living in London and we had friends in common. One day he confided that his mother had told him that mine was exactly the right answer.

At the end of three years, university graduation had finally rolled round. It took place in the June sunshine of 1976, amid all the splendid Cambridge architecture. Undergraduates were allowed to bring two guests. I made up my mind almost immediately that I wanted both my parents to be there, despite the fact that Daddy had shouted at and bullied Mummy and me for years, and that my parents had hardly spoken to one another since the divorce. My fiancé, Peter, who had known me since our schooldays, was quite fond of Mummy. After she had been in Huddersfield for a few years, he once remarked with affection that she had acquired something of a Yorkshire lilt. But Peter did not have much time for Daddy, so he implored me not to invite them both. He kept saying that if they both showed up, there was bound to be a row of some sort, but I would not listen. I felt strongly that, because it was such a momentous occasion and I would be the only Black person graduating that day, it was important to have my parents there to support me, and to demonstrate pride in who I was. Peter despaired, accepting with a sigh that he was not going to convince me to change my mind.

On the big day the weather was bright and sunny. My parents arrived together and both seemed proud to attend. After the ceremony in the university's eighteenth-century Senate House,

Newnham invited its new graduates back to the beautiful college gardens for a celebratory reception, complete with wine. It must have been quite intimidating for my mother, but she remained dignified. However, once we got to the event in the gardens, Daddy started to mumble, quietly at first, but then getting louder and louder. I was utterly horrified when he started to call the Newnham graduates 'prostitutes' – I had no idea why – and I was frightened that the other families might overhear him. I could not understand why he was embarrassing me and ruining my special day.

Looking back, I can see that he was secretly even more intimidated by the whole event than Mummy. If he had found parents' evening at school hard, this was a complete nightmare to him. There he was, a Black man who had left school at fourteen, surrounded by middle-class white people in the Newnham gardens in Cambridge. He must have thought – rightly so – that they would not want to talk to him, and so he dealt with his fear and anxiety by bubbling with anger.

Before he created a real scene, my mother and I ushered him back to my college room, where he seemed to calm down a little. Partly to distract Daddy, my mother suggested that we clear the room and pack up all my belongings into his car, starting with my books. Barely had we completed this, however, when there was some other altercation – perhaps me complaining about his awful behaviour at the post-graduation reception. Daddy stormed out of my college room, left the building and drove off, without me or Mummy, but with all my books.

I knew straight away that I would never see my precious books again and I was distraught. They were my most prized possession, and Daddy had driven off with every single book I had ever bought since childhood.

Mummy and I eventually got back to London on the train, and the next day Peter showed exemplary restraint in not saying, 'I told you so.' But what should have been a proud and happy day was marred by the loss of my books, for which I never forgave my father, causing a pain that still resonates in my memory.

Years later I learned that, despite appearances, Daddy was inordinately proud of me. He would carry a copy of my GCE results everywhere and (much to my brother's annoyance), given the slightest excuse, would whip them out to show whoever he was with. They were proof that I had listened to him in one regard: 'You should not just be as good as white people. You always have to be better.'

My relationship with Peter was not to last. As the time grew nearer for us to be planning our wedding, we both realized that marrying the first person you had ever slept with was not necessarily the wisest move. There was no falling-out as such, although it did not help that we both started to see other people, tentatively at first, and then more seriously. I had become friendly with Jack Pole's son, Nick, and eventually started dating him. Peter and I realized we both had ambitions that went beyond getting married in our early twenties and settling down in suburbia like our parents. In other words, we both grew up.

I was recruited by the National Council for Civil Liberties (NCCL) in 1978 as its race-relations officer. My role was to research and campaign around race issues.

3.   A Political Awakening

I never really had a clear-cut career plan for myself. To the extent that anything was planned, the path that I went on began in 1975, in my final year at university. Despite the fact that the 1970s are known for stagnation, strikes and the Winter of Discontent, for someone in their twenties graduating from university, there was still a certain optimism about the era. Though I did not expect a Cambridge degree to waft me magically into a high-paid profession, it was also true that I did not know anyone who wanted to work and did not have a job.

My parents, their friends and family members in Britain were not white-collar professionals – another generation would pass before seeing a Black person in most white-collar roles was not something to remark upon – but they worked hard. My parents' generation of Caribbean immigrants, often nurses or public-sector employees or factory workers, helped build institutions like the National Health Service (NHS) that Britain is so proud of today, though that was not properly appreciated by wider society at the time. For many of them, the public-sector roles in which they found themselves were part of their identity – jobs they could emphatically take pride in.

I embarked on my own working life with similar confidence, believing I would find a worthwhile job. Just as my mother had stepped into the world of work in Britain having arrived on a boat from Jamaica, so I stepped into the world of work having emerged from Cambridge University. The civil-service administrative traineeship, which I had jumped through so many hoops to pass, was purportedly a general graduate recruitment scheme, but it might as well have been an Oxford and

Cambridge scheme, judging by the large number of graduates from those two universities who joined it with me. The idea was that we would be on a smooth flight path to becoming senior civil-service officials.

Driven by the same sense of purpose with which my mother had begun working as a nurse, I embarked on life as a graduate trainee in the Home Office, a government department originally formed in 1782. Like all British government departments, it was led by politicians and staffed by officials. At the lower echelons, departments delivered services at a local level, and at the top tiers, officials gave advice to politicians with the aim of delivering policy. It was a monolith – an extraordinary place for a young radical Black woman to find herself in. Immigration, security, policing and all aspects of law and order came under the Home Office. All the officials were white and a large proportion of its clients were Black, which probably made it one of the most institutionally racist organizations in Britain. It was hardly a glamorous job, and it had certainly not been my lifelong ambition to work there, but women were just beginning in larger numbers to strike out into exciting areas of employment that were traditionally reserved for men. Job options for women graduates, even from Oxford or Cambridge, tended to be limited to conventional female roles such as teaching, publishing and the civil service. Of that year's intake of graduate trainees to the civil service, I was the only Black person. I had requested to go into the Home Office, remembering my hall tutor's advice that it was the second most powerful civil-service department. Power to me always held a glamour of its own. When I was a Cambridge undergraduate, my director of studies, Gill Sutherland, had written about me to the principal of Newnham, saying that I was interested in the mechanisms of power but inhibited in my approach to them, for fear I would be swallowed up by the establishment, the more so because I was a Black woman. I had taken my tutor's remarks seriously about how powerful the Home Office was, so it was not coincidental that my first job was so close to the heart of government. Just as my parents believed they could conquer Britain, I secretly believed I could conquer the Home Office.

Even if I had ignored the sage advice of the Cambridge selection board's advisor, I suspect I still would not have ended up in some subservient typewriter-bashing role. First of all, if there was one lesson Newnham undergraduates absorbed, almost from the walls of the place, it was that women were as good as men. Second, I did not have the kind of temperament that allowed me to slip unthinkingly into a glorified typist role. The civil service was the first institution – of a series, in the years to come – to discover that I was not easily squashed.

The Home Office was a dreary and stultifying place that put a heavy premium on conformity. Yet in its own way the civil service was meritocratic – that was the point of the elaborate administrative trainee scheme – at a time when many private-sector organizations were nowhere near as fair. Oxford and Cambridge graduates might have sailed through the administrative trainee scheme, but nobody rose to be a powerful government official simply because of whose son or daughter they happened to be.

It was a jolt for me to find myself there, on graduating from Cambridge in 1976. I did not support the elitism and class-based nature of the Cambridge system, but it was without question a lovely city, which I had become accustomed to in my three years studying there. I went from all that beauty to the Prison Department headquarters, which is where the Home Office had placed me. It had moved from its erstwhile location in Whitehall – the imposing and long-standing historical centre of the British civil service – to a shabby office in a tower block on Eccleston Square, at the back of Victoria railway station. It was physically run-down, with a tired, institutional look to it, but I soon learned that shabby buildings can belie the importance of the institutions they house. There was nothing tired about the way the Home Office wielded power. It believed in a command-and-control approach to bureaucracy, and while it was not the only set of civil servants to be dismissive of politicians, the Home Office certainly seemed to feel most strongly about marginalizing those who were elected to office.

However intimidated I might have been by this new job, it was undoubtedly a shock for the Home Office to 'welcome' the only Black person in the entire organization at administrative grade or higher. Almost everyone in the building was white. I once met a Black temporary secretary in the ladies' loo, an event that was memorable for its rarity; we both looked faintly uncomfortable and even embarrassed to see one another. Something about the forbidding atmosphere of the Home Office made reaching out to a fellow Black person seem inappropriate.

My role at the Prison Department gave me the opportunity to learn about other parts of the Home Office, including police and parole, since they were closely intertwined with criminal justice. It was not a department for exciting policy developments; since 1877, when the Prison Department was put under the control of the Home Office, its role has been to lock people up. For that reason, if everything is going well, the public will not hear anything about it. Some ministries, such as those of teachers or nurses, have a client base that will make a fuss if they are not happy with the way things are, but the Prison Department's clients are incarcerated men and women, and the vast majority of people will not listen to or care about them. So unless prisoners actually clamber onto the roofs of their prisons, their department may seem calm, even boring.

I'm not sure who was more surprised by the young Diane Abbott: me or my new colleagues. I ruffled a few feathers in my time there. My policy responsibility was young criminals, who in those days were held in a variety of places, including borstals, youth detention centres and young prisoner centres. Part of my job was to visit these prisons, accompanying a senior Prison Department official. On one of these trips the officers in charge of the main gate lifted it on our arrival to let the white male official in, but brought it down sharply to bar me, though I was only a few steps behind him. I was left with my nose pressed against the glass section of the gate.

Usually I tried on these visits to leave the talking to my senior colleague, but on one occasion the prison complained about me after we had left. Their complaint had no substance, which was unsurprising given that I had hardly said anything. What the prison officers seemed to be objecting to was the very presence of a Black female official. I later heard from a colleague that my seniors saw me as bright and intelligent, but also dangerous.

When I joined the Home Office in the 1970s the Home Secretary was Roy Jenkins (the very same Jenkins about whom I had been so rude – within earshot of his son – as an undergraduate at Cambridge). Working in the Home Office, however, I saw his merits as a forceful and reforming Home Secretary. Among other things, he had advocated strongly against capital punishment (which was abolished under Frank Soskice in 1965) and theatre censorship, as well as for the decriminalization of homosexuality; the banning of racial and sexual discrimination in employment (formalized in the Sex Discrimination Act 1975 and the Race Relations Act 1976); and the liberalization of abortion law and divorce law. During my first months in the job the National Council for Civil Liberties (NCCL), an advocacy group that campaigned against infringements of civil liberties, had published a report that severely criticized Jenkins for not fighting back against his officials on a number of human-rights issues: 'injustice in the courts, the abuse of police powers, repression in the prisons, the harsh operation of racialist immigration laws, intrusion into the individual's private life and the obsessive secrecy which covers the operation of government'. The same report said, 'Mr Jenkins prides himself on being a civilised man. There is nothing civilised about his decision to go ahead with the introduction of six months solitary in the control units for recalcitrant prisoners or his decision to increase the punitive power of unaccountable prison governors.' It was striking that Jenkins, considered by many a liberal, had been successfully brought round to senior Home Office officials' way of thinking on these issues. It was known that Labour Home Office ministers, in particular, were too easily intimidated by the smooth and confident Home Office mandarins, while at the same time always being anxious to be seen as reliably 'tough' on law and order. If even a clever and forceful politician like Jenkins could not fight back against the anti-civil-liberties bias of the Home Office, then there was not much hope for a less dynamic politician.

The more I understood about the role of unelected and unaccountable officials in the Home Office, the more concerned I became, because this department had responsibility for so many government activities that touch on the liberty of the subject, including prisons, probation, terrorism, immigration, drugs policy and criminal justice. Working for the Prison Department inculcated in me a strong support for civil liberties and the firm belief that it was wrong in principle that areas like these should be managed and directed in an undemocratic way.

This being my first proper office job, I also learned, mainly through observation, the niceties of office politics. The senior civil servants were government officials who had risen up the ladder to advise and support elected politicians. They generally had good manners and did not shout or bluster, yet they were ruthless about getting their own way and, if necessary, would thwart mere elected politicians. To some degree, senior civil servants were able to do this because they usually spent their whole careers rising to the top in a single government department, meaning that they knew more about it than elected politicians, who moved between government departments frequently, often before they were able to properly grasp what the department actually did. Furthermore, civil servants had the advantage of being able to focus on the work of their department. Whereas politicians are often distracted by what is happening in Parliament or even within their own political party, senior civil servants frequently excel at using their power and authority quietly behind the scenes. In fact it could be said that it is mostly career civil servants who run the country – and they do this while taking every care to pander to the vanity of their political masters.

It is easy for civil servants to get away with treating elected politicians as puppets, and this is particularly true of the Home Office. The department is so enormous and complex that it is very difficult to master, and it would be an unusual politician who took the trouble. Junior ministers often get moved around far too quickly to get to grips with such a large and sprawling department, so they fall into the habit of saying to themselves, 'If you don't understand an issue, just do what your civil servants tell you.' It doesn't help much that the media only give the Home Office their full attention when there is a prison breakout or a refugee crisis – otherwise, much of what the department does is considered boring by journalists. However, what I learned is that there is no issue so weighty or complex that it cannot be boiled down to a one-page memo. Even the act of thinking about the memo will have helped to clarify your approach.

On the job I spent a great deal of time reading files, partly out of necessity and often out of curiosity. Everything was stored in files made of brown cardboard, inside which would be months, if not years, of memos. Sometimes I read the files to research a topic or to obtain a specific piece of information. But on other occasions I would browse files to get a better understanding of the history of a particular policy, or simply out of general interest. There is one file I have never forgotten. It showed that Home Office civil servants were not merely dismissive of elected politicians, but were also unafraid to thwart them. It illustrated everything that was wrong with the British criminal-justice system and the way that the Home Office ran it.

I came across the file by chance and spent an afternoon reading every memorandum it contained. It was a few years old and the subject was the censorship of prisoners' letters. The very first minute on the file was a memorandum from a junior Home Office minister who happened to be a Tory. He had, unprompted, investigated the issue and decided that the routine censorship of prisoners' letters served no useful purpose whatsoever. When I first started reading the file, I naively assumed that this clear and unequivocal instruction from their minister would be enough to ensure that Home Office civil servants would scramble to implement his wishes. Nothing of the sort happened. Instead the original memo triggered a cascade of memos in response from middle-ranking and senior civil servants, some of which just tried to change the subject. Typically they rambled on about general issues, before saying anything at all about the minister's original memo. When they realized they had not been successful in deflecting the minister from his determination to abolish routine prison censorship of prisoners' letters, civil servants resorted to playing for time. The memo was passed up and down and all around the Home Office bureaucracy. A lowly administrative trainee like me was too junior to play a part in that process; I was only reading the file by accident. The original memo passed through the hands of a whole panoply of senior civil servants, from a Principal to a Senior Principal, to an Assistant Secretary, onwards to an Under-Secretary, ending up with the Permanent Secretary. Each senior civil servant who handled the file would add another memorandum.

By the time the file came into my hands, it was very fat indeed. At every single stage a civil servant had written, with great care and in elegant prose, why ending prison censorship was unthinkable in theory and completely impossible in practice. The junior Home Office minister was theoretically in charge of the Prison Department, but the file recorded how, in the end, he gave up and stopped talking about the topic altogether. Eventually he was moved to another ministry, which was convenient for the civil servants who were determined to kill off his idea. The moral I drew from that huge file was that it was virtually impossible for government ministers to get anything done if senior civil servants did not want it to happen. The Home Office, with its combination of secrecy and a bureaucratic class with a strong sense of its own omniscience, must be among the worst places for this.

Though it went through various reorganizations in the decades that followed, the Home Office has never strayed far from its core competencies of prisons, policing, immigration and security. It was the responsibility for these areas of government that earned it the name 'The Dark Department'. The Home Office is shrouded in secrecy. For instance, although it was set up in 1782, it was not until the 1980s that it released information on the number of Black people who were locked up in British prisons. And even though its clients in the criminal-justice system and the immigration service were often Black, the Home Office bureaucracy itself was overwhelmingly white. So heavy is the secrecy surrounding the Home Office and its activities that most people – including the majority of government ministers, Labour and Conservative alike – are unaware that in its cold heart the Home Office is an emphatically anti-civil-liberties organization.

Despite there being much to criticize about the Home Office, with regard to the internal bureaucracy it was a relatively fair-minded and meritocratic place, and I was fortunate in my managers. The department was no different from most public- and private-sector institutions of the time in terms of its employee demographic being overwhelmingly male, but by chance (or perhaps not), my boss at the Prison Department was a woman called Muriel Peck. She was the type of formidable senior female civil servant in whose footsteps I imagine my Cambridge tutor thought I might follow. Muriel was always conservatively dressed, with no apparent concessions to femininity or style. She was unsmiling and seemed a very serious and austere lady, though it turned out there was a softer side to her, and I learned that she was pleased to have another woman in the department. During the time that I worked for her, I took her to be committed to the single life, but after I left the Home Office I heard that she had gone on to marry another senior civil servant in the department, a Mr Wilfred Hyde. Imagine the flirtations going on behind the filing cabinets! Her nine-to-five austerity might have been her way of dealing with the oppressively male atmosphere of the Home Office.

My other boss in the Prison Department was a senior prison governor on secondment, Ian Dunbar. He was an attractive man, smartly dressed and far more relaxed than Muriel. It was impossible not to like Ian, and we got on well. He was cheerful, enthusiastic, energetic and genuinely wanted to reform the prison system. We talked a lot about the subject, though he never really confronted what was wrong with it. Despite being senior within the system, he did not stand up and challenge it – his approach was mostly to talk. After Ian's death in 2010 I discovered he had been awarded a scholarship to a college in Portland, Oregon, where he had met Martin Luther King and Paul Robeson, which had sparked a lifelong interest in civil rights. It was a sign of how highly regarded he was in prison policy that he was given an obituary in *The Times*.

I was one of two administration trainees who began working at the Prison Department at the same time. The other could not have been more different from me. Nigel Pantling was the archetypal high-flying civil servant: not only was he white and male, but he was also a former officer in the Royal Artillery. Although we may have seemed like chalk and cheese, I could not have had a more courteous and supportive colleague. We shared an office, and the layout meant that our desks were joined and we faced each other directly. In a time before computers and email, all non-verbal communications happened by minuting files and passing them on to colleagues or up the food chain to our superiors. Muriel was my boss and Nigel's, and she was determined not to discriminate in any way. She would come into our office with whatever file she wanted us to work on and, rather than favouring either Nigel or me, would hold the file equidistant between our adjoining desks and put it down. Then she would exit the office, leaving it to us to decide who did what work.

It was in 1977, while I was at the Home Office, that Daddy died at the age of fifty-four, from complications of diabetes. We were still estranged, but despite everything, I loved him. When I realized that he had died and I had not been there, I broke down. He had been harsh and controlling and had made my mother's life a misery; but certain decisions that he had taken, such as insisting I should stay in Britain rather than being sent to Jamaica to be brought up by my grandmother, and his choice to move our family out to suburban Harrow away from the racial disturbances of Paddington and Notting Hill, were important for my future. He had had a difficult life, like many Black men of his age; he had been made redundant from his factory work, went through a period as a minicab driver and then bought a shop in Northampton, which he worked very hard to keep going. Despite his many dreadful characteristics, he bequeathed me a stubbornness and determination that helped make me the woman I am.

When I graduated from Cambridge I moved back to London, and the first place that I lived was as a lodger in a flat in Pimlico, owned by a lovely Liverpudlian ex-actress called Sonia Lushington. It was Adam, my old Cambridge friend, who had connected us. When he realized that I was going to be in London for my Home Office job, his first thought was that she and I would get on. I learned later that she had rung Adam to say how much she would love to have me as a lodger, adding, 'It makes no difference, but you did not tell me Diane was Black!'

I had a very happy year with Sonia. Her flat was only a short walk away from the Royal Court Theatre, which had a reputation for daring new work and would feature Black playwrights when other theatres did not. One of the first plays I saw at the Royal

Court was in 1974: *Play Mas* by the Trinidadian playwright Mustapha Matura, which was about the links between the annual Trinidad carnival and the politics on the island. To me, theatre was always an important aspect of Black culture, which in turn is an essential dimension of Black politics.

I had enjoyed being Sonia's lodger, but she moved out of her flat to a house in Islington and I had to find somewhere else to live. The weekly listings magazine *Time Out* was the bible of young Londoners; much of it was taken up by entertainment listings and restaurant reviews. There was also a big section on rooms to rent and flat-shares. So I scoured the pages of *Time Out* for my next place to live and ended up in a flat-share in Belsize Park. My two flatmates were amiable white men in their twenties. We led quite separate lives, mainly because I was increasingly drawn into politics, so it was a rare occurrence when I and either one of them was at home in the evening. It was one such evening when one of them suggested that we go out for a drink at the pub. The evening passed unremarkably. Afterwards he said, unprompted and unexpectedly, that he felt that being seen out drinking with a Black woman gave him a tiny bit of status, a touch of excitement. Though not insulted, I was a little taken aback. It was the first time I had been objectified in such a brazen way.

I was still working at the Home Office, and my frustrations with the reactionary nature of the institution led me to dip my toe into political activity and join the Labour Party for the first time. I had never belonged to a political party while at Cambridge, mainly because I found all the young men and women there grooming themselves for parliamentary careers quite chilling, and I was not sure that they had any real political convictions. Joining the Labour Party was a minor act of rebellion: as a trainee senior civil servant, you had to ask permission to join a political party. Although nothing was explicit, it was understood that being a party member was unlikely to help you move up the career ladder. From then on, I pursued a twin-track career: by day as a Home

Office civil servant; and in the evenings and at weekends as an increasingly committed Labour Party activist. Living in Belsize Park meant that the very first local Labour Party I joined was the Hampstead constituency, which at the time was rather bohemian, with a largely intellectual, artistic, middle-class cohort of members.

It was here that I met Ken Livingstone. A Lambeth councillor and later the prospective Labour parliamentary candidate for Hampstead, Ken was not particularly bourgeois or artistic, but he was a big player in the London left. He knew everybody and everything that was going on, and he was the one who introduced me to left-wing London Labour Party politics. Ken was one of a cohort of young left-wingers who were then in the foothills of Labour politics in London, and I soon joined them. We had a distinct set of political views, including support for gay rights, race equality, feminism, campaigning for Palestine and support for a United Ireland. Support for gay rights was considered particularly extreme then; we were described as 'loonies', not just by the tabloid press but also by a great many Labour Party members, particularly outside London.

Our sympathy for the Irish republican cause was a position that few people in mainstream Labour politics had much truck with. The 1980s saw a series of bombings by Irish republicans on the British mainland. Targets included army barracks, top lawyers, the upmarket Harrods department store in Knightsbridge, and London parks such as Hyde Park and Regent's Park. It all culminated in the 1984 Brighton bombing, when an assassination attempt against members of the British government took place. Even in the late 1970s a glimmer of understanding of the Irish republican cause was wildly unpopular in all the major political parties. As someone whose parents were born in a British colony, it seemed obvious to me that if you were an unwilling subject of the British, then you had to fight for freedom.

In 1978 Ken and I went to the annual Labour Party conference, which that year took place in Blackpool. Like nearly every other Labour conference, it was held at a seaside resort because of the abundance of cheap hotel accommodation, though you hardly had time to focus on the sea. I was Hampstead's youth delegate, and Ken went in his capacity as the party-political candidate. It would be Labour's last conference as a party in government for nineteen long years, but it was my very first party conference and I loved it. I loved the way you were immersed in politics almost as soon as you got off the train. I loved the way political intrigue made the seaside air crackle with electricity. I was thrilled to glimpse the glitterati of the Labour movement, and I loved being able to observe the deal-making late at night in the back bars of conference hotels like the Imperial. It was here that I caught my first glimpse of important politicians in the flesh, such as the MP Tony Benn, and John McDonnell, who was elected onto the Greater London Council and then became Ken Livingstone's chair of finance. I also met Haringey councillor Bernie Grant – fearless, rumbustious and firmly on the left. Born in Guyana, he migrated to London in his twenties, became a trade-union official and then a councillor. We were all young Labour Party activists and part of a London left-wing insurgency, but I do not think any of us realized how often our paths would cross in the decades to come.

The party conference had a manic atmosphere – it was galvanizing and alive with possibility. One day, while hurrying between one meeting and another on the blowy Blackpool seafront, Ken introduced me to his long-standing friend and leading London left-winger, Jeremy Corbyn.

By then I had moved on from frilly smocks to jumpers and jeans. Warm clothes were essential against Blackpool's autumn chill. Jeremy was respectably dressed, also in warm clothes. The only mildly counter-cultural aspect to his appearance was that he wore no tie and had a beard. In an era when most left-wing men favoured jeans, tie-dye T-shirts and long hair, Jeremy's style was comparatively staid, if often untidy. This might have been because he started his working life as a trade-union official, and working-class people like their representatives to look respectable. Or it might have been because the Corbyns were a middle-class family. Or maybe, since his politics were so flamboyantly left-wing, he did not feel the need to advertise this with nonconformist clothing. We were drawn to one another from the moment we met: Jeremy saw me as energetic, determined and bright, and I found him funny and kind. I was impressed by his political commitment: he had long been a committed anti-racist and strongly opposed apartheid, so we had plenty in common and plenty to talk about. We discussed the Rivonia Trial that had taken place in apartheid South Africa in 1963–4, when several members of the African National Congress (ANC) were charged with militant acts of sabotage designed to 'foment violent revolution'. The outcome was the life imprisonment of ANC militants led by Nelson Mandela, who made a three-hour speech considered a key moment in the history of South African democracy, concluding with the words: 'During my lifetime I have dedicated myself to this struggle of the African people. I have fought against white domination, and I have fought against Black domination. I have cherished the ideal of a democratic and free society in which all persons live together in harmony and with equal opportunities. It is an ideal which I hope to live for and to achieve. But if needs be, it is an ideal for which I am prepared to die.' I was a schoolgirl at the time of this speech, but as I grew up, supporting the struggle against apartheid and campaigning for the release of Nelson Mandela became of great importance to me and, I soon learned, to Jeremy as well.

We were both surprised to learn that we had a Jamaican connection, too. My family of course hailed from Jamaica, and I visited the island most years. Jeremy, it transpired, had spent two years there as a young man on the Voluntary Service Overseas (VSO) scheme. He had taught at one of the top schools in the capital,

Kingston College, had volunteered at a small experimental theatre called The Barn and had helped at a rehabilitation centre for polio victims.

When we got back to London we started dating, and by November I had moved into Jeremy's house in north London. It helped that we were part of intertwined left-subcultures – Jeremy a councillor in Islington, me an activist in Westminster. Jeremy was easy-going and attracted to very strong-minded women. Early in our relationship he spoke admiringly about his first wife, Jane (from whom he had separated), and about how, when she was angry, she shouted so much that their dog Mango would race off into the back garden.

While Jeremy was absorbed with the Labour Party, I further explored radical Black liberation politics and expanded my interests and network in the anti-racism cause. In 1979 I attended the first conference held by the Organisation of Women of African and Asian Descent (OWAAD), a national umbrella group for Black women activists. I must have looked a little lost as I emerged from Brixton Underground station trying to find the venue, for a Black man with long dreadlocks deduced my situation and asked, 'Are you looking for the OWAAD conference?' I was amazed that he had guessed, but as it turned out there were a lot of Black women on their way to the conference that morning. The man offering assistance was Ricky Cambridge, one of the founders of the Black Unity and Freedom Party, who later became a friend and collaborator in radical politics. Ricky took me to the Abeng Centre that morning and the OWAAD conference commenced.

OWAAD, as the name suggests, aimed to unite Black and Asian women; it was the very bedrock of our politics. One of our slogans was 'Our Unity Is Our Strength'. OWAAD was established in 1978, and among its founding members were Stella Dadzie, Olive Morris and Gail Lewis, all well-known Black female activists at the time. The conference was a revelation; after attending mostly all-white Labour Party meetings, it was wonderful to be surrounded by other Black women, all learning from each other. It was the first time I had seen so many come together – more than 300 in one room. And it was the first time I had been in a meeting where everybody shared my perspective. Black liberation movements such as Frelimo in Mozambique were strong influences on our understanding, and we drew inspiration from international figures like the Jamaican prime minister Michael Manley, who served from 1972 to 1980 and again, from 1989 to 1992. He was a democratic socialist, a hero to the whole Caribbean and its diaspora – and, for his female admirers, it did not hurt that Manley was good-looking.

OWAAD soon inspired other groups to spring up, such as the Brixton Black Women's Group and Southall Black Sisters, which was established in August 1979 after the killing of the New Zealand teacher Blair Peach during a demonstration against a National Front rally at Southall Town Hall. After spending my childhood, adolescence and university life largely feeling quite isolated as a Black woman, I was blown away by OWAAD, and it remained my main Black political connection for some time.

There were five talks at the conference that day: on education, the law, healthcare, employment, and the anti-imperialist struggle. Black children and institutional racism in the British school system was by then already a key issue for the Black community – Black mothers in particular. In 1971 New Beacon Books had published an influential book by the Grenadian revolutionary and educationalist Bernard Coard, entitled *How the West Indian Child is Made Educationally Sub-normal in the British School System*. It had been written following a leaked report by the Inner London Education Authority in which it was revealed how the education system was discriminating against Black children, who were being pushed out of mainstream schooling and disproportionately sent to 'educationally subnormal' (ESN) classes, often based on IQ tests that were biased against Black migrant children. As a result of

Coard's publication, parents and educationalists sought justice, and one outcome was the establishment of supplementary Saturday schools, which were organized voluntarily; they might take place in people's homes, churches or any sort of community space available to them. The organizers aimed to support the children educationally and compensate for the institutional racism they faced in their schools during the week – all within the context of Black heritage. This might include African history, the history of the slave trade, the current struggle against apartheid, the campaign for civil rights in the United States and discussion of figures such as Martin Luther King.

We also talked about cultural matters. Times had moved on from the hair-straightening craze of my teens – wearing your hair naturally became not only fashionable, but a political statement. Our heroine was Angela Davis, the internationally known radical African American political activist and academic. For some time she featured right across America on Federal Bureau of Investigation (FBI) posters. And she was unmistakable with her big Afro.

OWAAD made the Labour Party look tame. We were committed feminists, but we were also trying to hammer out what a Black feminism would look like within the broader women's movement. We discussed prisons, policing, immigration, literature, Black history and revolution – and because of all these passionate debates, one of the earliest campaigns that I got involved in was the 'Scrap Sus' campaign. It was a fight against an early form of stop-and-search, led by ordinary Black mothers, in which we would march and go on pickets to protest at police harassment of, and brutality against, young Black men.

One of the important Black British figures of the time was John La Rose, founder of the radical New Beacon Books, the UK's first Caribbean publisher and bookshop, of which I was a regular customer. John La Rose came to Britain from Trinidad in 1961 and was a key figure behind many cultural initiatives, including the Caribbean Artists Movement (CAM), alongside writers Edward

Kamau Brathwaite from Barbados and Andrew Salkey from Jamaica. Other notable artists and intellectuals involved with CAM, which flourished mainly between 1966 and 1972, included the pioneering historian C. L. R. James, the cultural activist Stuart Hall and the poet James Berry. A younger generation inspired by CAM included Linton Kwesi Johnson, whose poetry and dub lyrics expressed the passion of his generation in terms of the struggle against racial oppression, and who published his collection *Voices of the Living and the Dead* in 1974.

Another prominent campaigner on behalf of the Black community was Darcus Howe. I first became aware of Darcus in the early 1970s, when he was making headlines as one of the 'Mangrove Nine', a group of young Black activists who had been arrested on charges of riot, affray and assault after a protest about the Mangrove Caribbean restaurant in Notting Hill being targeted with constant drugs raids by the police. A demonstration by 150 people at the local police station ended in violence and Darcus was arrested, together with Barbara Beese, Rupert Boyce, Frank Crichlow, Rhodan Gordon, Anthony Innis, Altheia Jones-LeCointe, Rothwell Kentish and Godfrey Millett.[1] Darcus, a former law student, chose to defend himself in what became a landmark trial lasting fifty-five days at the Old Bailey, the Central Criminal Court of England and Wales. I was in the upper-sixth form at the time and went on a trip to the Old Bailey to sit in the public gallery and watch some of the trial. In the end Darcus was acquitted of all charges. This is on record as the first time that a judge, in his summing up, acknowledged that 'evidence of racial hatred' had played a part – and it was no accident that the trial received wide interest as being symbolic of the relationship between Black people and the state. Darcus went on to edit *Race Today*, which became the leading voice in radical Black political journalism, chronicling the struggles of immigrant communities in Britain. As an anti-authoritarian Marxist publication, *Race Today* reflected Darcus's mentor (and uncle), C. L. R. James.

His orientation was towards independent political action, self-organization and the democratic proposition that 'every cook can govern'.

Black activists such as John La Rose and Darcus Howe made an enormous impression on me because they opened up a way of thinking and writing that was completely different from Cambridge academia; and their cultural work ran alongside politics. They helped to shift white left politics in Britain from being purely about class and trade unionism, towards reflecting the concerns of Black people. For the first time Black people were visible in mainstream left politics as something other than victims. A new Black politics was emerging. Up until the mid-1970s it had been very much about those who had been born abroad and the anti-colonialist battles they fought, and that still shaped their worldview. But now Black politics was increasingly about the Black men, women and their children who had been born in the UK, and while anti-colonialism was still important, issues such as education and policing rose up the agenda.

It was not inevitable that I would join the Labour Party. Many Black politicos of my generation steered clear of it, believing that the left tended to subordinate the politics of race to class politics. Instead Black political activists of the seventies and eighties devoted themselves to community politics. If I had not been in a relationship with Jeremy, I might have drifted away from the official Labour Party, but he drew me in and infected me with his love and enthusiasm for the party. I had never met anyone so absorbed by it. By day he was a full-time official for the National Union of Public Employees (NUPE), the predecessor trade union to today's Unison. His evening and weekend hours were taken up with being a Labour councillor in the north London borough of Haringey. Whatever spare time Jeremy had was consumed by being a volunteer organizer in various local Labour campaigns, and I could not help but get caught up in his whirlwind of activism.

When not going to meetings and on marches, I read Black newspapers such as the *Caribbean Times*, *West Indian World*, the *Jamaica Gleaner* and, from 1982, *The Voice*. This was before the existence of online communication and when mainstream newspapers carried virtually nothing about Black people, unless we were rioting or mugging. So Black newspapers were the only way to find out what was going on in the community. I also read a lot of the left-wing press, including *Tribune*, the *New Statesman* and *London Labour Briefing*. The satirical magazine *Private Eye*, although it was not politically left-wing, was rude enough about Tories and the establishment to suit me.

Having been to Cambridge and having worked as a Home Office bureaucrat, I had always remained very questioning of the establishment. This was, to some extent, because of how much it contrasted with my upbringing in a working-class Black community. People react in different ways to finding themselves thrown into a particular discomfiting situation. Some try to bury their origins and fit in with whatever institution they find themselves in. However, for me the same determination that made me want to go to Cambridge in the first place, despite my teachers not being encouraging, had made me question some of the thinking and assumptions that I found when I got there. Through my reading, hanging out in Black bookshops, going to meetings, talking to my girlfriends and to Jeremy, week by week I learned more about the social and political issues of the day. Whereas at Cambridge much of my time had been about academic learning, now I was beginning a lifelong course in political learning.

In many ways it was a great time to have this awakening, for it was a period when the left was on the rise, including inside the Labour Party itself. The left in the Labour Party had historically been based on the industrial trade unions, such as the mineworkers. There were also middle-class activists, often full-time union officials or lawyers and sometimes writers. During my early years in the Labour Party, Michael Foot was the Labour leader. He was a lovely man, a writer and journalist, and his passion was the Campaign for Nuclear Disarmament (CND), of which he had been a founding member in 1957. The dropping of the first atomic bomb by the United States on the Japanese city of Hiroshima in 1945, which killed thousands of innocent civilians, left people all over the world with an acute fear of nuclear war. At one point there was a lot of talk about 'tactical' nuclear weapons; German peace activists used to say, rather darkly, 'The more tactical the nuclear weapon, the deader the German.' The British left, both inside and outside the Labour Party, rallied around CND, which organized huge anti-war events – and although the sentiment was well supported by ordinary Labour Party members, the leadership regarded the anti-war movement with horror.

Alongside the political causes we were committed to, Jeremy and I had continued our romance, and in the summer of 1979 we went on a camping holiday in the South of France. We travelled by motorbike and, Jeremy being Jeremy, it was a socialist motorbike, an East German model. It broke down regularly on our trip south, which I found rather irritating, but lovingly repairing his motorbike by the side of the road was Jeremy's happy place. When we reached the campsite I perked up. As well as enjoying the French countryside, I was looking forward to some delicious Gallic cuisine. I was horrified when Jeremy unpacked his motorbike saddlebags to reveal a week's supply of instant macaroni and other processed foods. After much discussion back and forth, I was able to argue for at least one restaurant lunch.

At Christmas that same year I learned where Jeremy got his personal austerity from. We spent the festive season with his mother and father, who lived in a pretty cottage in Shropshire. They were a lovely couple who could not have been kinder or more welcoming to me, but they practised true socialist frugality. I was used to jolly Jamaican Christmases, with all the customary foods (though better seasoned), plus all the Caribbean specialities, including rice and peas (with scotch-bonnet peppers, pimento, thyme, garlic and coconut milk), spicy stewed chicken, curried goat and rum cake. To drink, there would be a ruby-red sorrel drink made with hibiscus petals and spices; and my favourite Caribbean drink, carrot juice with lashings of condensed milk, vanilla, nutmeg, cinnamon and a touch of rum. There would also be plenty of alcohol on the Christmas table. Christmas at Jeremy's family home was quite different, his mother and father being more abstemious, moderate consumers to a fault. Dinner seemed mostly about boiled vegetables; a turkey was their sole concession to the festive season. The house was freezing and there was no alcohol.

Around that time I began to realize that, realistically, ours was not a match made in heaven. We were too different. I had a range of interests and enjoyed reading and the theatre, but Jeremy was 99 per cent absorbed in party politics. The only other thing I remember him spending time on was growing vegetables in his back garden. Once, after I lamented our lack of social activity as a couple, he pondered it for a few days and told me we were going out. Feeling excited, I dressed up nicely and we bundled into the car. I couldn't wait for this surprise and had no idea where we were going – perhaps a nice wine bar? It turned out that Jeremy's idea of a social outing was to drive me to Highgate cemetery and proudly show me the tomb of Karl Marx.

Our affair continued for a short while longer, conducted mainly in between attending meetings, before gradually collapsing. It was not an acrimonious split; Jeremy does not do acrimony. A couple of our mutual friends – the Haringey councillor Bernie Grant and Islington councillor Keith Veness – helped me move my belongings out of Jeremy's house. There were no regrets for either of us: for me, meeting Jeremy in 1978 had steered my political life in a new direction, and for that I was grateful.

As an administration trainee at the Home Office, I was moved annually from department to department. I did not have a choice of department and in my second year I was sent to the Parole Board. Although it was still part of the criminal-justice system, it was quite different from the Prison Department. There I had been directly involved in long-term policy decisions, and together with my colleagues I was at one remove from the men (and women) in the system.

By contrast, the Parole Board could not have been more engaged with the lives of individual prisoners. It was an advisory body made up of people such as judges, probation officers and psychiatrists. They made recommendations to the Home Secretary about whether and when prisoners should be released. Typical of the Home Office of the time, it was a process totally lacking in transparency and with no right of appeal. Every week small groups of members of the Parole Board met in a different part of the country and I was their one-woman secretariat, getting on the train to travel to their meetings, listening (but not contributing), taking the minutes and going back to headquarters to action the decisions. It was an interesting switch: at the Prison Department I had been concerned with keeping criminals in prison, and with the Parole Board I was involved in letting them out. Reading all those files about individual prisoners humanized them for me and left me with the lasting conviction that, unless someone is violent or a physical threat to others, sending them to prison does not necessarily solve much.

I was at the Parole Board for a year and I began to get itchy feet. Although my time at the Home Office was certainly formative, and I liked some of the people I worked with, in the end I could not wait to leave. I appreciated what I learned about government, but the longer I worked there, the more I realized that I hated what I had to do. The ethos of the Home Office was completely contrary to what I believed in; I could not visualize spending the rest of my working life locking people up, crafting racist immigration legislation and generally infringing on civil liberties.

So in 1978 I was recruited for an organization at the other end of the political spectrum: the National Council for Civil Liberties (NCCL), later renamed Liberty, which had historical links to the trade unions and fought against unjust laws, the over-mighty state and any infringement of civil liberties, speaking up about human rights long before this was fashionable. It recruited me as its race-relations officer – the first one it had ever had. Up until then the NCCL had dealt largely with civil liberties from a white perspective, but this was a time of change and it wanted to engage more fully with Black perspectives, issues and people. When it came to hiring me, it probably helped my chances that I had gone to Cambridge (in fact the general secretary of the NCCL, Patricia Hewitt, had also gone to Newnham). There were not many Black people working in professional roles in the late 1970s, even in the voluntary sector, and this continued into the following decade.

When I joined the NCCL it was having a debate about ethnic monitoring. 'Old school' NCCL employees were fiercely against it. They thought collecting data like that was giving too much power to the over-mighty state and was an intrusion on people's privacy. In my new role I was able to successfully argue that, without collecting data on ethnicity in relation to issues such as employment, it would be impossible to plan strategies to fight racism. The NCCL had Black people on some of its committees, but I was its first paid staff member dealing solely with race. As Patricia Hewitt noted in hindsight, my decision to leave the Home Office and join the NCCL caused such a stir at the Home Office that it let me leave all but immediately. I was one of the few – perhaps its only high-flying Black graduate recruit – and it was not happy that I was leaving, especially to go to an organization that it thoroughly disapproved of.

I had to get used to my new surroundings. The NCCL's were dilapidated and occupied a warren of cramped offices up a flight of stairs in a seedy building in a rundown part of King's Cross. With just fourteen staff members and two lawyers, the NCCL was a much smaller organization than I was used to from my time at the Home Office, which employed tens of thousands of people nationally. The only thing the two organizations had in common was that I was the sole Black person in the building.

The NCCL was frequently at odds with the Home Office, no matter which political party was in power. It was not afraid to be critical of Labour Home Secretaries, who tended not to be particularly interested in civil liberties; they seemed to think that an over-mighty state was not necessarily a bad thing, so long as it was in Labour Party hands. The NCCL had a major impact on public debate, because the arguments were on its side, its members were effective campaigners and additionally had a useful network of contacts, including in the media. The NCCL had a close relationship with the trade unions, going back to the hunger marches of the 1930s, and had been a strong supporter of the 1984–5 miners' strike when the miners' leader, Arthur Scargill, was being demonized by the media. To the Home Office, the NCCL was public enemy number one – which was why I was so pleased to join.

When I began working there, the NCCL already had a reputation as a nursery for people who went on to be prominent figures in the Labour movement. One of these was Martin Kettle, the research officer at the NCCL, whose parents had been distinguished members of the Communist Party. Our paths crossed very briefly: as I was arriving, Martin was leaving the world of left-wing advocacy to go into journalism. He always looked pained when I was around and, according to my NCCL colleagues, he did not really approve of me. Perhaps he thought me not left-wing enough, or maybe too smartly dressed. The NCCL in the late 1970s was a strongly feminist organization, at a time when feminism had not reached some parts of the Labour movement. This owed something to the presence of some notable feminists, including Patricia Hewitt and Harriet Harman. I was already a supporter of women's rights, and the feminism of the women with whom I worked and campaigned at the NCCL reinforced that. Up until now, feminism had not been on the agenda for most male progressives; for too many older left-wing men it was as if giving women the vote was the beginning and end of the conversation. When I went to work for the NCCL, however, progressive women (and some men) were insisting that organizing working people should include women. There was a push to put feminism on the agenda of the left, including of the Labour Party.

When I joined NCCL, Patricia Hewitt had already become something of a star in left circles. Born in Australia, she had come to Britain to study at Cambridge and had quickly lost her Australian accent, acquired a British partner and lots of British friends. Maybe it was because she was originally an outsider to society in the UK that she had a cutting edge when it came to criticizing institutions of the British state. She also used her charm, media skills, persuasive powers and considerable campaigning ability to build both her own and the NCCL's profile.

When I first met Patricia, she was not just a feminist, she was left-wing – so left-wing that MI5 suspected her of being a communist sympathizer. A strong supporter of Tony Benn, she publicly condemned those Labour MPs who claimed to be on the left yet had abstained in the hotly contested 1981 deputy-leadership battle between Tony Benn on the left and Denis Healey on the right. It was believed that, under the collegiate system of electing Labour leaders, Benn would have won, had a handful of Labour MPs not abstained. Left-wing Labour Party members up and down the country were furious, and Patricia waded in to attack the guilty MPs. But even then everyone at the NCCL knew that Patricia was looking for a parliamentary seat: the joke among colleagues was that some elderly Labour MP only had to look a bit poorly and Patricia would be on the train to his constituency the next day.

The organization pursued some high-profile campaigns for

female equality. One campaign that the NCCL backed to the hilt was the Grunwick strike, a dispute at a film-processing plant in north London that soon became a cause célèbre on the left. It involved 440 women workers, 80 per cent of whom were Asian and 10 per cent Black. A dispute on this scale, especially one that was all about ethnic-minority women, was unheard of. The strike was triggered by the sacking of Devshi Bhudia, a male worker, for allegedly working too slowly. Workers were also angry about the low wages and long hours. The average wage was £28 a week (while at that time the average national wage was £72 per week) and working overtime was compulsory. But as the unofficial strike leader Jayaben Desai said, 'The strike is not so much about pay, it is about human dignity.' The women stayed out on strike between 1976 and 1978, and Harriet Harman, who was the NCCL's legal officer at the time, gave it every support. However, the Grunwick strikers were eventually driven back to work.

Another challenge taken up in 1982 by Anna Coote and Tess Gill, who served on the NCCL committees, was a little more trivial, but attracted a huge amount of publicity. Anna and Tess wanted to stop a wine bar called El Vino's, much frequented by lawyers and journalists, banning women from standing at the bar and being served. Women had to sit in a back room and wait for a barman to come and take their order. It sounds ridiculous now and was ridiculous even then, but Tess and Anna nevertheless had to take their case all the way to the court of appeal. All three High Court judges who heard the case had to declare an interest because they all drank at El Vino's, which goes to show what an elite watering hole it was. Nevertheless, the judges still found in Anna and Tess's favour and proved the effectiveness of the 1975 Sex Discrimination Act.

Coming from a Home Office background, I was very much gamekeeper-turned-poacher at the NCCL. I was proud to go and work there, because the NCCL had a stellar reputation for campaigning on civil liberties and human rights. At the Home Office there had been individuals personally committed to reform, including my former boss Ian Dunbar, but the job at my grade and above was to implement what top Home Office officials (as opposed to elected politicians) thought best, to run the Prison Department as it had always been run and to collude with the veil of secrecy over the 'Dark Department'. It was ultimately too frustrating to be working on policies that I did not support and in ways I did not believe in. At the NCCL I was empowered to take dead aim at the Home Office and its abuses, and I was happy to do that; in the beginning I was simply relieved to have escaped the Home Office. Gradually, however, I began to understand that being a Black person in a left-liberal organization had its own challenges.

In one way the NCCL was more radical than the Home Office. It usually took the opposite view to the latter on anything to do with law and order. But as a Black person I felt oddly vulnerable. In the Home Office there was a structure, everything was done on paper and there was a process. Precisely because the NCCL was not structured in that way, it created a feeling of vulnerability. I thought the NCCL was going to be some nirvana of progressivism, but attitudes to me framed by race were still an issue there, if more nuanced. I had expected it at Cambridge and at the Home Office, but I was surprised to find it at the NCCL. The main issue was that it was accustomed to treating Black people as victims rather than equals. Its members were more used to emoting over pictures of fly-blown African babies than engaging with a real live Black woman bouncing around, who clearly thought she was equal to them all. I had ruffled feathers at the Home Office, albeit unwittingly, but I was surprised that I caused my colleagues at the NCCL a similar sense of unease. I don't know what I could have done about it, since my mere presence seemed to make for a combination of a vague sense of threat and a general feeling of discomfort. Some of my colleagues appeared to think I was not a 'deserving' sort of Black person – they thought me too confident, too smartly dressed. Initially I felt quite isolated, having not much in common with them, but I was determined not to let myself be put off and I threw myself into my job.

Fortunately we shared the building with the Institute of Race Relations (IRR). Previously it had been an academic organization with strong links to the government, but in the early 1970s most of the members and the staff began to question whether working so closely with politicians and the government would actually help the people and communities whose interests it was supposed to be serving. It was a clash between an essentially paternalistic model and the members and supporters who wanted the organization to speak for Black people and be a hub for activism. The internal struggle in the IRR effectively led to a coup, and the day-to-day running of the organization was now in the hands of its chief librarian, Ambalavaner Sivanandan, usually known as Siva. A handsome, charismatic man born in Sri Lanka in 1923, he had arrived in Britain in 1958, in time to witness the Notting Hill race riots. Siva later wrote, 'I knew then I was black . . . race was a problem that affected me directly.' On becoming the director of the IRR, he turned it into a radical Black think tank and continued to build up its library with books on colonial politics, Black history and Black literature.

Not too surprisingly for someone as wedded to books as I was, on discovering the IRR, I quickly acquired the habit of slipping downstairs to that library. Research was a significant part of my role at the NCCL and I would often spend hours there reading. The IRR published a journal on racism, empire and globalization called *Race and Class*. There were pamphlets and reports on issues including racism and the press, Black deaths in custody and school exclusions, and books such as *How Europe Underdeveloped Africa* by Walter Rodney. Then there were the autobiographical novels of Buchi Emecheta, *In the Ditch* and *Second-Class Citizen*, the latter described in a *Race and Class* review as 'something of a revelation', since its author was a Nigerian Igbo woman, whereas 'of the scores of books about race and black communities that had appeared during the 1960s and early 1970s, the great majority are written by white academics ultimately concerned with the relationship between white society and black "immigrants".' The reading that I did at IRR had a lasting influence on my politics: it was all writing that was not available in the libraries at Cambridge, that the Home Office probably considered subversive and that could not be found in the bookcases upstairs at the NCCL. It was also a relief to be able to speak to Siva, and the other Black people who worked at IRR as volunteers, about my role at the NCCL.

The NCCL had set up a race-relations committee two years before I started there. Part of my job was to facilitate the committee and work with its members. The committee included Paul Boateng, a socially committed young lawyer of Ghanaian and Scottish origin, who worked at Paddington Law Centre. Like any ambitious lawyer, he was customarily attired in a smart suit and tie; less typically, he sported a sizeable Afro. Another luminary on the committee was Trevor Phillips, who was well known even then as the first Black president of the National Union of Students. The race-relations committee's major campaign was a call to scrap the 'sus law', which allowed a police officer to stop, search and even arrest anyone suspected of breaching Section 4 of the Vagrancy Act 1824. It was an archaic law that had long been in disuse, but the Metropolitan Police revived it in the 1970s, using it as legal cover to stop, search and detain young Black men simply 'on suspicion'. As Paul pointed out, the first time there was any parliamentary discussion of these concerns we had support from David Pitt – whom Harold Wilson appointed to the House of Lords in 1975, making him the second peer of Afro-Caribbean heritage after the cricketer and politician Sir Learie Constantine – and from Eric Lubbock (a former Liberal MP who also served in the Lords, having inherited a peerage), but no support at all from Labour, who were in government. The Minister for Police answered the debate in the House of Lords and was actively hostile. It was clear, therefore, that we were not making any headway, despite the fact that the issue was of huge importance in many Labour MPs' constituencies.

After hearing about the campaign against the sus law via a leaflet in New Beacon Books, in 1978 I began to attend meetings of the Black People's Organisations Campaign Against Sus (BPOCAS). The twin aims of the campaign were to scrap that law and to demand an independent inquiry into police relationships with Black communities. The campaign was a crucial one, begun by working-class Black mothers distraught about how their sons were being harassed by the police; they were determined to do something about it. Radical lawyers and organizations, including the NCCL, took up the campaign to 'scrap sus' after these mothers had got it going. I had joined the campaign while I was at the Home Office and worked on it with even more passion at the NCCL.

One of the initial tasks in my new job was to organize a race-relations conference. It was the first one the NCCL had ever put on, and my colleagues' initial suspicion of me meant they were surprised that I had had the wherewithal to organize it. The conference was about both race relations and racial discrimination and was part of a strategy of reaching out to the Black community. It included sessions on immigration and nationality, discrimination in housing, local government, education, policing and 'scrap sus'. Speakers included young up-and-coming campaigners like Trevor Phillips and Paul Boateng, and prominent race-relations campaigners of the time, some of whom represented a more paternal old guard, such as Ann Dummett, one of the founders of the Joint Council for the Welfare of Immigrants. The conference broadened and deepened my understanding of race issues and confirmed that there was a new generation of Black activists coming forward. It was a pivotal period in the politics of race: campaigners were moving on from simple opposition to fascist organizations such as the National Front, to the more complex battle against institutional racism. Working at the NCCL opened up a whole new world of volunteering to me: it was a good fit for my political activities outside the office, as it enabled me to meet and learn from people who shared my values and campaigning instincts, many of whom I would work with for years to come.

In general, too, there was increasing evidence of organization within Black communities. In the late 1970s the Standing Conference of Afro-Caribbean and Asian Councillors (SCACAC) was formed by Russell Profitt, a councillor in Lewisham, and Phil Sealey, a councillor in Brent. In 1979, a couple of weeks before the general election, SCACAC called a conference where a 'Black People's Manifesto' was issued, laying out sixteen demands that were being made in the interests of Black and Asian voters. SCACAC's hopes of seeing this through were soon dimmed by the election result of May 1979, which ousted James Callaghan's incumbent Labour government and brought in the Conservative Party, led by Margaret Thatcher.

I was at the NCCL when Thatcher became the first woman ever to hold the role of British prime minister. She famously said on the day of her election that she would take inspiration from St Francis of Assisi and 'where there is discord we will bring harmony'. In fact, for her entire premiership she did the complete opposite.

In the voluntary sector we quickly realized that Mrs Thatcher was not a friend to the issues that we were campaigning on. This was partly because of her emphasis on free markets at the expense of community-based organizations; moreover, we saw from the beginning a number of clues as to how her political project was going to move forward.

In 1978, three years after she became leader of her party, she said, 'People are really rather afraid that this country might be rather swamped by people with a different culture and, you know, the British character has done so much for democracy.'

Unfortunately, her popularity soared after this speech. Those of us on the progressive side of politics saw this as dog-whistle rhetoric aimed at those who were uncomfortable with Britain gradually becoming a more multiracial society. It also became clear that Thatcher was prepared to use the police to clamp down on Black communities. Whether you were a Black activist in the community, a white ally or someone working for a voluntary organization, this was galvanizing.

The contours of her policies on a whole range of domestic issues also began to become clear, from slashing benefits to presiding over a steep rise in unemployment. Thatcher clearly represented a break with the British post-war social democratic consensus and became a figure detested by the left.

As the Thatcher era dawned, I was broadening and deepening my understanding of the politics of race. Within the NCCL itself, I increasingly had misgivings about being surrounded by white liberals oozing concern over me, but I could happily have stayed in the voluntary sector addressing the issues I cared about. However, my career took a swerve that I had not anticipated when I had been at Cambridge pondering what to do next. I was still at the NCCL when I embarked on an affair with a television executive. We had met at a party; after all, notwithstanding my political activity, I was still going to the occasional smart party. As always, I talked a lot, and he said later that he found me flirtatious. We embarked on an intense relationship that both of us found exciting, although we had virtually nothing in common apart from sexual attraction. He happened to be married, but I do not recall that bothering either of us. I was young and reckless, and I imagine it was not his first extramarital relationship.

One day, as we were lying in bed together after making love, he said idly that he thought I would make a good television researcher. I was not yet experienced enough to understand that men say that sort of thing when they are having an affair with you. Had my lover been a cattle breeder, he might have asserted that I would be great at breeding cattle. But, partly because he himself was so successful in television, I took him completely seriously.

So it was that in 1979 I began preparing to take the next step in my career: becoming a television journalist.

I joined Thames News in the spring of 1980. I loved the hurly-burly of a busy newsroom. I also became involved in the media trade union, the ACCT (the Association of the Cinematograph Television and Allied Technicians).

4. Making the News

After a childhood spent voraciously reading any book I could get my hands on, and my teenage years consuming radical politics in magazines, it was in many ways predictable that media became a large part of my adult life. None of my tutors and careers advisors had suggested media of any kind to me as a possible career path while I was a Cambridge undergraduate, but a few years out of university, here was this tentative job offer in television. I was approached by a London Weekend Television (LWT) producer by the name of Michael Attwell, who wanted to sound me out about working on programmes for young Black people. He broached the idea of me presenting a programme called *Babylon* that was intended to be all about London's Black community. In the all-white media landscape of the time, *Babylon* was a radical idea. As it turned out, I did not get the job. A dashing young man called Lincoln Browne became the presenter and *Babylon* became a six-part current-affairs series, broadcast between 1979 and 1980, aimed specifically at young Black Londoners.

On a personal level, I was becoming increasingly certain that the time had come to move on from the NCCL. I was looking at other jobs in the voluntary sector but, encouraged both by my close encounter with the job at London Weekend Television and following on from my boyfriend's casual remark, I also began studying job advertisements in the media section of *The Guardian*. When I spotted a promising ad for researchers at ITV's London station, Thames Television, I applied. Much to my surprise and delight, I landed the job and in the spring of 1980 started work on *Thames News*, the daily news programme for the London area.

Thames Television represented a major change in my work life, not least because it was more glamorous than my two earlier jobs. These were the golden years of ITV, in which their companies were making a lot of money; Thames was particularly lucrative, with a turnover of hundreds of millions of pounds a year. It delivered well-known and money-spinning light entertainment and drama series, such as *The Sweeney*, as well as comedy shows featuring stars like Benny Hill and Morecambe and Wise. These were made in Thames's studios' main production base in Teddington in west London, whereas I worked in their corporate base and current-affairs headquarters on the Euston Road in central London. Somehow Thames's more pedestrian news and current-affairs programmes basked in the reflected glow of its money-making and exciting light-entertainment division. Companies made all their own programmes, instead of commissioning them from under-funded independents, and employed ample quantities of permanent staff rather than freelancers. In the pre-Thatcher era, the closed shop and tough union negotiators meant that terms and conditions for employees were excellent, even for entry-level journalists like me.

I took to my new job from the beginning. I liked the fast pace and the fact that each day was different. The pressure of putting out two daily shows – a lunchtime bulletin and the main programme at 6.30 p.m. every weekday – meant working at speed: from 8 a.m. until the programme aired, the pace in the newsroom did not slacken. To produce the bulletin in the middle of the day, lowly researchers such as me had to work through our lunch hour. The kindly Thames management provided us with lunch at our desks: sandwiches, accompanied by several bottles of wine. It was a hard-drinking regime and it was unthinkable to have a meal without wine to wash it down. I am embarrassed to say that, for someone who considered herself a socialist, I settled quite quickly into this lavish regime.

Though I was enjoying myself, this was not a typical experience for others like me in the field; it formed a strong contrast with what many other Black people in television were experiencing at the time. With exceptions such as ITN's iconic Trinidadian-born news presenter Trevor McDonald and, a little later, BBC newsreader Moira Stuart, Black people in TV either worked on 'ethnic' magazine shows or in children's TV. These were great journalists and many of them became my friends; but those 'ethnic' shows usually went out weekly, rather than daily, and bore no resemblance to a fast-paced newsroom putting out two bulletins a day. Nor did they offer a way up the journalistic ladder or a route into mainstream television.

I realized I had had a lucky escape by not getting the job on the 'ethnic' programme at LWT. At *Thames News* I was tipped into the hurly-burly of a busy newsroom from the beginning and did not do ethnic anything. Every morning my fellow news-desk journalists and I came in early, picked up by a car paid for by Thames. This was before the internet was universal, so when we got in to work we had to read every single newspaper, open mounds of post and go through all the press releases. Then we rang round the police, fire brigade and ambulance service to find out what crimes, fires and deaths had happened overnight. This all happened under the eagle eye of our news editor, a hard-bitten journalist who had come into television from newspapers. The information that we news-desk journalists put together was the basis of the *Thames News* morning meeting. There, the editor and other producers decided what would be in the show that night, and which reporters and journalists would get which stories. Then it was our job to round up the reporters and the camera crew and brief them on whichever story we were running.

In the 1980s *Thames News* was only just moving on from a system where short films in news programmes were made under the film agreement of the film technicians' union (the Association of Cinematograph Television and Allied Technicians, or ACTT). This meant that even five-minute films required a director, producer's assistant (PA), sound man, lighting man, researcher, reporter and unionized company driver. The leader of a film crew was normally the cameraman – and it always was a man. The first question he would ask you was the full address of the shoot. Then he would consult his Michelin restaurant guide to find the nearest three-star restaurant. Only then would he ask any practical questions, such as whether the shoot would require interior lighting.

The provision for expenses at Thames was astonishing. A few weeks after I started, my news editor asked me sternly if I had claimed my expenses. I was a little puzzled; there had been no such thing as expenses at either the Home Office or the National Council for Civil Liberties, so I innocently said no. He sighed and handed me an expenses form. I laboured over that form for some time and eventually produced a claim for a Mars bar and some bus tickets. I will never forget the way he shook his head mournfully, sat me down, took his wallet out of his back pocket and produced some carefully folded restaurant bills, then proceeded to draft a new – and almost completely fictitious – expenses claim.

In many ways the *Thames News* newsroom could not have been more different from either the Home Office or the NCCL. It could even boast a little more diversity: for once, I was not the only Black person in the building. There was one other journalist of colour: the tall and elegant reporter Sandra Naidoo. However, I recognized that this was not nearly enough and there was still a problem, so in 1981 I helped to set up a new campaigning organization called the Black Media Workers Association (BMWA). I thought it would be good to bring together the few Black people who *were* employed in film and television, if only to exchange gossip and support each other. My response to injustice of any kind is always to organize, and the BMWA was an early attempt to challenge institutional racism in the media. Thames was one of the biggest independent television companies in the country with thousands of employees, and it could still only claim a handful of Black employees. 'Diversity' and 'inclusion' were not recognized as issues to be concerned about, and

Thames management gave the impression of being blissfully unaware that there was a problem.

We called our organization 'Black' because in the 1970s and 1980s there was a notion of political Blackness, based on the unifying experience of British colonialism; the term embraced Africans, West Indians, Indians and South Asians. We quickly made links with the big media unions, such as the National Union of Journalists and ACTT (which later became BECTU), and we met their officials in order to discuss training. They also granted BMWA some funds, and Black media creatives were glad to reach out to other Black people through BMWA. These included Mike Phillips, a well-known print journalist (better known at the time than his younger brother, Trevor); Julian Henriques, later a professor at Goldsmiths, University of London, working on cultural studies and scriptwriting; and Parminder Vir, a successful film-maker and television producer who later produced *Babymother*, a reggae musical with a west London setting. BMWA lasted about five years as a formal organization, but we all stayed friends and valued the support we had been able to give each other.

BMWA intersected with the political interests that I continued to engage in outside my work in television. Working at Thames also enabled me to stay politically active in the evenings and at weekends, which is why I was able to tell my producers at Thames, fully a year in advance, that the left of the London Labour Party was poised to take control of the Greater London Council (GLC) at the 1981 elections. The GLC was an elected London-wide council that covered thirty-two boroughs, each of which elected a councillor. Before those elections it was not known as a hotbed of activity or controversy. It was run by the Tories, with sixty-four Tory councillors to just twenty-eight Labour councillors, and was led by the Thatcherite Horace Cutler. He was keen on getting media coverage, so he invested in dedicated studios to enable live radio and television broadcasts. The GLC was supposed to be responsible for strategic services such as the fire service, emergency planning and waste disposal in the greater London area, and it shared responsibility with London boroughs for providing other services, such as roads and housing.[1] However, being a council associated with the capital city, with a copious budget to match, the GLC was under the nose of the national newspapers. In the right hands, it had the potential to attract a lot of media attention.

After much cajoling, I was eventually given permission to be based semi-permanently at the GLC headquarters at County Hall, from where I would cover unfolding events as the 1981 election came nearer. By this point, County Hall had been the headquarters of local government for fifty-nine years. It was in a very central position on the South Bank and lay bang opposite the Houses of Parliament.

The GLC was definitely not as hectic as the Thames newsroom; things were more tranquil even though the elections were on the horizon. The mornings were often quieter, though events would heat up in the afternoons, when I had to research stories and arrange filming for the *Thames News* evening bulletin. I began my day rather later than I was used to at Thames, and the first thing I did was go to the GLC press office to collect the day's press releases and glean information about any significant goings-on. The chief press officer was the dynamic and glamorous Mary MacKenzie, who was rumoured to be having an affair with the Tory leader of the GLC, Horace Cutler. By coincidence, the same year that I began covering the GLC for Thames, Mary's son, Kelvin MacKenzie (who was just as dynamic as his mother, though not particularly nice), was promoted to editor of *The Sun* newspaper – which perhaps foreshadowed the totally malign influence that he would later have on the British political scene. Every morning, after collecting Mary MacKenzie's press releases and gently skirmishing with her, I would go for lunch in the County Hall dining room, usually with the two other journalists whose full-time job (like mine) was covering the happenings at the GLC. One was the *Evening Standard*'s correspondent, and the other was there for the *Evening News* (now defunct) – they were two amiable middle-aged men who were good pupil-masters for someone younger, like me. Long before evening papers were a mix of show business and gossip, I learned the ropes from these vastly experienced journalists, who were always kind and cooperative and never competitive.

Although I did not have the knowledge and experience of my evening-paper colleagues, I had one advantage over them, because I knew what was going to happen before too long. When I started covering the GLC for Thames, it was a resolutely right-wing administration controlled by the Tories; cutting spending, selling council houses and neglecting London Transport were on the agenda. It was a programme that benefited the wealthy parts of London at the expense of everybody else. But, just as I had prophesied to my bosses at Thames, in the 1981 GLC elections the Labour left swept to power.

The left in London had quietly planned this for some time, with a strategy called 'Target 82'. It was so called because the aim was to take control of the GLC by 1982, to replace some of the centrists and right-wing councillors and put left-wingers in their place. It was not led by any one person, but by a group of activists from all over London – most prominent among whom was Ken Livingstone. The strategy involved left-wingers meeting in groups in their borough. At one point Ken thought I should run for the GLC in the 1981 election, but I felt I was too young. The first stage of the Target 82 campaign was making sure that left-wingers were selected as Labour GLC candidates in as many constituencies as they could manage. Then they worked hard to get their people elected. So the morning after the election, London woke up to find out that Labour had not only defeated the Tories by fifty to forty-one, but that there were many more left-wing Labour councillors than anyone had expected. The next step was the key: Labour councillors on the GLC had gone into the 1981 election led by a dull, but completely un-frightening, centrist called Andrew McIntosh. But the day after the election, left councillors voted him out (as planned) and made Ken Livingstone leader of the GLC. It was a triumph for the left in London. The left-wing publication *London Labour Briefing* celebrated with a victorious headline on its next front page: 'London's Ours'.

As a television journalist by day and a Labour Party activist by night, I knew many of the left-wingers who had got themselves elected to the GLC, and above all I knew Ken Livingstone from my earliest involvement with the party. I had been his ward agent when he ran as the Hampstead candidate in the 1979 general election. Two years after this, the left had taken control of the GLC and County Hall. Old-guard Labour councillors were swept out of power and left-wing councillors took over the key committees. Nobody had heard of these politicians – not even of Ken himself. Up until this point he had been an obscure councillor for Camden and Lambeth and had been entirely unknown outside London, but now he burst onto the national scene in a blaze of publicity and was instantly labelled 'Red Ken' by the tabloid media. Not all the publicity that Ken and his GLC received was positive, but no one could now say he was obscure.

Ken immediately made changes at County Hall. When I was first based there, working for Thames Television in anticipation of the 1981 council elections, the corridors, meeting rooms and the chamber were entirely populated by middle-aged white men. Ken brought about a rapid transformation: more women and more Black people, and the average age of councillors on the GLC appeared to drop. The most important thing I learned from Ken was his idea that you could get the white working class to agree to a progressive line on issues like gay rights and Black rights if you delivered for them on a basic level. Accordingly, the two policies that he insisted on in the early years of the left's control of the GLC were cutting the price of school dinners and cutting transport fares. The authority was no longer concerned only with emergency planning, housing and the fire service; under Ken, it became a nationally recognized, powerful vehicle for flat-out opposition to Margaret Thatcher.

Like every London left-winger, Ken saw Thatcher as the enemy. So virtually every day he did or said something to antagonize her and attack everything she stood for. In a stroke of genius, he once put up a huge billboard displaying London's unemployment figures on the side of County Hall, opposite Parliament, where you could not miss it. When the unemployment figures went up, as they did almost every month of Thatcher's premiership, Ken put these new figures on his billboard. He also used his new position as the leader of London local government to stage a meeting with Gerry Adams of the Irish republican party, Sinn Féin.

Funnily enough, though Margaret Thatcher and Ken Livingstone's mutual enmity made sense, the Labour Party leadership was hardly more friendly towards him. For Neil Kinnock and the people around him, Ken represented everything they hated about the Labour left, and the London left in particular. Local-authority politics in London had been dull to the point of soporific, until the left took over the GLC. Once Ken Livingstone took charge, there was an explosion of interest in the GLC from the national media. Ken brought the long-standing social concerns of the London left onto the national stage, speaking up for women's rights, LGBT people, ethnic minorities, republicanism and a united Ireland. Just as importantly, he funded organizations campaigning on many of these issues. This all made the Tories and the national media apoplectic, and very soon the *Daily Express* was describing him as an 'IRA-loving, poof-loving Marxist'. In 1986 the *Daily Mail* told its readers, 'The GLC has made London the laughing stock of local government by opening its doors to every no-hoper, Marxist trouble-maker, political scrounger, foreign terrorist and sexual pervert who wanted a public handout.' But Ken's willingness to speak up for minorities was always going to be part of his 'brand' and, as time went on, it became a major source of his popularity.

I was not only at the heart of the story, going into County Hall every day to plan and research items for *Thames News*, but I also had a better understanding of what was going on than most mainstream journalists. Up until Ken became the leader, most of them scarcely knew what the GLC was, let alone what it actually did. That was valuable for Thames when it came to pitching these news stories more broadly. I also got to spend time informally with John McDonnell, Paul Boateng and Jeremy Corbyn, who were all either GLC councillors or activists who spent a lot of time there.

Eventually, however, when Thames management discovered that I was going to put myself forward as a potential Labour candidate running for Westminster Council, they decided (not unreasonably) that I was too politically involved to work in the news and current-affairs department any more. I was moved off *Thames News* altogether and transferred to the factual-programmes department, based in offices on Tottenham Court Road, round the corner from the Thames corporate HQ and news centre. The factual-programmes department was known derisively by news journalists as 'soft furnishings', perhaps because it was close to the well-known furniture store Heal's. I felt that I had been relegated to a programme-making backwater. No longer was I involved in putting together at least one news bulletin a day. At 'soft furnishings' the pace of life was so slow that I cannot remember a single programme I was involved in that was actually put on air. I missed the pace and immediacy of live television, and I knew I had to move on.

I also wanted to do things that were a corrective to the relentlessly corporate and materialistic ethos of commercial television, and be involved in media that better reflected my values. Apart from bringing Black programme-makers together through BMWA, I began writing for left-wing magazines, especially because I was keen to write about matters that were not getting covered in the mainstream media, in particular issues of concern to Black people and work by Black activists. I wrote occasionally for *London Labour Briefing*, a left-wing publication with the slogan 'Labour Take the Power', about the anti-racist campaigns that I was involved in. Ken Livingstone was one of the founders, and the magazine was very much at the centre of London Labour left campaigning, particularly Target 82. Ken wrote one of the magazine's first editorials, saying that the publication was intended to keep 'active militants inside the Labour Party and the unions in London in touch with each other and up to date on what is happening in the various battles across the capital'.

Another publication that I wrote for was the weekly political magazine *The Leveller*. I began writing for it late in 1979 and ended my involvement in 1981 – the early years of Margaret Thatcher's Conservative government. The *Leveller* collective was a group representing a coalition of various left and progressive movements: socialists, feminists and others. Members included Steve Bell, in the early stages of his impressive career as a political cartoonist for *The Guardian*, and already a brilliant iconoclast; and Jane Root, one of the few other female members, who later became the first woman to be a channel controller for the BBC.

The Leveller was very different from Thames Television. Whereas Thames had smart offices, good pay packets and an elaborate organizational hierarchy, *The Leveller* was run by a collective who worked for free and met every week in a tatty basement on the Caledonian Road. Getting a job at Thames Television meant studying the recruitment ads in newspaper media pages, submitting a CV with your qualifications and going for an interview. By contrast, all you had to do to join the *Leveller* collective was turn up at any of the weekly meetings; there was certainly no interview or selection process. The content of *Thames News* was decided by the editors and senior journalists – researchers and low-level journalists like me could make suggestions, but we had no say in the content of the programme. By contrast, any member of the

Leveller collective – which comprised an eclectic mix of Marxists, anarchists, feminists and radicals of no fixed political abode – could make editorial suggestions, then go away and work on them. With no editor, there was no chain of command, and the magazine's content was ultimately chosen by the collective.

The election of Mrs Thatcher had given debate on the left a particular urgency. Issues such as gay rights and feminism were increasingly on the left agenda, and *The Leveller* was reflecting that ferment. Cover stories at the time included 'Gays Coming Out' and 'Bringing it all back home' (on Northern Ireland). It represented a liberation from the conventional perspective that was required to write three-minute items for the evening news at Thames. I felt that my colleagues in the collective were raising issues and enabling voices that would not otherwise be heard, and that their ethos was centred on challenging the conventional. Many members of the collective saw themselves as being to the left of the Labour Party and, despite my own membership of the party, I identified with this position and found *The Leveller* decidedly exhilarating.

With there being no editor, final decisions on the magazine's content were made by whoever turned up for that week's meeting. This was very democratic in many ways, and was certainly better than the top-down hierarchy at Thames Television. However, it was at *The Leveller* that I began to notice the contradiction between counter-cultural rhetoric and left-wing practice. Despite the radical verbiage, left-wingers could unknowingly reflect the racism and sexism of wider society. The collective was virtually all white – and informal ways of working often enabled white men to dominate a situation, even as they masked that dominance with left-wing rhetoric. The only other person of colour involved in *The Leveller* that I recall was H. O. Nazareth, known as Naz, a clever and acerbic Indian film-maker, writer and journalist.

My first article for *The Leveller* in 1979 was about Labour Party democracy and reflected my involvement in the Labour Party at that time. In 1980 I was writing about the rioting that erupted in St Pauls, Bristol, and put urban insurrection 'triumphantly back on the political agenda'. In my article I said that 'The front-line is located where people are in struggle; where working people under all types of pressure, racism, capitalism in crisis, clash with the forces of the state.' I concluded the article by talking about the reverberations the riots had in the Black community, using my own mother as an example of how Black people had been politicized by the riots. Mummy was a respectable middle-aged woman nearing sixty, and I had never suspected her of having a radical bone in her body. To my surprise, she was pleased and excited by the ITN film of policemen running away from Black youth and said firmly, 'It shows they can't push us around any more.'

Another story that I reported on for *The Leveller* was the 1981 Black People's Day of Action, a protest march following the tragic New Cross house fire, which happened at a house-party in New Cross, south-east London, in the early hours of Sunday, 18 January 1981. Thirteen young Black people, aged between fourteen and twenty-two, were killed in the fire, and another twenty-seven youngsters were seriously injured. Two years later one survivor took his own life. Racial tensions were running high in New Cross anyway; the far-right activity that my parents lived through in 1950s west London was very much still around, most prominently from the National Front. The deaths and grave injuries caused by the New Cross fire shocked and horrified the Black community London-wide.

When there were no arrests following the deaths, and the inquest recorded an open verdict, rage swept through the Black community. Black people were convinced that the fire was caused by a white racist arson attack and could not believe that the Met Police could not find a single suspect, and voiced their horror at being over-policed as citizens and under-policed as victims. The community was also upset by the apparent indifference of the white population and accused the Metropolitan Police of covering up the cause of the fire. A New Cross Massacre Action Committee (NCMAC) was set up, chaired by John La Rose and formed by an alliance of the Black Parents Movement, the Black Youth Movement, Bogle-L'Ouverture Publications and the *Race Today* Collective. It was set up at first to provide immediate support for the grieving families and very quickly went on to campaign for the police to be held to account for both their inaction and their failure to open an investigation. In an attempt to make wider (white) society take the cataclysm of the New Cross fire seriously, NCMAC organized a 'Black People's Day of Action' on 2 March 1981. About 20,000 people marched through London for eight hours, carrying placards with slogans such as '13 Dead, Nothing Said'. It was the first major mobilization of the new Black politics, instigated by young Black people and centred on their relationship with the British state.

I went on the march, taking the number thirty-six bus from Paddington to New Cross. As the bus made its way across London, I observed white passengers getting off to go to work as increasing numbers of Black people boarded the bus on their way to New Cross. Something was on the move, both literally and in the sense of the mobilization of the Black community. Men in bookie shops left their betting and joined the march; people in doorways were drawn along; and schoolchildren whose school gates had been locked specifically to stop them getting involved jumped over the walls to join the march.

When I arrived at the gathering point for the march, I was awestruck to see coachloads arriving from everywhere in the country for this unprecedented national protest. It was the biggest Black march that I had ever been on. Up until then, demonstrations in Britain that Black people were involved in had been about decolonization and freedom struggles. It felt now as if we were part of a revolution, like the ones I had read about at Cambridge, except that this was on the streets of London. It was amazing to be with so many who understood intimately why we were all there, because so many of the challenges we had experienced were related to our ethnicity. I will not forget how it felt to be moving steadily forward alongside so many like-minded participants – not only seasoned Black activists, but ordinary people on a march for the first time in their lives. All of us were determined to demonstrate our outrage at thirteen young people dying in that way, with nothing being said or done about it by wider society or the government.

From New Cross, we marched over Blackfriars Bridge and made our way through the City of London. When we swung down Fleet Street (in those days the heart of the newspaper industry, where all the major national papers had their offices), there were no doubts about what media reporters thought of Black people: journalists were hanging out of windows shouting racist abuse, making monkey noises and throwing banana skins.[2] But we marched on, past Scotland Yard and the Houses of Parliament, heading to Hyde Park. All along the way others were joining us.

The press coverage in the following days was among my earliest introductions to the sad fact that, when it comes to Black people, the mainstream media has no problem simply making things up. I had taken part in a very large, peaceful and dignified march, but coverage of the event in the tabloid press bore scant relation to what had happened. The next day's newspapers bore sensationalist headlines, including 'The Day the Blacks Ran Riot', 'Black Day at Blackfriars' and 'The Rampage of the Mob'. On the day of the protest – 2 March 1981 – the tabloid newspaper narratives of crazed Black people rioting were dominant.

I was still working at Thames Television and had taken the day off to go on the march. Thames had reporters and camera crews covering it, yet they did not capture any images of Black people rioting. This was, of course, because there were no riots. The following day, when I went into work, I found the *Thames News* reporters and journalists fretting because they believed the lurid tabloid headlines and thought that Thames had missed the story. I tried to tell them that I had been on the march and it was nothing like the newspapers described, but my colleagues were unmoved. At best, they thought I had missed the riots; at worst, they did not believe me.

In 1981 I wrote my last article for *The Leveller*; it was a review of *Sizwe Bansi Is Dead*, a play by the South African novelist Athol Fugard. The problem with the play was that it dealt with a single legal aspect of apartheid, the pass laws, and by focusing the audience's anger on a single instrument of apartheid rather than on the illogicality of the system, Fugard stopped short of locating the roots of apartheid that had caused the most damage.

There had been complete media misrepresentation of the protest march, which was called to express community anger about the thirteen young people who died in the New Cross fire and the apparent lack of interest by the police and authorities. This was the type of incident that led BMWA to monitor the depiction of Black people in the media. Such biased journalism demonstrated the need for more Black people to be involved in all areas of media work. In 1982 we published a report titled *Black Workers in the Media*, which was based on research carried out by the professional broadcaster Marina Salandy-Brown and provided evidence of how tiny the numbers were. Marina's figures found that of the entire workforce of British mainstream newspapers and television, Black workers accounted for just 0.07 per cent.

The most empowering cultural event of 1982 was the inaugural International Book Fair of Radical Black and Third World Books, set up as an annual event by three Black-led organizations: New Beacon Books (founded by John La Rose and Sarah White), Bogle-L'Ouverture Publications (founded by Guyanese-born Jessica Huntley and Eric Huntley) and the *Race Today* Collective (encompassing activists such as Darcus Howe, Leila Hassan and Linton Kwesi Johnson). The Black Book Fair, as it became known, was a formidable undertaking that took place every year for more than a decade and was described as a 'meeting of the continents for writers, publishers, distributors, booksellers, artists, musicians, film-makers, and the people who inspire and consume their creative productions'.[3]

That first book fair was held in Islington Town Hall in 1982 and was opened with an address on 1 April by the radical Trinidadian historian C. L. R. James (who was spending the last years of his life in Brixton, in a flat above the *Race Today* office). There was an energizing buzz in the atmosphere, and it was electrifying to be in a space filled with bookstalls displaying publications, every one of which was likely to be of interest, and which would not have been found in the dominant high-street shops such as W H Smith. The book fair came with a week of cultural and political forums, concerts, films, poetry readings and art exhibitions. The excitement of it all was palpable, with more than 6,000 people attending the festival week. An opening event at University College London's Bloomsbury Theatre featured several films with subject-matter that resonated powerfully with Black audiences: Imruh Caesar's *Riots and Rumours of Riots*, Menelik Shabazz's *Blood Ah Go Run*, Lionel Ngakane's *Jemima + Johnny* and Franco Rosso's *The Mangrove Nine*. In the panel discussion that followed, 'A Forum on Black Films in Britain', I participated alongside such key Black practitioners as Horace Ové and Yvonne Brewster and spoke about my experience of working in television, as well as my activities in the Black Media Workers Association.

By the early 1980s I had become increasingly involved in the Labour Party, having been radicalized by my campaigning on issues like feminism and race. Over the course of the preceding decade or so, Tony Benn had emerged as the commanding figure on the left of the Labour Party. He had begun in the centre of the party and had even been a minister in Harold Wilson's government from 1964 to 1970, going on to serve in Wilson's Cabinet from 1974 to 1979. Over time, Benn gravitated more towards the left and, when asked why, he cited a number of issues: the way the civil service thwarted elected politicians; the power of Labour leaders; the power of industrialists and bankers; and the power of the media. Benn backed all the left-wing issues, including nuclear disarmament and the right to strike. He was later an unyielding and passionate supporter of the 1984–5 miners' strike, in contrast to the then Labour leader Neil Kinnock who, although he was the son of a miner and represented a mining constituency, adopted the view of the political establishment and was strongly against the strike. Benn also supported Sinn Féin, the Irish republican and democratic socialist political party. Left causes in the Labour Party became known as 'Bennism' and his supporters were called Bennites.

Benn was a great orator. Right from my earliest days in the Labour Party, I was in the audience for many of his speeches and found them compelling. I admired his principles and his belief that 'we are not just here to manage capitalism but to change society and its finer values'.

There could not have been a greater contrast between my involvement in so much interesting community activism and politics in this period (together with the writing that I did about it, outside normal work hours) and my daytime employment at Thames TV, stuck in a programming backwater, far removed from my beloved news and current affairs. My work life was increasingly dull and slow-moving. Then, in 1983, a job came up that was anything but dreary.

TV-am was Britain's first-ever commercial breakfast broadcaster. I was one of its earliest hires as a reporter/researcher. I was mostly working behind the scenes as a journalist, but TV-am gave me my first opportunity to appear in front of a television camera. Although this was undoubtedly because it did not have as many staff as Thames, and so everybody had to double up, it was still exciting and new to me. TV-am was a young company, except for the star presenters – and was all white, except for me. It was a radical venture, though not so radical as to think of hiring more than one Black person. As always, I did not let this bother me and just got on with the new challenge.

In some ways it was the perfect job for me. Unlike at Thames TV, the management did not care that I was going to be a Labour councillor, so long as my political commitments fitted around the hours of the job. Doing a live breakfast show usually involved working overnight, but it also meant that I had my days free for council work and other political activities. It was an exhausting routine – for years afterwards I only had to hear the TV-am jingle to feel the sudden Pavlovian response of my body telling me that I had been up all night.

TV-am's purpose-built production centre was in Camden Town, the epitome of metropolitan chic. The management of TV-am had commissioned Terry Farrell, then Britain's leading postmodern architect, to design its building. It was probably meant as a physical expression of how contemporary the company and its programmes were. The building had many dramatic features, including twelve enormous teacups on the roof. Inside, the studios were on the ground floor and the journalists worked in a spacious open-plan newsroom on the first floor. The offices for managers and star presenters were located around the perimeter of the first floor, with floor-to-ceiling inner walls made of glass. These walls were a stylish architectural feature, but also meant that the journalists bashing away at keyboards in the newsroom could look up and see straight into the offices of our elders and betters. As the TV-am internal dramas unfolded, we could see much of whatever was going on, and although we obviously could not hear anything, body language spoke volumes.

As part of the earliest tranche of journalists hired by TV-am, I witnessed its rise and precipitous fall. The main selling point of TV-am in the early days was its line-up of star presenters, known as the 'Famous Five'. Michael Parkinson, David Frost, Angela Rippon, Anna Ford and Robert Kee were all among the most high-profile television presenters of the time; Anna and Angela were particularly notable, as women pioneers. In charge of everything was Peter Jay, the founder, chairman and chief executive of the company.

Jay was the son of a former Cabinet minister and was married to Margaret Callaghan, the daughter of one-time prime minister James Callaghan. He was widely considered one of the cleverest men in Britain and was famous for his theory of TV current affairs' 'mission to explain'. This was something he mooted in 1972 in a series of articles in *The Times* co-authored with his friend John Birt, then executive producer of the current-affairs programme *Weekend World*. Their first article had stated that 'There is a bias in television journalism. Not against any particular party or point of view – it is a bias against understanding.' Their argument was that analysis had been dropped in favour of visuality, and they felt that TV journalists and documentarians should write their plans out before recording anything with a camera crew. However, this was a controversial position in the industry and was mostly seen as pointless and pretentious.

Apart from TV-am's star presenters, the original journalists hired were a youthful bunch and many of us went on to distinguished careers in media and public life. But in the early months TV-am was in turmoil. The management did not know where it was from one moment to the next, and in such a flat organizational structure, with a lack of any discernible support system, we journalists had to seek support in one another. People I worked with at TV-am included Sue Inglish, who went on to work at ITN; Jackie Ashley, who became a successful newspaper journalist; and Adam Boulton, who became a current-affairs star. Adam was the political editor of Sky News for twenty-five years and covered five general elections, but for me he will always be the scruffy young ex-public-school boy, with his shirt hanging out of the back of his trousers and dubious table manners.

In 1983, before TV-am went on air, Peter Jay gave all the rank-and-file journalists what was clearly meant to be a stirring oration.

He delivered the speech in the open-air atrium at the centre of 'Teacup Towers', as the TV-am building was known. Jay stood at the top of the central staircase, as if on the bridge of a ship, and we journalists crowded below on the ground floor looking up at him. Before he began speaking, we were each handed a specially printed and hand-signed copy of an essay that he had written, with the title 'What is news?' The essay began, 'Those of us that read PPE at Oxford in the fifties . . .' I don't recall anything else that was in this essay, but I do remember thinking – even as a Cambridge graduate myself – that his opening line was ridiculously pompous. The speech that Jay went on to deliver was obviously designed to enthuse his listeners. He assured us that we had been hired because we were the best and the brightest. Nobody was persuaded by this; we all suspected that, having spent so much money on big-name presenters, TV-am had hired its troop of young journalists because we were cheap. Peter Jay also told us, 'The next weeks and months are going to be among the most hectic and demanding of your lives. We are asking one hell of a lot of you. In return and above all, we want you to have fun.'

He was right about one thing: the early months of TV-am were not only hectic, they were chaotic. Before the station went on air, it was exciting. It had all the energy of a start-up and was produced at an even speedier pace than my old programme, *Thames News*; furthermore, we were producing many more hours of television. TV-am was confidently expected to be a huge success – the 'Famous Five' alone were supposed to guarantee this. Instead it quickly became clear that the revenues were a quarter of the sums that TV-am management had predicted. Worse, Jay turned out to be a hopeless executive, not a businessman at all. He paid the Famous Five astronomical salaries and hired far too many people. His theories about current-affairs television turned out to be completely irrelevant to breakfast TV, and it soon became apparent that those watching television in the early morning mainly wanted something light and undemanding. The Famous Five might be very high-profile, but most of them could not do light and fluffy. Before long, TV-am was heading for disaster. One of the lowest points was when the men from the London Electricity Board came to turn off the company's electricity supply because the management had not paid the bill.

Within months, Jay was ousted in a boardroom coup. The leader of this intrigue was the suave Tory MP Jonathan Aitken, who then replaced Jay as boss of the company. Soon after Jay left, I was in the TV-am newsroom tapping away at my computer. A member of the company board strolled past and we got chatting. After a while he said, 'Funny thing about Peter Jay, the board knew that he knew nothing about business but we thought he knew all about journalism.'

I stopped typing, looked up and replied, 'Funny you should say that; we knew that he knew absolutely nothing about journalism but we thought he knew all about business.'

Jay may have been living proof that you really can fool all of the people all of the time. In the aftermath of his sacking, with the company facing financial peril, I had a series of meetings with Jonathan Aitken – he in his role as temporary CEO, and me as the company's trade-union representative for my journalist colleagues. To our mutual surprise, we got on pretty well. TV-am was teetering on the brink of disaster, but in the end it was saved by the dumping of Jay's pretentious idea about a 'mission to explain', getting rid of almost all the Famous Five presenters, sacking journalists and bringing in a hugely popular puppet character called Roland Rat.

I had been working for TV-am for a few months by the time of the 1983 general election. The Labour Party was led by Michael Foot, who was by then in his late sixties and was widely respected by the Labour Party grass roots. However, his twin political passions, the Campaign for Nuclear Disarmament and British withdrawal from Europe, marked him out as a left-wing extremist, in the eyes of the media and the right wing of his own party.

Despite all the ups and downs, I was pleased to have the opportunity to work in television news and current affairs. It might not have had the status of writing columns for *The Times*, but it taught me how television journalists see the world, and not to be afraid of cameras. After an exciting and even perilous time at TV-am, I left the company in March 1985 for a new job as equalities officer with the film technicians' union, the ACTT, which was affiliated with the Labour Party. This was completely the other side of the fence from the big television companies that I had been working for up until then. It was my first experience of being a paid full-time official in a national Labour-movement organization – until then, most of my experience of the Labour Party had been as a local councillor who wrote about the GLC.

The general secretary of ACTT was Alan Sapper. He was very left-wing and a tough negotiator for his members. Sapper was on the council of the Trades Union Congress (TUC), the national trade-union organization to which most unions belonged, and during the miners' strike I saw a number of trade-union bosses gathered in his Soho Square office, plotting how best to support the miners. In my new job I was covering for Sandra Horne, who had been seconded to another role in the union. She was the very first ACTT equalities officer and one of a handful of women doing that job in the whole trade-union movement – in fact she was the only female official at ACTT. Though I was filling in for her role, she was still around, and I learned a lot from her about functioning in an all-male environment. She was clever and funny and was very committed to women's issues.

It was remarkable that ACTT had an equalities officer at all; it was a male-dominated, right-wing union and was militant in terms of looking after its own rights in the industry. That said, at the very top it was surprisingly liberal on such issues as women's rights. The deputy general secretary was Roy Lockett, who was genuinely interested in equalities. This was not the case in the trade-union movement as a whole and certainly not the case in the

ACTT, but Roy backed me up, both with the men in our own union and dealing with male officials in other unions.

The ACTT headquarters were in seventeenth-century Soho Square, which had traditionally been the heart of the British film industry. It was a small union, the type of craft union that nowadays would be swallowed up in the bigger general unions. But before Margaret Thatcher legislated to limit unions, a combination of the closed shop and highly skilled union negotiators made the ACTT very powerful in the film and television industry. It was due to its negotiating skills that I had enjoyed such lavish working conditions at Thames TV.

For a craft union, the ACTT was a radical organization with an interest in equalities long before some of the bigger unions; for instance, it had appointed the first trade-union researcher into discrimination against women. I had been a member of the ACTT for a while, and my involvement in it increased when I was attempting to bring together Black people working in film and television. The national Labour Party had been suspicious of efforts by me and other Black members to organize within the party, so it was a pleasant surprise to find that ACTT officials such as Roy Lockett and Sandra Horne were not only genuinely interested in race and gender issues, but were comfortable with women and Black people organizing within the union. It was helpful, in my new paid trade-union role, that I had already been working with officials there on training, employment and equalities as a lay member, and my new job brought together my interest in politics and my working life within the media. There were hardly any Black female full-time officials at the time, and what clearly made me even more unusual was that I was not the client of some powerful trade-union boss. I was my own woman.

In an interview with the Equal Opportunities Review I explained my plans for the union. I had seen with my own eyes how only a handful of Black people were getting through the recruitment process to work in mainstream television. I was intent on creating an open and fair system of entry, first by setting up technical training specifically for women and ethnic minorities. Even when women and minorities had the training, however, it was still very difficult for them to get into film and television. One policy that the ACTT was promoting, to crowbar open entry for under-represented groups, was the Workshop Declaration. I had worked on this as a lay member of the union, and as a full-time official I was able to help take it further. The Workshop Declaration was designed to get round the fact that at the time you had to be a union member to work in film or television. Yet the only way that you could get union membership was if you already had paid employment in the industry. Many film-makers, especially Black creatives, were therefore stuck in a vicious circle: they could not get union membership without a job, but they could not get a job without union membership. The excuse that potential employers were making for not employing them was that they were not union members, so most Black people who wanted to work in film or television laboured unpaid, often in the community sector with non-profit voluntary groups, frequently with a social purpose.

The ACTT Workshop Declaration meant that Black film-makers could come together in groups (workshops) and apply for membership collectively, and each member of the workshop would also get their individual membership. It was a great breakthrough for Black would-be programme-makers and film-makers, who were now able to cut through a system that had effectively excluded Black people until that point. Many of those who got their union membership through workshops were then able to launch their careers successfully, and several became internationally known film-makers. One group was the Black Audio Film Collective (BAFC). Founded in 1982, it included the likes of John Akomfrah, Lina Gopaul, Trevor Mathison and David Lawson, and produced what the British Film Institute described as 'some of the most challenging and experimental documentaries in Britain in the 1980s'.[4] Another initiative was the Sankofa Film and Video

Collective – taking its name from the Ghanaian concept of *sankofa*, meaning 'return and fetch it', to represent the idea that recovering knowledge from the past is of benefit to the future – which was founded by Isaac Julien and other art graduates (Martina Attille, Maureen Blackwood, Nadine Marsh-Edwards and Robert Crusz) in 1983 and, like the BAFC, focused on exploring Black culture and identity within the British context.

Sankofa's first production, and Julien's directorial debut, was *Who Killed Colin Roach?* (1983), a poignant reflection on the true story of the young Black man in his twenties who had been shot the previous year in suspicious circumstances at the entrance to Stoke Newington police station. The Hackney community exploded in intense anger at this killing, and tragically Roach proved to be one of a series of young Black men who died in the custody of Hackney police officers. In 1986 BAFC made a stand-out documentary called *Handsworth Songs*, which explored memories and experiences of race and immigration; it was later commissioned by Channel 4 for its series *Britain: The Lie of the Land* and won several international accolades. The documentary featured newsreel and archive footage from the civil disturbances in Birmingham and London in the autumn of 1985, which arose partly through simmering racial tensions between the police and the local Black and Asian communities. John Akromfah and Isaac Julien went on to become very distinguished film-makers, creative artists and knights of the realm, and I was glad to have given some support in their earliest film-making years through my role in the union.

From 1986 to 1987 I was the head of press and public relations at Lambeth Council, a role based at the town hall in Brixton. Brixton was like a home-from-home for me, and I loved working in that part of London. It had incredible energy and I knew it well. It was an area of London where masses of Jamaicans had settled following the arrival of the *Empire Windrush* in 1948, and I had plenty of friends and relatives there. Although I was born and raised in west

London and had represented the Harrow Road ward for years, I was regularly in Brixton for political meetings, to see friends or simply to hang out. There were a number of important Black community organizations based in Brixton, including *Race Today*, edited by Darcus Howe.

Lambeth Council was one of the leading local authorities at that time for progressive politics. Left-wingers of all races clustered around the council, either as elected members or involved in community campaigns. The leader of Lambeth Council from 1986 and 1988 was Linda Bellos, who was a hate-figure for the mainstream media. As a lesbian woman, she pushed all their buttons. Although she was a local-authority leader in London, Linda became a national figure because of the malign attention of the media. She was routinely described in the press as one of the 'loony left', but in reality Linda was saner and more capable than her detractors. Much of my time was taken up with countering media attacks on her, though I sometimes dealt with less inflammatory matters. One year Lambeth Council supported a fund-raising bike ride from south London around the Midlands. Many of the cyclists were white, but there were also many who were Black or Rastafarian. Residents and home-owners in middle England were somewhat surprised to see Rasta cyclists pedalling furiously down their roads and country lanes with their locks flying in the air. But that didn't affect the sponsored bike ride, which ended up raising a lot of money.

Lambeth Council was frequently associated with fierce attacks on the Thatcher government, but Linda also worked hard to promote initiatives, such as the sponsored bike ride, which involved the whole Lambeth community. Many of these initiatives were interesting and fun, and it was my job, with my little band of press officers, to try and get them in the national press. Sadly, most of the media were only interested in stories about Lambeth that fitted their 'loony left' paradigm.

Linda Bellos and I had already known each other before I went to work for her as the head of her press office. Our paths had crossed through our mutual involvement in London-wide left politics and I liked and respected her. Working for Lambeth Council rounded off my experience in the media, beginning on one side of the fence as a journalist working for national broadcasters, and eventually crossing over to work for a media trade union and Lambeth Council, which was very much the type of organization that was either ignored or subject to hostile coverage in the media. I didn't know it at the time, but a comprehensive understanding of how the media worked was to be helpful to me in the future.

An historic night. I was elected MP for Hackney North and Stoke Newington on 11 June 1987 – the first Black woman to be elected to Parliament.

5.   A Feeling about Hackney North

In the early 1980s I plunged into Labour Party politics with energy and enthusiasm. When I originally joined the Labour Party, as an act of rebellion against the Home Office where I was then employed, I joined the Hampstead branch, which was then not as posh as one might imagine. In fact it had a proud left-wing history, being the party of Michael Foot, the distinguished left-winger who served as leader of the Labour Party from 1980 to 1983.

Foot, who started out as the MP for Plymouth Devonport and later for Blaenau Gwent, was a passionate orator and an un-ashamedly leftist leader. He was sixty-seven when he was voted in, and was famously dishevelled with flyaway grey hair. From the beginning of his tenure the media were cruel to him, calling him 'Worzel Gummidge', after a scarecrow character from a popular children's series of the time. When Foot was elected I was only casually involved with the Labour Party, so it did not impact on me too deeply; however, I did understand that his election was seen as a decisive turn to the left for my party. In the months before the 1983 general election, Kelvin MacKenzie – the editor of *The Sun* newspaper – summed up the general opinion of the media by running the headline 'Do you seriously want this old man to run Britain?' The Labour manifesto drawn up under Foot's leadership was described by the right in the Labour Party as 'the longest sui-cide note in history' and the party lost, in an unprecedented defeat.

I was the only active Black member of the local Labour Party, but it was strongly left-wing and had a history of trying to advance Black representation. It was inordinately, and justifiably, proud of the fact that in 1959 it had selected the first Afro-Caribbean to run for the British parliament: Dr David Pitt, a local GP. He had lost in that election, which took place just a few months after the racist killing in west London of Kelso Cochrane, and a year before the Notting Hill 'race riots'. Pitt weathered racist abuse and threats during his campaign, but did not withdraw from the contest. The fact that this amiable man with strong local roots and excellent political credentials could not get elected deterred local Labour parties from selecting Black candidates for decades to come. In the end, David Pitt did get into Parliament, though not via an election: in 1975 Harold Wilson made him Lord Pitt of Hampstead.

In 1980 I moved into a flat-share in Paddington with a Nigerian actress called Joy, and we quickly became good friends. A year later I bought my first flat in Lanhill Road in Maida Vale, with £1,000 that my father had left me and a mortgage from Westminster Council. This was at a time when local authorities offered mortgages, and property prices were not as extortionate as they later became. Being back in Paddington, where I had spent so much time when I was growing up, meant that in order to continue my Labour Party activism I had to transfer my membership to that constituency Labour Party (CLP). First I tried ringing the secretary of the local party and asking for the time and place of my Labour Party ward meeting. I did this repeatedly, and the secretary always promised to ring me back, but never did. It was puzzling, but I assumed that she was busy.

Trying a different tack, I spoke to friends I knew from Cambridge who happened to live in the area and were local Labour members. They found out the day, time and place of my local ward meeting and told me, so one evening I turned up uninvited for the meeting, which was being held in a local sports centre on the Mozart Estate. As I ventured through the doorway, I was shocked to see an anxious-looking white man rush up and hold out his arms to stop me entering. After a bit of a kerfuffle, the members in the meeting reluctantly let me come in and sit down.

I later learned that local Labour members had been told that a scarily radical Black woman had moved into the area and might try to join the party – and they were determined to keep me out. The Labour Party in Paddington could always rely on a big vote from the Black community, which it seemed to take for granted; but the idea of a Black person actually *joining* the party was intrinsically suspicious to them. As a Black woman, I was used to covert – and overt – hostility, but I also felt strongly that there were changes I wanted to see in the world that could only be achieved by working alongside or inside the Labour Party. Black concerns were forcing themselves onto the left agenda.

Perhaps the most important event at the time were the Brixton riots of April 1981, a series of violent clashes between Black youths and the Metropolitan Police. They were triggered by Operation Swamp 81, a ten-day action in which more than 100 local plainclothes officers stopped and searched almost 1,000 young Black people and made 150 arrests. This operation was the result of increasing tensions between the police and Black people all over London, which were in turn a response to racist policing. The uprising in Brixton resulted in 279 injuries to the police, forty-five injuries to members of the public, more than 100 vehicles burnt out and more than 150 buildings damaged. I visited Brixton the day after the rioting and it was eerily quiet, with smashed buildings, broken glass in the gutters and smoke in the air. I had never seen scenes like these on the British mainland. They were reminiscent of the scenes of disorder and violence in Northern Ireland that were all over the media then, with the British Army ruthlessly crushing the Catholic insurgency. The Brixton riots were not quite on the scale of a civil war between young Black people and the British state, but it felt like the beginning of one.

Politicians of all parties were very shaken. They had not expected, and did not understand, young Black people exploding with anger like this. It was a long way from smiling waiters in the Caribbean sunshine, singing calypsos and serving rum punch. The

British political class felt bewildered and threatened, and so great was their alarm that, just two days later, the Tory Home Secretary Willie Whitelaw commissioned the Scarman Report, an inquiry led by a High Court judge, Lord Scarman, whose terms of reference were 'to inquire urgently into the serious disorder in Brixton on 10–12 April 1981 and to report, with the power to make recommendations'.

The Scarman Report was published in November and was the first report of its kind. It was led by a judge and, because of that, British politicians had to pay attention. Among other things, Scarman concluded that 'racial disadvantage [was] a fact of current British life' and that 'urgent action [was] needed if it is not to become an endemic, ineradicable disease threatening the very survival of our society'. Although most of the urgent action that Scarman recommended was not implemented, his report was a milestone because it was the first time that a government inquiry had spoken about police accountability, racial disadvantage and inner-city decline. These were tumultuous times in race debates, but they represented progress.

I was making personal headway by running for selection as the Labour candidate for the Harrow Road ward in Paddington, which was part of the Westminster local authority. Becoming a council candidate was a competitive process, and it was the first step in going on to be elected as a local-authority councillor by the public. The fact that I had the opportunity to be selected at all meant that my fellow Labour Party members had moved on from their initial suspicion of me becoming a member and were prepared to see me representing local people on the council. I had worked hard to allay their concerns about my radicalism by faithfully attending local meetings, getting involved in local campaigns and going out leafleting, and I did my best to be pleasant and non-threatening to the other Labour members. That year I ran for the Westminster City Council elections and there was more campaigning and leafleting than ever. The local Labour Party had put forward candidates for the ward who were almost a cross-section of local residents: Joe Glickman, a jolly semi-retired taxi driver; Paul Dimoldenberg, an activist (and a councillor there to this day); and me. My leaflets stressed my commitment to race equality. The slogan was 'Giving Black People a Fair Share' and it went on to say that 'Black people have not had a fair deal when it comes to council services, particularly housing. I want to fight that kind of racism.'

On election night I went to my first-ever election count. Physically counting the votes is an aspect of electoral politics that never changes, and watching the ballot papers piling up on the trestle tables is always nerve-racking for the candidates. However, my strong anti-racist message had not seemed to put off Paddington voters, and Paul, Joe and I triumphed against the Tory and SDP–Liberal Alliance candidates. A few days later in a *Guardian* article about how little progress Black people had made in the election, it was noted that I was 'the first black [person] to win a seat on the strongly Conservative Westminster City council'. I was particularly pleased to become a councillor for the Harrow Road ward because it was the same area that my family used to live in, and it was where my mother had given birth to me at Paddington Hospital, Harrow Road.

My first council meeting took place on 17 May 1982 at Westminster Council House, where meetings of the full council were held – and it was not without its challenges. Security at the door initially refused to admit me, assuming that a Black woman could not possibly be a councillor, and only after some persuasion was I allowed to enter. Westminster is like a lot of London boroughs, with a diverse mix of areas: it contains affluent localities such as Mayfair, but also poorer areas such as Paddington. The northern part of Paddington bordering on Brent had large numbers of Caribbean and Irish voters, who had traditionally voted Labour; but when I became a member of Westminster Council, it was firmly in the hands of the Tory Party. By 1983 Shirley Porter was its leader. Shirley was the daughter of Jack Cohen, the son of a

Polish Jewish immigrant who began by selling groceries from a market stall in Hackney and eventually built his business up into the biggest supermarket chain in the country: Tesco. Cohen had a brilliant internal motto: YCDBSOYA ('you cannot do business sitting on your arse'). His daughter had the same approach to politics and treated the whole of Westminster Council as if she were managing a giant supermarket. Shirley had no patience with local democracy and ran the council on a strict command-and-control model, and we clashed on almost everything, from her adoration of Mrs Thatcher to her reckless privatizations. One of the most grotesque of these was selling three Westminster cemeteries for five pence each to ruthless asset-strippers. The cemeteries were attached to valuable land and properties, and the developers realized the profit from these and then promptly abandoned the cemeteries to vandals, drug addicts and fly-tippers.

That was bad enough, but Porter went too far when she tried to implement a ruthless gerrymandering policy. In the 1986 local-council elections the Tories won Westminster only very narrowly; if 106 votes had gone the other way, Labour would have won. A panicked Shirley Porter brought in a policy that she called 'Building Stable Communities', which was really about dumping homeless people outside the borough and having a big drive to sell off council houses within Westminster, with the intention of bringing in people more likely to vote Tory. In the short term the policy worked, and the Tories won Westminster in the 1990 local elections by a landslide. Eventually, however, the District Auditor found the policy to be illegal, and Porter and five others were ordered to pay a surcharge of £36.1 million (though in the end the final settlement in 2004 amounted to only £12.4 million).

Although Shirley Porter was a whirlwind of right-wing activity, I did glimpse another side to her. Once she mentioned in passing how for two years she had campaigned successfully against racism in golf clubs. She had found that many clubs would claim they were full whenever a Jewish person applied to join, and that – as the *Jewish Chronicle* reported – in some cases, clubs had a quota for Jews. This conversation confirmed something that I had always thought: anti-Black racism and anti-Semitism were in many ways part of the same ultimate struggle against injustice.

Aside from this interaction, I was never able to relate to her. It was not so much that Shirley was a Tory; rather, it was her brutal and uncaring attitude towards ordinary people in Westminster. Apart from mistreating the homeless and stealing elections, Porter's main political preoccupation was fighting my erstwhile Labour Party conference companion, Ken Livingstone. As leader of the GLC, he was shifting it firmly and defiantly to the left. Margaret Thatcher was infuriated both by the policies and the political resistance. Her solution made Shirley Porter's gerrymandering look tame: in 1986 Thatcher decided simply to abolish the GLC. It caused a huge political row that rocked London for months. Most ordinary Londoners were on Ken's side, but Thatcher did not care. She was prime minister and she drove the necessary legislation through. Shirley Porter, a devoted follower of Thatcher, supported her enmity with Ken to the end.

I liked being a local councillor, and the fact that I was representing the corner of Paddington where I was born gave me enormous pleasure. Politics is a people business and being a councillor is all about engaging with people and families, and it was here that I learned how important it was to listen. I came to realize that the people I represented found engaging with authority far more difficult than residents in more middle-class areas. This might be because English was not their first language, or maybe they did not have the confidence. Quite often they would come to me with one problem, but only by being patient and listening would I get to what was really worrying them.

My work on the council prompted me to link up with other Black councillors and we began to campaign and organize, to try and convince the Labour Party that Black people should have representation at every level of the party. I started to wonder whether I should not try to get elected to Parliament myself. Most people would have thought this was a completely unrealistic aspiration; there were hardly any Black people running for Parliament at the time, and no Black man or woman had ever been elected. Being a woman made the idea even more unfeasible, because there were no Black female Labour candidates at all. Twenty years previously, David Pitt had run and lost in my old constituency of Hampstead. In 1983 Paul Boateng ran and lost in Hertfordshire West. It was not a happy experience; local Labour Party members were not wholly enthusiastic about his candidacy, he had doors slammed in his face and even dogs set on him. Russell Profitt, a respectable head teacher who was popular locally as a Lewisham councillor, was also looking for a seat. In 1984 Labour members in the Lewisham East constituency selected him as their parliamentary candidate, but the national party blocked his candidacy on the pretext that he had been selected from an all-Black shortlist. It would never have occurred to them to block a candidate selected from an all-white shortlist, as 99 per cent of the Labour candidates were. The opposition at the top of the Labour Party to selecting Black men and women as MPs was visceral.

My reaction to this was shaped by an inspirational book published in 1984 by an English writer called Peter Fryer, *Staying Power: The History of Black People in Britain*. It was a revelation. Fryer's interest in Black history had been sparked in 1948 when, as a journalist with the *Daily Worker*, he had covered the arrival at Tilbury docks of the *Empire Windrush*, bringing to Britain one of the most sizeable early groups of post-war Caribbean migrants. *Staying Power* was written in the wake of the 1981 riots in Brixton and elsewhere and pulled together fragmentary sources to produce a coherent narrative about Black British history. Until the publication of this book, the focus of Black history was predominantly on African Americans or the Caribbean. Fryer's work is responsible for many people beginning to understand there was such a thing as Black British history, because he definitively put on record information about the Black presence in Britain going back to the Roman conquest. Among those he wrote about were the British-based African abolitionist Olaudah Equiano (c.1745–1797), the mixed-heritage Jamaican agitator Robert Wedderburn (1762–1835/6), the Black Chartist leader William Cuffay (1788–1870) and the Indian communist Shapurji Saklatvala (1874–1936), who was first elected to the British Parliament in 1922 (and who was defined as 'Black' by the terminology of the time, which included those of Asian as well as African heritage). With this book, Fryer had recovered the tradition of Black British rebels. It made me realize that I was not merely an isolated and aberrant figure, but was walking in the footsteps of earlier generations of Black British radicals.

Becoming a councillor in Westminster had made me realize quite how under-represented and marginalized Black people in the Labour Party were. The party historically had structural methods of empowering minorities; the idea was that by working together in these separate sections, minorities could support each other and find a voice, while remaining firmly part of the wider Labour Party. Under the broad banner of the party, there were women's sections and young socialists, but I – along with other Black activists – felt that Black members were not empowered enough. I began by setting up an informal Black caucus in Paddington, so that we could provide support for one another. Then, together with activists including Bernie Grant, Sharon Atkin, Marc Wadsworth and Narendra Makanji, I helped to set up the Black Sections campaign, which was designed to bring together and empower Black members in the Labour Party.

We wanted Black Sections to become an official part of the Labour Party, with more representation at local-authority level – more Black councillors and more representation among the unpaid officers in local CLPs. We also wanted more Black Members of Parliament. There were very few Black members of the Labour Party and it was easy to feel isolated, particularly if you lived outside London. These seemed reasonable enough demands, yet the Labour Party leadership thought that Black Sections were completely unreasonable, not to mention dangerous. When we tried to table a Black Sections resolution at the Labour Party conference that year, we were roundly denounced by the great and the good from the conference platform. Senior people within the Labour Party could not see the contradiction between supporting Black self-organization in South Africa and being vehemently opposed to it in the British Labour Party. Neil Kinnock was particularly opposed to Labour Party Black Sections, which seemed to him like dangerous radicalism. He appeared to think that his occasional expression of concern for Black people far away, such as campaigners against apartheid in South Africa, meant that he could dismiss the concerns of Black people on his doorstep.

It didn't help that we couldn't always count on the support or the confidence of other Black members in the Party, and of key Black figures in society. Some Black party members even openly opposed Black Sections. Trevor Phillips, who years before had been elected as the first Black president of the National Union of Students, did not believe that we would see Black Members of Parliament in our lifetime, and he probably wasn't the only one. Nonetheless, we fought on. A group of us, including Bernie Grant and other Black councillors, went to see Labour Party officials in order to press the case for there being more Black MPs. We argued that 80 per cent of Black and brown people voted Labour, so it was only fair that we had some representation at parliamentary level. Officials were dismissive, insisting that it was impossible to get Black MPs because there were not enough of us coming forward for selection. We decided that if, as the officials claimed, there were not enough Black people coming forward who wanted to be MPs, then we would put ourselves forward. Initially I tried running for selection in Brent East, but the established left candidate was Ken Livingstone – leader of the GLC, one of the most powerful Labour politicians in London and, until this point, a friend and ally of mine. Livingstone's eye had been on Brent East for some time; he had assiduously directed attention and resources to it, as well as building close links with the Irish community and rallying supporters on the ground. I might as well have thrown myself under the wheels of a tank rather than challenge the mighty Livingstone machine in London. I had taken very poor advice from people in the constituency who disliked me personally, and it was one of the things I will always regret. Ken was understandably furious when I entered the race, and his anger that year coloured his attitude towards me for years to come.

I grew increasingly upset and dispirited as the situation became more and more unpleasant – I could not even get the women's section in Brent East to vote for me. One evening, as I was walking across Westminster Bridge from County Hall on my way home, Jeremy Corbyn was heading towards me on his way to a meeting. Seeing a friendly face, I burst into tears, oblivious to all the passers-by.

'Why doesn't Ken Livingstone like me?' I sobbed piteously.

Poor Jeremy was too kindly a man to make the obvious point: that all is fair in love and parliamentary selections. Eventually he calmed me down, saying, 'Never mind, duck, these things happen. Get your head up, do it again and you'll get selected.' Predictably I was roundly beaten in Brent East, but I took Jeremy's advice, raised my head and tried again.

Among the Black MPs who were campaigning for Black Sections there was a tacit agreement that we would not contest the same parliamentary selections. Bernie Grant was given a clear run in Tottenham, where he was leader of Haringey Council, and I was expected to be the only Black person to run in Westminster North, the constituency where I was now a councillor. Once again, I lost. It was painful to see those I thought were friends organizing feverishly against me and swinging behind another woman candidate, Jennifer Edwards, whom I had first met when we were both Cambridge undergraduates. What made it hurtful was that these were people I had campaigned and socialized with for years, and Jennifer was a friend – or so I thought – whom I had brought into the Labour Party. It was at this stage that I discovered the truth of US President Harry Truman's dictum 'If you want a friend in politics, get a dog.'

By the autumn of 1985 I was thoroughly disheartened by parliamentary selections and had virtually given up on becoming an MP. I was tired of being the token Black woman on the shortlist and tired of being humiliated. At the time I was working at the ACTT trade union and my efficient and supportive secretary, Pat, was a Labour stalwart who used to scan *Tribune*, a weekly newspaper that was then the most widely read left-wing publication. One day she saw a notice in the paper that Hackney North was inviting people to apply to be their prospective parliamentary candidate. When Pat first told me about it, I said gloomily that I was not interested. But she insisted, bustling off to draft the letter of application to the Hackney North Labour Party, then plonking it on my desk in front of me for signature.

Taking the line of least resistance, I signed, not very hopefully.

Pat kept saying, 'I just have a feeling about Hackney North.'

Hackney North was an optimistic move. It was not a part of London that I knew well; most people who wanted to become the Labour Party candidate there were content to wait for the sitting MP, Ernie Roberts, to retire. He was seventy-three years old, mildly left-wing and not unpopular locally. I would have to deselect him, which seemed unlikely given that the majority of local Labour Party wards had nominated him, and his established successor was the left-wing leader of Hackney Council, Hilda Kean. In the run-up to the selection conference, a long-standing Black party member took me to one side and gently informed me that I was not going to win. But now that I had entered the race, I wanted to go hell for leather.

Gathering support was an uphill battle. Most of the white left, particularly the men, thought I was too right-wing. This was not an opinion based on fact, but I had come across such assumptions before: a Black woman who was articulate, had graduated from Cambridge University and dressed nicely was automatically suspect, to a certain kind of left-winger. It seemed like a particularly British attitude. Nobody in Black America, Africa or the Caribbean thought there was a contradiction between a Black person being educated, well turned out and on the left of the political spectrum – and I did have a lot of Black support within the party. One enthusiastic supporter who was instrumental in gaining support for my selection was the charming, gregarious and hyperactive Patrick Kodikara, a one-time Hackney councillor, chair of Hackney social services, member of the Community Relations Council and of Hackney Committee against Racism. The problem was that, despite Black people making up a substantial section of Labour voters in Hackney, they were very under-represented within the local Labour Party itself. And even among that small group of Black activists, the men regarded me with a touch of misogyny. There was something about a young Black woman with long braids that they found hard to take seriously.

As the selection came nearer, I fell back on my long-standing belief in the importance of history, and to encourage myself I went to Hackney Central library to read about the borough and absorb myself in its history. At that point my knowledge of Hackney was confined to the culinary; it was the home of the famous Ridley Road Market in the centre of Hackney, opposite Dalston Kingsland station. From the 1950s onwards, and even after Caribbean food was more widely available, Caribbean people used to head there from all over London to shop for staples such as breadfruit (a doughy vegetable), yam (a starchy tuber), green banana, callaloo (a version of spinach), okra and sweet potato. I wanted to know more about other aspects of its history, and in the library I read about how Hackney had always welcomed migrants, including thousands of Jews from Eastern Europe at the turn of the century; about cultural icons like the Hackney Empire, a famous music hall that is still famous for its pantomimes and artistic events; and about famous people born in Hackney, such as the notorious East End gangsters, the Kray brothers. Going through those archives confirmed what I had always thought about the importance of history; I had known, from my early days studying it at university, that every happening and every struggle in politics has its roots in some kind of history, and this knowledge strengthened my resolve to go forward.

The selection conference itself took place in the council chamber in Hackney Town Hall, which had been built in the 1930s. There were more than a hundred people present. Although the result was assumed to be inevitable, there was still a buzz of anticipation. My fellow candidates could not bring themselves to speak to me: Ernie because I was challenging for his seat, and Hilda because I was a threat to what she probably considered her God-given right to succeed him. I was standing in the hallway outside the council chamber, waiting for the selection to begin, when two of my female supporters came up to me and said quietly, not unkindly, that if I came a good second then I would have done well.

I was scheduled to be the last person to deliver my speech to the assembled Hackney North members. Waiting nervously, I paced up and down the corridors. After a while I looked up and realized that on the walls were a series of black-and-white photographs of former mayors of Hackney, dating back to before the Second World War. These past mayors were mostly the children of immigrants from Eastern Europe. After a time it seemed as if they were all whispering to me: 'We did it,' they said, 'our parents were immigrants; we achieved, and you can do it too.' Those repeated whispers were not only reassuring; they also reminded me of the importance of self-belief. I made myself think of my family – in particular of aunts and cousins who had endured hard lives and had died prematurely – and I realized that I was there for them.

Finally I went into the council chamber. Knowing that almost all the people who were in the room did not think I could win, and were in any case mandated to vote for someone else, I delivered the speech of my life. I talked about Uncle Charlie, who had migrated from Jamaica to Florida to be a farm worker, and told the story of how he had challenged the system by entering the office to collect his pay. I was trying to establish the theme of my speech, which was about racial justice, and talking about my family steadied my nerves and gave me strength. Powering on to my conclusion, I told the rapt audience of Labour Party members that twenty-five years of history and the transformation in the racial demographics of Hackney were catching up with them that day. They could run from it, but they could not hide.

I looked out at the faces of the party members who made up the audience and I could see them struggling with the increasing realization that, whomever else they had promised to vote for, on the basis of this performance they might have to vote for me.

Finally, I told them they had a choice. They could look to the past and continue as the party of white working men, or they could embrace the future by selecting a candidate who represented Hackney's growing ethnic community. I brought my speech to a climax by quoting the poem of the African American writer Maya Angelou, 'Still I Rise'.

I think all those former mayors of Hackney whose portraits hung on the corridors outside the chamber would have been proud of me. I left the room to prolonged applause and I knew that, whatever happened, I had given it everything I had.

I won on the second ballot, by forty-two votes to Ernie Roberts's thirty-five. When we were told the result, I do not know who was more shocked: me or the Hackney North members who had been swept up in the moment and had voted for me. The local party officers, who were solid Ernie supporters, looked devastated.

The paid party official in attendance that evening was also distraught. As the meeting broke up, he blurted out, 'We did not think you could win. Otherwise we would have done something.'

Ernie Roberts, the sitting MP whom I had deselected, was beside himself. There was a lot of talk about a Black woman being an electoral liability. Ernie told the *Hackney Gazette*, 'It was an unfair result that underlines the need for one member, one vote. I was rejected because I was not Black, and I am not a woman. But if the Party is going to be divided on the basis of colour, sex and witch-hunts, then we shall lose the next election.' He stormed out of the town hall before the official announcement and did not congratulate me, either then or ever. By contrast, many ordinary members crowded up to me in the council chamber to shake my hand.

I rang friends and family, and went to an impromptu celebration party in a supporter's house in Stoke Newington. All the while I was saying to myself, 'I can't believe it.' I ended the evening taking a cab to friends in south London, where there was champagne and further congratulations. I spent the night with them, and when I picked up a copy of *The Guardian* on my way to work the following morning, 9 December 1985, there on the front page was a photograph of me, with the news of my selection under the headline 'Leftwing MP unseated by black woman'.

At work, where there were more hugs and more champagne, I spent the day coping with a barrage of press enquiries and giving media interviews. By the time I finally returned to my flat in Maida Vale that evening I felt completely exhausted, almost too tired to be euphoric. An appalling anticlimax brought me abruptly down to earth. The evening of my selection meeting, the woman in the flat below mine had called the police because she saw a damp patch on her ceiling. The police turned up and, without even bothering to consult me first, completely overreacted by kicking down my front door. It had been off its hinges all of Sunday evening and all day Monday, and nobody had told me. I felt vulnerable, terrified and helpless with anger. My little flat, which was all the security I had in the world, had been torn open like a sardine can. I went to spend the night with another friend who lived nearby. She said grimly, 'This is just the beginning. It is going to be hard and lonely.'

The news of my selection was not greeted with much acclaim by the mainstream media, notwithstanding the *Guardian*'s article on the day after the meeting. The *Daily Express*, *The Times* and the *Sun* all described me as an extremist, with the last-named reporting the result under the headline 'Black Diane "won after vote swap"', making it sound as if I had won by some nefarious means. All it really meant was that many of the delegates at the selection conference chose to vote for me rather than Ernie, even though their branches had expressed a preference for him. Meanwhile Ernie took his bitter complaints about 'malpractice' all the way to the Labour Party's National Executive Committee (NEC). They ruled, however reluctantly, that the selection process had been carried out properly, and my selection would have to stand. This confirmation provoked a hostile leader in *The Times*, in which I was denounced for my rhetoric of class struggle and skin-colour consciousness.

At the time I had not spoken to my brother for many years. When I was selected as the prospective parliamentary candidate for Hackney North, with every prospect of becoming the first Black British female MP, I did not tell him. I didn't even know where he lived, although I knew it was outside London. However, nothing defeats our intrepid tabloid press when they are looking feverishly for dirt on their latest target. One of the more scurrilous Sunday papers found out where Hugh lived and turned up on his doorstep. They knocked on his door and asked, 'When did you last see your sister?'

In truth, it had been many years, but Hugh instinctively went into protective mode and said that he had last seen me the week before. Then he rang me to tell me all about it.

The photographs taken of me on election night are a testament to the unifying power of family: my brother Hugh, together with our mother, standing proudly beside me and sporting a socialist red tie.

Not every Labour Party member in Hackney was happy with my selection. Labour-supporting journalist Fiona Millar wrote a scathing article in the *Express*, saying that Black Sections were the 'new albatross' around Neil Kinnock's neck. She went on to insist that I and others were 'loathed by provincial MPs who had nothing in common with their extremist views' and added, 'Most opinion polls now register an obsession with minority interests such as gay, black and lesbians as one of the chief reasons for disillusion with Labour.' It is safe to assume that her views reflected those of the Kinnock inner circle; she was close to Neil and Glenys Kinnock, and later Tony Blair's spin doctor Alastair Campbell became the father of her children. So while the national Labour Party could not block my selection, it was more successful in taking out two other Black women selected as parliamentary candidates around that time. One was Sharon Atkin, a clever, ebullient Lambeth councillor, who was selected in Nottingham East. The selection was run entirely properly, but soon afterwards Sharon was at a public meeting and in her response to a goading question she blurted out, 'I don't give a damn about Neil Kinnock and the racist Labour Party.' It might not have been polite, but she had broken no rules. Yet that was all the excuse the national party needed to remove her as a candidate.

The other candidate whom the Labour Party eliminated in a Vauxhall by-election a couple of years later was Martha Osamor, a lovely woman who had migrated to Britain from Nigeria. She was a great campaigner and had been very involved in community politics in her home constituency of Tottenham. Martha became particularly active after the Broadwater Farm riots in Tottenham, which happened after the wrongful arrest of a young Black man called Floyd Jarrett in October 1985, about a month before I was selected for Hackney North. Martha was a founding member of the Broadwater Farm defence campaign, and spoke all over London, organizing demonstrations and producing a 'manifesto for the movement for civil rights and justice'.

Nearly every ward in Vauxhall CLP nominated Martha. But the Labour Party did not bother to give a serious reason for blocking her candidacy. That she was Black, female and left-wing was enough. Roy Hattersley, deputy leader of the Labour Party at the time, was incredibly patronizing about her, reportedly telling the NEC, 'If there was ever anyone who has been used by extreme elements it is Martha Osamor. She is a simple woman of that sort. She could never have got elected to Parliament.' When some of us lobbied Kinnock on Martha's behalf, he wrote to us saying: 'I am sure that you will see the NEC's shortlist for Vauxhall as reflecting a serious commitment to having a candidate who will be in tune with the electors.' There was no doubt that by a candidate 'in tune with the electors', Kinnock meant someone white.

Miraculously, in this extremely hostile climate at the top of the Labour Party, I hung on as a candidate. I was in no doubt that, if the national Labour Party could have found a way of removing me, they would have done so. I was the only Black woman who got through in the 1987 election cycle. But three Black men were also selected for safe Labour seats. One was Bernie Grant, whom I had known for years. Another was Paul Boateng, who had been the only Black member of the Greater London Council. Though he had lost the Hertfordshire West seat in 1983, he benefited in 1987 from the activism around the Black Sections movement and the general wave of support for the left in London, and was selected as the candidate for the safe Labour seat of Brent South.

The final member of the quartet of Black Labour candidates elected in 1987 was Keith Vaz, a suave, ambitious young lawyer who had come to Britain as a child in the 1960s from Yemen. Though he was of South Asian heritage, Keith was considered to be Black like us. He lived in west London, but unlike Bernie, Paul and me, he was not a member of the London left that revolved around Ken Livingstone's GLC. In 1985 Keith had been selected for Leicester East and moved up there, away from the controversies that regularly swept through the London Labour Party. His greatest political asset was his mother, Merlyn Vaz, who adored her son. It would be hard to imagine anyone who less resembled the stereotype of a quiet, shy, retiring South Asian woman. A member of Leicester council, she rushed around to political meetings, got involved in campaigns and had shrewd political instincts. I do not doubt that had she been born a few years later, she would have been an MP.

The four of us were set to be candidates in the 1987 general election. We were all standing in safe seats, but there was no expectation that we could definitely win. Black candidates had lost safe Labour seats before, notably David Pitt in 1970 as the candidate for the perfectly safe seat of Clapham. Perhaps it was the idea that selecting a Black candidate was tantamount to throwing your constituency away that made Labour Party members so reluctant to select one for years after that.

My campaign in 1987 was stormy. I received a barrage of racial abuse by post and telephone. A brick was thrown through the window of my campaign headquarters, and the Tory candidate in Hackney North, Oliver Letwin, described me as 'a revolutionary with no genuine allegiance to parliamentary democracy'. The SDP (Social Democratic Party) candidate, Simon Taylor, told the *Hackney Gazette* that an issue on which his campaign would be fought was my extremist views. A number of senior Labour Party figures refused to be seen with me, and Neil Kinnock himself presumably shared the view of the Tories and the SDP that I was a dangerous extremist, as he never visited Hackney North and sent no message of sympathy and support when my campaign headquarters were attacked.

During the campaign I was invited to speak to workers at the Ford plant in Dagenham. The Transport and General Workers'

Union convenor steward at the Ford factory was a Black man called Joe Gordon, and Ford had a large Black workforce. Bryan Gould was the MP for Dagenham and was Labour's national campaign organizer; he was horrified when he heard I was coming and tried to block the event. Gordon stood up to him and the event went ahead. Gould made a point of sitting far away from me, for fear that we might be photographed together, whereas Gordon pronounced my candidacy 'a tremendous step forward for the Labour Party as far as black people were concerned'.

Back in the constituency, my supporters flung themselves into the campaign to elect Britain's first Black woman MP. I had a brilliant campaign organizer, John Burnell, who fought the campaign as if for a marginal seat. I lost almost 2,000 votes to the SDP, possibly from white Labour voters who could not bring themselves to vote for a Black 'extremist' but did not want to vote Tory, either. Overall the Labour vote held firm and, thanks to the work of John Burnell, Peter Kenyon, US Congresswoman-to-be Terri Sewell and others, it only went down by 3.3 per cent.

After all the losses and false dawns of the past, it seemed that on Thursday, 11 June 1987 voters in Brent, Tottenham, Hackney and Leicester were finally ready to elect Black MPs. On election night at Hackney Town Hall I was wearing red, and my hair was a mass of long braids. The red was for socialism and the braids were a nod to my African heritage. It was an incredible night. As the ballot papers were counted at long tables in the hall, I watched in amazement as the piles of papers with X marked against Abbott gradually rose higher, and I slowly realized that I really was going to win. I could feel the excitement surging around me.

It was a long night. The Hackney returning officer did not finally declare until three in the morning; and that was the point when I allowed myself to believe that I actually had won and was going to become Britain's first Black woman Member of Parliament. When the returning officer announced the result, I was swept away in the excitement of the moment. I could hardly get the words out, but I said something about it being 'a victory for faith, a victory for principle and a victory for socialism'. It was a triumph not only for me, but for the local party members who had selected me, believed in me and worked their socks off to try and deliver victory against the odds.

As well as jubilant local Labour Party members, personal friends who had spent weeks knocking on doors for me were there, and acquaintances from university whom I had not seen for years were in the town hall to see me get elected. My old friend Adam, who had said years earlier that he knew I was going to become Britain's first Black woman MP, was there, pleased and proud to have been proved right. And despite all the family rifts, my brother and my beaming mother were beside me on the Hackney Town Hall stage. In some ways the person I was most pleased for was my mother. She could not have dreamed when she came to England from rural Jamaica all those years ago that her daughter would become a British Member of Parliament. It reminded me of a saying that my friend Anni would sometimes repeat: 'If you are working-class, being an MP is the job your parents always wanted for you – clean, indoor work and no heavy lifting.'

When the sun came up and all the formalities and jubilation were over, I walked home on a high. My campaign manager had insisted that if there was going to be a Black woman standing for election, everyone was going to know it, so all the campaign posters that I walked past had big photos of me smiling out from them. It felt surreal to see my face on those posters and to realize that I really had been selected by the people of Hackney.

In the days that followed I met many older West Indians who told me how proud it made them feel to see someone who looked like them in Parliament. I thanked everyone for their good wishes, and for weeks to come I was moving around in a daze. But even in that daze, reality cut through. I was under no illusions as to what the attitude of the national Labour Party would be to the election of me and my Black colleagues. It was summed up by what had happened a year earlier, before I got elected. The BBC had invited me to go on their flagship evening-television politics programme, *Question Time*. It was unusual to have someone who was still only a parliamentary candidate on the programme, but perhaps they thought that if I did win, I would be a history-maker. The programme always featured national politicians and was chaired by the intimidating Robin Day, notorious for his abrasive style of interrogation, delivered as he peered down over heavy-rimmed spectacles, wearing his signature polka-dot bow tie.

I am naturally a confident person – at least that is what I look like from the outside. But I was definitely nervous about going on *Question Time* for the first time. Because I had worked in television news and current affairs, I knew that any Labour Party representative appearing on a show like that always got briefed by the party beforehand. So in plenty of time – four weeks ahead, to be exact – I contacted Peter Mandelson, who was then the party's Director of Communications, for my expected briefing. Weeks passed and no briefing came. With just a week to go, I was beginning to panic, so I rang him once more, but still Mandelson did not send a briefing. The day before filming I called him again in a real panic and we had a perfunctory conversation. He obviously was not interested in helping me and did not care if I made a complete fool of myself. So it was a very nervous woman who arrived at BBC Television Centre to appear in front of the cameras on a national news and current-affairs programme for the first time. I had been given no briefing, no coaching and no support whatsoever from the Labour Party nationally.

Despite this lack of support from Peter Mandelson and the party, I must have done reasonably well, because I then became a *Question Time* regular. There were periods when I went on even more frequently than some shadow Labour Party ministers. However, it was that first experience with Peter Mandelson that made me wise to the fact that those at the top of the party wanted it both ways: on the one hand, they insisted that Black candidates were a liability; on the other hand, they tried to ensure that we failed, by offering us no help whatsoever.

It was historic for four Black MPs to be elected for the first time, but we were not allowed to bask in the glory of our achievement. The Labour Party officials and the Labour Party leader, Neil Kinnock, did not see it as a triumph and noticeably did not celebrate it as such. Kinnock thought of his Black MPs as an embarrassment. We were the embodiment of the 'loony left', and this was precisely the image he was trying to get away from. *The Times* reported that he was considering purging the party of Bernie Grant, Paul Boateng, Jeremy Corbyn, Ken Livingstone and me, to counter what he and his advisors regarded as the 'disastrous' London effect.

Kinnock was not the only one wary of the election of four Black MPs for the first time. Bernard (known as 'Jack') Weatherill, Speaker of the House of Commons, was a kindly man who meant well, but he seemed to think the election of four Black MPs was akin to the advent of barbarians. He called together a group of trusted MPs from all parties for a private meeting, to discuss how Parliament would meet this challenge. Many existing non-Black MPs thought that we would be like the MPs of the Irish Parliamentary Party under Charles Stewart Parnell, who found ingenious ways of disrupting the Commons, like engaging in endless filibusters to keep MPs up all night. One of the MPs whom a terrified Speaker Weatherill called to his preparatory meeting was the Tory MP Jonathan Aitken, who had been my boss when I worked as a journalist at TV-am. As the only MP at the meeting who had met any of us personally, he was able to reassure Jack and the others that I was not such a dangerous radical as all that, nor did I have plans to burn down any buildings. At the end of the meeting they concluded that everyone should be cautious, but they should all do their best to make us welcome.

When I stepped into Parliament for the first time as an MP on 17 June 1987, it was a little like the first day at school. While I may have sounded coherent, I was still in a bit of a daze from the night I had been elected a Member of Parliament. Of course that didn't mean I had not thought carefully about what I was going to wear. For such an important occasion I wanted a unique outfit, so I commissioned a skirt suit made to measure from a satin material. The jacket was of fabric that the dressmaker herself had designed, blue with a swirly pattern that was reminiscent of African textiles. The skirt and the lapels of the jacket were black, and I finished off the look with a gold-coloured neckpiece and large gold earrings, with my hair styled in shoulder-length braids. Bernie wore a spectacular agbada – a long, flowing traditional West African robe; we made an eye-catching pair. Our MP friends, including Jeremy Corbyn, made a point of coming up to us, perhaps innocently trying to be friendly, but I always had a slight suspicion that they wanted to be in the iconic, history-making photographs.

On my first day in the House of Commons I sat in the seat where Enoch Powell always used to sit, which felt appropriate. Despite the bravado of my outfit that day, in the weeks to come I sat on the green benches in the chamber of the House of Commons scarcely able to believe that I was an MP. Everything about Parliament was designed to overawe and bring home to a young Black woman that somebody like me was not supposed to be there. They did not even have Black waitresses. The architecture was intimidating: the building was constructed in 1870 in the Gothic Revival style, with 1,100 rooms, 300 staircases, three miles of passageways, innumerable dining rooms, bars and a smoking room. There was even a rifle range. More intimidating than that was the fact that round every corner were attendants wearing black tailcoats, who took even longer than our MP colleagues to become accustomed to the Black newcomers. Bernie, Paul and Keith could not have looked more different, yet they were regularly confused with one another (though any such confusion was avoided in the cloakroom, which had a named hanger for each MP). When I was first elected, every hanger had a long loop of red ribbon, which was traditionally for MPs to hang their swords from, never mind the fact that no one had worn a sword in Parliament for 700 years – it just went to show how long it can take Parliament to adapt to change.

The wider world also had difficulty adjusting to the idea that Black people could be MPs. By this time my brother was a civil engineer and, not long after my election, when attending an Institution of Civil Engineers dinner at the House of Lords, he mentioned in passing to a fellow diner that his sister worked in Parliament. 'So she works in the kitchen?' came the reply.

The rituals and language of Parliament took a lot of getting used to, and Parliament itself had the feel of an old-fashioned gentlemen's club. In some ways it had always been one. Historically, Parliament has been a part-time job organized to facilitate working in business or practising as a lawyer. The House of Commons begins its debates in the middle of the day precisely in order to give MPs time to do much of their work before coming in. The hours were particularly convenient for lawyers. What mainly contributed to the sense of a gentlemen's club was that it was the most overpoweringly male place I had ever worked in. I had attended an all-girls' grammar school and had moved on to Newnham, an all-female Cambridge college, before working with a fair number of women during my time in the media. In Parliament, however, the numbers of men were overwhelming. The most powerful female presence in the House of Commons was the prime minister, Margaret Thatcher; needless to say, she and I had completely different political perspectives. In 1987, out of 650 Members of Parliament, there were only forty-one women. As a Black woman, I was of course completely on my own: just me, out of 650 others.

As a new MP, I gravitated towards parliamentarians whom I already knew— all London left-wingers, with one notable exception: Jonathan Aitken, MP, my old boss at TV-am and a Tory who would become my voting pair. 'Vote pairing' is a tactic whereby two Members of Parliament of opposing parties agree to abstain from voting during legislature if the other one is unable to attend, this being done with the consent of their party whips, whose task it is to ensure party discipline.

One of my best friends in the early years was Tony Banks, MP; he is there in the corner of a photograph of the four Black MPs on the day we were sworn in, and in the months to come he took it upon himself to show me the ropes. On my first day he took me into the Members' Smoking Room, which was yet another bar, and he made a point of ordering a bottle of champagne to celebrate my victory. The Smoking Room was a favourite haunt of Tory MPs and as we sipped our champagne, they looked on with scarcely concealed horror. Tony told me afterwards that it gave him huge pleasure to see the look on their faces.

Tony was a stalwart of the London left, an acerbically witty man who was popular on both sides of the House. He had been chairman of the GLC when Ken Livingstone was leader and was a devoted Bennite. Years later, when he became chair of the Commons Art committee, he insisted on commissioning a portrait of me. Normally the Commons does not commission portraits of mere backbenchers, but Tony was insistent. 'You are history,' he said. The painting hangs in Parliament to this day.

In my first year in Parliament I also spent time with other left-wing MPs, including Jeremy Corbyn and Ken Livingstone – although Ken never really forgave me for attempting to challenge him in Brent East – and I joined the Socialist Campaign Group (SCG), a left-wing group in Parliament that met every week. The SCG was a group of MPs who supported Tony Benn, who usually attended our meetings. We would look at the debates for the following week and discuss them, sometimes inviting an expert to brief us on upcoming business or issues. Speakers would come to us from national campaigns, and often we would plan rebellions against the Labour leadership. When I entered Parliament, the SCG revolved around Tony Benn. This was fine by me because, like most ordinary party members, I adored him and had nothing but admiration for the way he stuck by his principles. He was not quite so popular with his fellow Labour MPs.

My immediate challenge as a new MP was to get an office, since MPs were not automatically allocated one. Office accommodation was scarce, as this era pre-dated the smart new parliamentary buildings such as Portcullis House. Handing out offices was a piece of personal patronage by the Labour whips – a power they guarded jealously. The Labour whip responsible was a dour Welshman called Ray Powell; Ken Livingstone later described him as 'a right-winger who rewarded loyalists and punished rebels'. Being unaware of this, however, I innocently tried to contact Mr Powell. I repeatedly went to the whip's suite of offices, but somehow he was never there – or so I was told. After finally managing to catch him, I asked politely about the possibility of an office and, with a perfectly straight face, Powell said that I was second to bottom on his list.

Still politely, I asked him who was at the bottom of his list. He replied, 'Ken Livingstone', and the realization dawned on me that failing to give me an office was not an accident, but a purely polit-ical decision on his part, designed to punish me for being one of the much-disliked and feared group of left MPs elected that year.

There were other difficulties too, of course. Many Labour MPs from outside London were convinced that we MPs from the cap-ital had lost Labour the election; nor did all Labour MPs have a particularly multicultural outlook. That year I was standing in the queue in the Members' Tea Room, chatting casually with the Labour MP ahead of me about Christmas. When I said I was thinking of going to Jamaica to visit family, he looked at me incredulously, saying, 'Do they celebrate Christmas in Jamaica?'

Soon after being elected, I was invited onto the BBC's *Question Time* for a second time. As before, I was given no support or media training from the national Labour Party. My fellow panellists this time were the Liberal MP Cyril Smith, Tory minister Michael Heseltine and *Sunday Times* editor Andrew Neil. Cyril Smith did not waste time before sticking in the knife. The polls, he said, showed that Labour was unelectable, and one of the reasons for this was me, and people like me. The white audience erupted in applause; and it was a view shared by most Labour MPs and political lobby journalists, too. One explanation for why other Labour MPs were so hostile was because they feared that the four of us would bring issues of race and immigration into mainstream political discourse. It turned out to be as bad as they feared.

I made my maiden speech in the House of Commons a few months later, on 16 November 1987, in a debate about proposals for an amended Immigration Bill. My mother was sitting in the Visitors' Gallery of the chamber, looking down proudly. The other Black MPs who had been elected alongside me – Bernie Grant, Paul Boateng and Keith Vaz – were in the chamber with me, to give moral support and administer a verbal slap-down to Tory MPs, if required. It was essentially a debate about tightening immigration legislation. After more than two hours of lively exchanges, preserved verbatim in Hansard (the official transcripts of parliamentary debates), it was 6.49 p.m. by the time my opportunity came to voice my views against the bill. Drawing on personal experience, I said:

> I have the distinction of both being the daughter of immigrants and representing a constituency in north-east London which, for more than a century, has been a classic centre where immigrants have been welcomed. My parents came to this country in 1950 as immigrants from rural Jamaica. Contrary to what Conservative Members might have us believe, they came – a whole generation of black and ethnic minority immigrants came – not to sponge, not to swamp anyone else's culture, not to provide objects of derision for Conservative Members, but to work. They came for a better life for their children. They also came with pride, as citizens of Britain and its Commonwealth, and believing in that citizenship.

In the quarter-century that has elapsed since 1950, to see what has happened to that notion of citizenship of Britain and its Commonwealth – that once proud ideal – is very sad indeed . . .

Above all, in the past quarter-century we have encountered the notion that immigrants, far from being people who cross the oceans in good faith seeking to work and seeking a better life, are a kind of plague or contagion. No measure is too botched, too legally illiterate or too racist to attempt to keep them out.[1]

I also spoke about the inefficiency and incompetence of the immigration authorities. Although I was a new MP, I already had a big caseload of immigration cases and I drew on my experience of dealing with those to speak about the chaos in the system. Despite all the immigration legislation passed since the Second World War, 1987 was the first year that a child of Black immigrants took part in a debate on immigration in the chamber of the House of Commons. It was a nerve-racking event. Traditionally maiden speeches are heard in respectful silence, though a few Tories could not resist making some polite but patronizing remarks.

The other major event in my first few months was going on a bill committee. When legislation has been debated for the first time in the House of Commons, it goes into committee, where a much smaller group of MPs debates it clause by clause, amending it if necessary. I was put on the 1987 Finance Bill committee, which was quite prestigious and was normally barred to left-wingers.

Nick Brown, an MP from the North-East, was the whip in charge and, although the whips' office was generally hostile to me and other London left-wingers, Nick and I became friendly. Later he explained that he was looking out for bright people to serve on the Finance Bill committee. He wanted MPs who could speak and not be intimidated, and he guessed that I was one of those. Nick knew that I always spoke from a left perspective, did not necessarily take the party line and made my own arguments, but none of that bothered him. He later described me as 'disobedient but fun'.

Sitting in a committee room in Parliament with self-important male colleagues on all sides debating clauses on VAT seemed a long way from Hackney and the grass-roots politics that I was used to, but I enjoyed it.

From my earliest time as an MP, I wanted to organize events in Parliament for my Hackney constituents, the Black community and other groups who could not in their wildest dreams have thought they would see the inside of Parliament. It was not always easy. One of my first receptions started late, because House of Commons security flatly refused to let my Black guests in. On another occasion, officials presented me with a bill for cleaning the carpet in the room where the reception had been held, though it goes without saying there was no unusual need to clean it. All my Black colleagues experienced these problems. It served to undergird the unspoken belief of the House of Commons authorities that somehow Black MPs were not legitimate MPs.

In August 1987 the *New Statesman* asked me to interview the American Black radical icon Angela Davis. I was thrilled to get the chance to engage with one of my heroines. We discussed patriotism, coalitions and hope. Although Angela herself would never have got involved in electoral politics, I was surprised to learn that she saw a role for it. She said, 'I think that the work of the fifties, sixties and seventies is now seeing fruits with the progressive Black candidates: the Congressional Black Caucus is the most progressive body in Congress.' She was reluctant to describe herself as a feminist, saying, 'I am wary of the historical connotations. It originated in white middle-class circles and for a long time was used to connote women who worked on issues which concerned only them – isolated from the wider context.'

As a new Parliamentarian, I found Angela Davis inspirational and a reminder of a wider political world outside the British Parliament. Meanwhile the institution began to get used to me and my three Black colleagues, and we got used to Parliament. Speaker Weatherill was relieved that we were not as scary as he had feared, and even invited Bernie Grant for a glass of port in his private apartments some evenings. Certain problems persisted, however, one being the petty harassment of our Black guests; we gave it some time to see if matters improved and, when they did not, the four of us felt obliged to write a letter in 1988 to the parliamentary authorities about the way our visitors were being treated. In it, we talked about being 'challenged by attendants as to our identity in unsubtle attempts to embarrass us', and furthermore that these occurrences were 'too frequent and had been going on for too long'. After our letter, things did change a little; yet to this day, the occasional Black guests get hassled by House of Commons security in a way that seems unnecessary.

In 1989 I joined the Treasury and Civil Service Committee. As an unreconstructed left-winger, I would not normally be put on one of Parliament's most prestigious committees, but the whip involved was my friend Tony Banks. Individual whips took it in turns to nominate MPs to whatever Select Committees they chose, and at this point in time these nominations were almost always confirmed by the cross-party Committee of Selection, which meant that the whips' control was considerable. So when Tony's turn came, he nominated me to the Treasury Committee.

Kinnock's office blew a gasket when they heard the news. In those days, however, the whips' office was its own centre of power. Whatever Chief Whip Derek Foster thought of Tony Banks's nomination, he was determined to safeguard the authority of the whips' office and so he threw his weight behind the decision. Ken Livingstone told me later that Kinnock's people only calmed down when they were told it was a choice between me and him. The Treasury Select Committee had oversight of government economic policy and held weekly sessions, where we took evidence on economic matters. Among those who came in front of our committee were Treasury ministers, Treasury officials, the Governor of the Bank of England, academics and economists. I am not sure why Neil Kinnock was so hostile to me going on this committee. Perhaps he thought I would not take the official Labour Party line on economic policy, or maybe he simply believed that I was too stupid. If it was the latter, I like to think I proved him wrong. Cambridge had taught me how to absorb information; my time at the Home Office meant that I knew how officials thought and how to question them; and my media experience had helped to burnish an existing confidence, so I had no trouble asking officials difficult questions.

The year 1989 also saw the inaugural activities of the Parliamentary Black Caucus, which had been launched the previous year by Bernie Grant. It was modelled on the American Congressional Black Caucus (CBC), which had been founded in 1971: a group of Black Congressmen and women who worked together to wield influence. Their slogan was 'Black people have no permanent friends, no permanent enemies, just permanent interests.' In Britain our attempt at a Black caucus foundered from the beginning. Mrs Thatcher was no friend to Black issues – so much so that I criticized her directly on the floor of the House of Commons during a debate on the Commonwealth Heads of Government conference held in Kuala Lumpur: 'Does the Prime Minister agree that, notwithstanding her ritual condemnation of apartheid, her performance at Kuala Lumpur demonstrates what everybody, particularly black South Africans know – that she is and remains at every international occasion that she attends an indefatigable fifth columnist for apartheid?' Unsurprisingly, Mrs Thatcher did not agree.

The other main problems were our tiny numbers and the hostility of the Labour Party leadership. The American caucus on its launch had thirteen members; by 2019 the membership had grown to fifty-five. There being so many Black Congressmen and women, they could afford to have a few colleagues who chose not to join. In Britain, however, there were just the four of us. Paul Boateng refused to get involved from the outset; I was never sure why, but perhaps he wanted to be a bit more mainstream than was implied by being in a Black Caucus. This cut our numbers by 25 per cent straight away. It was obvious that we could be more effective working together, so we recruited a member from the House of Lords. Lord David Pitt had been the second Black man to become a member of the House of Lords; in fact he was the first person to greet me when I entered Parliament in 1987. He was happy to be a member of our Parliamentary Black Caucus, so Bernie, Keith, David and I ploughed on with setting up the caucus. I tried to get financial support from business, as the CBC in America had successfully done, but in Britain business told me, 'We want customers, not shoplifters.'

Nevertheless we managed to have a high-profile launch. A delegation of African American politicians flew over to support us, including Congressman Ron Brown, chair of the Democratic National Committee; Congressman Mervyn Dymally; and former Congresswoman Shirley Chisholm. With so many notable US politicians supporting our UK caucus, even Neil Kinnock had to dial down his opposition. We went on to lobby on a series of race-related issues, including the slanted coverage of race in the mainstream media. In 1989 I joined the CBC's annual conference in Washington DC, and the following year my Black colleagues and I met the iconic American civil-rights leader Jesse Jackson. At that time Jesse was a more high-profile figure than any elected American Black politician and it was exciting to meet someone who had been so deeply involved in the US civil-rights struggle since the 1960s. He had been there when the internationally acclaimed civil-rights leader Martin Luther King was assassinated.

In 1990 Nelson Mandela – the man Thatcher had called a terrorist – was released from prison. The images on television that showed him walking free after twenty-seven years, having served the majority of his time on Robben Island (the maximum-security jail for political prisoners), were unforgettable and incredibly moving. Anti-apartheid campaigns and the slogan 'Free Nelson Mandela' had been one of the most important international movements of my adult life and had essentially become part of left-wing popular culture. For Mandela finally to have been freed, after all these years, confirmed that progressive forces could fight and win. It was particularly emotional to witness Mandela come out of prison hand-in-hand with his formidable wife Winnie, each with a fist raised in a powerful image of political triumph.

Meanwhile the tabloid press still continued to depict me, and my left-wing colleagues, as a threat to civilization. In 1991 Neil Kinnock had been engaged in a years-long battle to expel what he regarded as an unacceptably left-wing faction called Militant from the party. The *Evening Standard* responded by devoting a whole page to photographs of me and my fellow Socialist Campaign Group MPs, with the headline 'Why won't Kinnock purge all these extremist MPs too?'

In that same year I was learning a lot from Jesse Jackson. He did not consider me and my Black colleagues 'extremist'; rather, he was an internationalist and wanted to reach out. In his 1994 presidential bid, Jesse built what he described as the Rainbow Coalition. This was an attempt to bring together not only African Americans, but also Hispanics, Native Americans, family farmers, the women's movement, anti-war campaigners and the LGBT movements. I was very interested in this unity politics and it greatly influenced my worldview. Outside the Labour Party, I was very much focussed on Black politics, and Jesse taught me the importance of bringing together strands of progressive politics. He became a good friend, and for years we would meet every time he came to Britain.

With only three members in the House of Commons and no funds, the Parliamentary Black Caucus could not survive. To this day, I think it was a lost opportunity.

From my earliest days as an MP, Margaret Thatcher had completely dominated national politics and the chamber of the House of Commons. At the 1982 Conservative Party conference, she had boasted, 'We have done more to roll back the frontiers of socialism than any previous Conservative government.' That was true then, and it was even more true by the time I was elected in 1987. From the beginning she had waged war on her perceived enemies, foreign and domestic. In terms of foreign policy, she was an enthusiastic supporter of the US Cold War and the arms race with the Soviet Union. Domestically, she believed in free markets. Her belief that the private sector was always preferable to public ownership led to a huge wave of privatization, for organizations including British Steel, British Airways, British Gas, British Telecom and the rail and water companies. Even other Tories called these privatizations 'selling the family silver'. One of her hallmark policies, and the one that did most to win her support from working-class voters, was council-house sales. Thatcher believed that home-owners were more likely to vote Conservative and, as always, she believed in private ownership as a point of principle. The lucky buyers were purchasing their homes at a considerable discount, but the policy decimated social housing.

Thatcher was not seen as someone who was interested in good race relations. Early on, she made her infamous speech about Britain being 'swamped' by people from different cultures, which was understood as a coded reference to the sense of threat that white racists felt about Black people in the UK. She was a looming right-wing presence that represented everything that the left – both inside and outside the Labour Party – was battling against. In 1982 came the Falklands War, a dispute with Argentina about two islands in the South Atlantic that few people had ever heard of. But they were British dependent territories, and Argentina invaded and occupied them. Mrs Thatcher responded by sending a naval task force to tackle the Argentinians and within seventy-four days they had surrendered. This played to the nationalism of many British voters and was widely seen as a triumph for Thatcher.

From 1984 to 1985 she embarked on one of her biggest domestic fights: taking on the National Union of Mineworkers (NUM) and its leader, Arthur Scargill. It was an important fight for Thatcher because it symbolized her total enmity to trade unionism. This strike had a huge effect on the left, even those of us far away from a coalfield. The mass pickets that the NUM mobilized, although criticized in the press, seemed emblematic of working-class solidarity. Thatcher did not even pretend that the battle was between the National Coal Board and the NUM. She explicitly framed it as a battle between herself and Scargill. He rose to her challenge and, at the 1983 NUM conference, said, 'I am not prepared quietly to accept the destruction of the coal industry, nor am I willing to see our social services dominated . . . Faced with the possible destruction of all that is good and compassionate in our society, extra-parliamentary action will be the only course open to the working class and the labour movement.' Ultimately, though, Thatcher was able to defeat the miners in what was a major triumph for her and the Conservative government. In 1983, before the strike began, Britain had 175 working pits. By 2015 every pit had been closed. Whatever anyone thought about the way Scargill conducted the strike, his prophecy that the future of the coal industry was at stake was proved absolutely correct.

As well as her determination to smash the power of the trade-union movement and her programme of privatization, Thatcher was intent on cutting public spending. The first line of her very first public-spending White Paper was 'Public expenditure is at the heart of Britain's present economic difficulties', and much of her drive to slash public expenditure was about cutting benefits. In 1979, when she came to power, the post-tax income of the top 10 per cent of the population was just five times that of the people at the bottom, but by 1997 the gap had doubled.[2] Thatcher was deemed by those on the right to have won a series of political victories, but her hold on national politics began to weaken, starting with public opposition to her poll tax. This was a per capita local-government tax that she introduced in 1990 and which was extremely unpopular, to the point that there was a huge demonstration against it in London on 31 March that year, where it was estimated there were 70,000–250,000 impassioned protesters around Trafalgar Square.

Public opposition to the poll tax seemed to embolden Thatcher's opponents in the Tory parliamentary party. Even though I was a member of the Labour opposition, I could feel the buzz of mounting disaffection on the Tory side, and I began to suspect, without even needing to talk to Tory MPs, that what we were seeing was the final act of the Thatcher drama.

In 1990 Parliament and the media were full of rumours that Michael Heseltine, MP was going to challenge her. He was a charismatic minister, a high-profile member of her Cabinet who was frequently at odds with her. Their main point of difference was on Europe: he was very pro-European, whereas Thatcher was Eurosceptic. Heseltine also considered himself a 'One Nation' Tory and less divisive than Thatcher. He became a vocal critic of her, and the possibility of a leadership challenge from him seemed increasingly imminent. I said in the chamber, rather mockingly, that if Heseltine became leader, the best Thatcher could hope for from his administration was 'mayor of Dulwich' – the suburb where she had bought a house. She did not laugh.

As the feeling continued to mount among MPs that Thatcher was on her way out, the final blow was delivered not by Heseltine, but from an unexpected source: Geoffrey Howe, who was Thatcher's deputy and her one-time Chancellor of the Exchequer. Although he was a notoriously dull politician, his resignation speech electrified the chamber of the House of Commons. It was pure theatre, and the most momentous parliamentary event that I had been a witness to. Howe's closing words were: 'The time has come for others to consider their own response to the tragic conflict of loyalties, with which I myself have wrestled for perhaps too long.'

Within weeks, Thatcher was gone. Her own MPs had turned against her. Those were the days when prime ministers were meant to take a hint and, if they were told verbally that most of their

MPs were not prepared to support them, they would go; they did not need to wait for mass resignations of their senior colleagues.

A tearful Margaret Thatcher left Number 10 Downing Street for the last time on 28 November 1990. Many would argue that among the legacies she bequeathed British politics and society were much greater inequality, a bloated financial sector, shrunken manufacturing and the beginning of large holes in the social safety net. But she also took with her the record of having been the longest-serving British prime minister of the twentieth century and one who, for good or ill, left a mark on her era. Parliament had expected her demise for such a long time, but when it finally came, MPs on both sides of the house could hardly believe it. It had the most dizzying effect on Tory MPs, who were giddy about what they had done. It was as if they had massacred matron.

Lord David Pitt was the first Black person to be a Labour Party parliamentary candidate in 1959. He was also the second Black man to become a member of the House of Lords and the first person to greet me when I entered Parliament for the first time as an MP.

6.   What Makes Us Free

By the early 1990s Mummy was dying of cancer. I was glad to spend time with her in the final months and was pleased that I was able to bring her 'home' to Jamaica for a long holiday towards the end. We stayed with her brother, Uncle Len, at his home in the hills of Kingston, to enjoy the peace and the Caribbean sunshine. My uncle knew this was going to be the last time he saw his beloved sister. We did not talk about it, but we all three understood the reality. Nobody was sad or mournful; Fred, the houseman, prepared and served delicious food; Mummy and my Uncle Len spent every day reminiscing about the good times when they were children. When Mummy and I left Uncle Len's house that final time, she turned to him and said, 'See you soon.' Both he and I were almost in tears, because we knew they would never see each other again.

Mummy and I returned to England and, soon afterwards, she passed away. She had always been very definite that when she died she wanted to be cremated, so I organized a quiet funeral and had her ashes packed in a plastic urn. Later that year I took the urn back to Jamaica, to Smithville, the countryside village where she had been born. I buried her next to her beloved mother, Miss Di.

It was a time of deep sorrow, though I was able to take some solace from the fact that we had been together for the final months of her life. Mummy was not aggressive, like Daddy, and was more softly spoken, but in her own way she was a very determined woman. Coming from Jamaica to Britain on her own showed that; besides the fact that, after sixteen years of marriage, she was able to gather her courage in her hands, leave Daddy, leave London and build a new life many miles away in Huddersfield. It always made me sad that while I was very close to Mummy, my brother was not. I never discussed it with Hugh, but I think maybe he thought she had abandoned the family. He did not seem able to comprehend the pressures that made her do that. And he has never really explained to me why he cut off all communication with Mummy, except to say that he found it the 'stress-free' option.

My parents' volatile marriage had a lasting effect on how I viewed relationships. On the one hand, I had a fear of being trapped in a marriage, as Mummy had been for so long. For years I thought Daddy was a monster, and it was only later in life that I realized what made him so angry about the society he was living in, and about the limitations and pressures of his own life. There was no safe way for him, as a Black man of his time, to express that anger, so he brought it home. Yet despite our problematic relationship, my father helped make me who I am.

The relationships I saw around me then were a million miles away from the romance that animated the historical fiction I had loved to read in my early teens. With my first real boyfriend, Peter, I built something that was not like anything in a historical novel. We were very close in a conventional way; Peter had to be extremely patient with me because, maybe owing to the emotional scars from my parents' difficult marriage, I was always doubting whether he really cared. The relationship lasted through sixth form, university and miles of separation; when it finally crumbled, it was not an unpleasant break-up, as my parents' had been. Peter was not that kind of person, and I had learned from observing my parents that this was not how I wanted a relationship to end.

It might be that their disastrous relationship made it more difficult for me to build relationships as I matured. There is a lot about being an MP that causes relationships to be difficult – Parliament's erratic hours not least among them – and being a woman MP makes them especially challenging. The female colleagues that I know with stable partnerships almost invariably got together with their partners before they became MPs, and some are even married

178

to other politicians. The fundamental problem for a man married to an MP is that the traditional balance of power is turned upside down. Some of these spouses are quite self-effacing and placid, don't feel threatened and have strong feelings of self-worth and careers of their own. Some couples even institutionalize the power relationship by having the husband work for the wife; personally, I would find that a little claustrophobic. One has to be calm to deal with a partner who's an MP, because politicians tend to lurch from crisis to crisis.

In 1990 I had met a Ghanaian architect, David Ayensu Thompson, through mutual friends who fancied their hand at a little match-making. We began a relationship that was somewhat fractious and not particularly close, but the following year, to our surprise, I fell pregnant. David's less-than-romantic response was to ask how he would know that it was his, so I duly prepared myself for being a single parent. It might have been the 1980s feminist in me – or maybe it was the example of my grandmother Miss Di, who never got round to marrying any of the fathers of her children – but somehow I was not that bothered about getting married.

My friends had other ideas. They felt it was simply not appropriate for Britain's first Black woman MP to have a child out of wedlock. Ros Howells, a good friend of mine, phoned me a few weeks into the pregnancy. She was older than me and came from a middle-class background. She was very ladylike, extremely kind and a determined fighter for racial equality, who later went on to be appointed to the House of Lords. I had met Ros originally through her campaigning work on race relations.

'I have been thinking,' she said to me. 'Who is this David Thompson anyway? You're pregnant – he has to marry you.'

Her firmness took me by surprise. Ros instructed me to arrange a meeting between her and David, which I obediently did; and by the time he emerged from that meeting we were engaged. It was not the most auspicious beginning for a marriage and, unsurprisingly, it did not last. It did, however, give me my wonderful son, James, who was born in October that year at Homerton Hospital in Hackney.

There was no such thing as maternity leave for MPs, no doubt because there were so few MPs who were women of child-bearing age that it had never occurred to the House of Commons authorities (who were all male) that it might be needed. All the way through my pregnancy I had to go into Parliament and vote. Some individual party whips tried to be helpful, but the whips' office insisted that I work until the Thursday before my due date and be back in Parliament eight days later. Childbirth truly brought home to me that, as an MP, you are never off-duty.

In the final hours, as I was flat on my back on the hospital bed in Homerton, convulsing with contractions and with my legs up in stirrups, the midwife in attendance saw her chance and began to lobby me about a pay dispute that the nurses had with the hospital.

I wanted to burst out, 'Can't you see I'm in labour here?' Instead I was obliged to listen patiently and give birth at the same time.

James was christened in the chapel of the House of Commons, at the suggestion of my voting pair, Jonathan Aitken, who became his godfather.

Although I considered myself to be a sturdy feminist, it did not occur to me to challenge the experience I had gone through. I just accepted the system. Being a single mother in Parliament was tricky; there was no other woman MP who was both single and had a small child, and Parliament made no allowances for bringing up children on your own. It routinely sat even later into the night than it does now, and there was no crèche. My son got to know many of the women who worked for me when he was a toddler, because they had to take it in turns looking after James. I had to physically read all my briefings and correspondence, and almost all meetings had to be conducted in person.

There was certainly no getting out of the Queen's Speech, where the government sets out its programme for the session. I ended up going through the voting lobby with my two-week-old son strapped to my chest, and to this day James holds the record for being the youngest person ever to go through a division lobby in the House of Commons. Other MPs were not impressed. One Tory said, 'This is an outrageous breach of the rules. It is bad enough having David Blunkett's dog trooping through the lobby, never mind babies.' Days later the Serjeant-at-Arms, a House of Commons official, told me that I had broken the rules and that I should not do it again. Don Dixon, MP, one of the Labour whips and not a particular friend of mine, said in exasperation, 'What is Diane supposed to do? Leave her baby lying around on the green benches?'

In those early years of juggling being a mother and an MP I soon realized that most whips were more willing to help women MPs, by permitting them to miss a vote, if they saw you as generally compliant. Initially I brought over a cousin from Jamaica to live with me and help look after James. An MP's life is not nine-to-five, so it seemed like a perfect solution. If I had to stay in Parliament voting until after midnight, I did not have to worry about James; he would be safely tucked up in his cot at home, with someone I knew looking after him. But when my cousin went back to Jamaica, things became nightmarish. I spent half the time thinking I was a terrible mother, and the other half thinking I was a terrible MP. Although I never took my son through the voting lobbies again, I would sometimes bring him in on a Friday, which was usually a quiet day, so that I could get through some work. My secretary would keep an eye on him.

One Friday, when I was walking through the Members' Lobby carrying James in my arms, the Tory MP Nicholas Soames spotted us and nearly fainted. It was not so much the sight of a baby that shocked him, but he was incredulous that I did not have a paid full-time nanny to look after my son. That was obviously taken for granted in the circles in which he moved. Matters improved a little when Nick Brown became Deputy Chief Whip in 1995; he was the first, in my time as an MP, to take seriously the question of accommodating mothers, and he was particularly lenient about letting me go home if he suspected that I was going to vote against the government.

In 1992, very much on the fringes of the Labour Party, I was increasingly looking outwards from Parliament and reaching out to the wider community. I set up Black Women Mean Business (BWMB), an initiative aiming to support, encourage and celebrate Black businesswomen. There was nothing like it at the time; no one was organizing events on the scale that I and my team did, and certainly not in the grand surroundings of the House of Commons. There were not very many Black female professionals at that time outside the music and entertainment business, but I corralled friends in areas like PR and marketing to come and speak for us. I even convinced the famous BBC newsreader Moira Stuart to address one of our annual conventions. We organized workshops and seminars on such topics as 'Building a Black Business', 'Marketing and PR' and 'Global Business'. The women who came were thrilled to be in the House of Commons, for almost all of them had never visited before. Often they would be the only Black face in their organizations, and they enjoyed networking with so many other Black women who shared their aspirations and had faced the same challenges. The initiative soon spread outside London, to places such as Bristol and Luton, with events that were all organized without a penny of funding.

In the same year that I set up BWMB there was a general election, which was a lot quieter for me than my first election in 1987. Commentators had come round to the view that you could elect a Black woman to Parliament and the heavens did not fall in. I also had a baby to look after, which limited me a little more in what I could do, and in the number of hours that I could be knocking on doors. It seemed I was no longer such an unwelcome novelty, and I faced fewer personal attacks and bricks through my headquarters' windows. On election night I won comfortably for a second time, and it was reassuring to realize that the electorate in Hackney North was not only willing to elect a Black woman as its MP, but was also prepared to elect her again, together with a baby. My majority even went up a little, to 10,727.

However, like all Labour MPs and supporters, I was shocked and upset by the result of the 1992 election. Seeing Mrs Thatcher ejected from Downing Street led us to think we were on a roll and that victory was within reach. John Major was seen as so unutterably dull (a view that was not restricted to the Labour benches), by comparison with his electrifying predecessor, that he was bound to lose. Furthermore, the opinion polls consistently put us on level pegging with the Tories, and even (occasionally) ahead. We didn't set much store by sarcastic tabloid headlines like The Sun's 'If Kinnock wins today, will the last person to leave Britain please turn out the lights.'

So it was with immense disappointment that we all woke up on the morning after the election to find that Labour had lost. Some thought that Kinnock had precipitated the loss with an ill-judged speech at an 11,000-strong rally in Sheffield, in which he had repeatedly shouted, 'We're all right'; many commentators said he had struck an overly confident tone. Whether or not this actually contributed to the shock result, Kinnock felt the need to resign, and John Smith took over as Labour leader. Smith was from Scotland, which at the time was a Labour bastion; he came from a distinctively Scottish Labour tradition that produced a number of prominent Labour MPs of the time, including Donald Dewar, Robin Cook, Alistair Darling and Gordon Brown. Back in 1981, four prominent MPs (David Owen, Shirley Williams, Bill Rodgers and Roy Jenkins) had left Labour to set up the Social Democratic Party, partly in protest at what they considered the unacceptably left-wing views of the then-leader, Michael Foot. Smith, although undoubtedly on the centre-right, had stayed put. When asked why, he said, 'I am comfortable with the unions. They [the others] aren't. That's the big difference.'

The SDP, although much lauded by the media, collapsed in 1988 when Kinnock was still leader of the Labour Party. So once John Smith became Labour leader, Gordon Brown and Tony Blair – close allies in wanting to get on with 'modernizing' the party and introducing their New Labour project – became increasingly frustrated by Smith's caution about weakening the party's link with the trade unions, moving away from Labour's historical commitment to public ownership and changing in ways designed to strengthen the party's appeal to middle England.

In 1994, across the oceans, something more momentous than the internal manoeuvring of the British Labour Party was happening: the defeat in the South African government of the all-white National Party, which had ruled the country since 1948 and was the architect of the brutal and racist apartheid system. All my life I had been a supporter of the anti-apartheid movement. 'Free Nelson Mandela' was a slogan that all wings of progressive politics could agree on; there was even a best-selling record with that title – that was how much the campaigning for Mandela's release had become a part of popular culture, although Margaret Thatcher, predictably, opposed economic sanctions against South Africa to the end.

The ANC, which had been banned since the 1950s for opposing apartheid, was at last able to take part in 'free and fair' elections, which it won, and that year I represented Parliament as an observer at those same elections. It was moving to be present at an event that so many of us had campaigned so long for. I noticed that when Black voters moved forward to put their ballot in the box, they would pause and look behind them for the last few seconds, as if they thought – having struggled so long for the right to vote – that even at the last minute some agent of apartheid would stop it happening. Nelson Mandela was duly elected president of South Africa on 10 May 1994.

Back in Britain, the Labour Party suffered the unexpected death of its leader, John Smith, after fewer than two years at the head of the Labour Party. After being frustrated for so long by Smith's caution, Tony Blair found the prize of the Labour leadership dropping into his lap at the relatively young age of forty-one. It meant that he and his close colleague Gordon Brown were able to go full steam ahead with their 'New Labour' project, and it marked the beginning of a completely fresh era in the history of the Labour Party.

Blair consciously regarded himself as a break with past Labour governments, whether it was Attlee's (which had created the welfare state) or Wilson's (which had refused to send British troops to fight alongside the Americans in Vietnam). New Labour was a response to the catastrophic election defeat of 1992, and Blair felt that for Labour to win again, it had to reach out to middle England in a way it had never done before. The idea of 'New Labour' was initially seen as a branding exercise, but it began to develop into a series of concrete changes in policies and orientation. As part of emphasizing the break with past Labour governments, there was a degree of continuity with Thatcher's policies. None of her privatizations were reversed; and her agenda of clamping down on trade-union freedoms, financial deregulation and almost no council-house building went completely untouched. Britain under New Labour was a better and more socially liberal place than it was under the Tories, but Thatcher herself said that one of her greatest achievements was the creation of 'New Labour'.

Blair was certainly a different generation from the recent Labour leaders. Michael Foot, Neil Kinnock and John Smith had all, in their own ways, had deep roots in the Labour movement, and it was impossible to imagine any of them as Tories. But Blair himself said that he could have joined any party. One of the first policy proposals he made as the new leader was the revision of Clause 4 of the party constitution, which struck me as symbolic of his determination to push the Labour Party in a centrist direction. Clause 4 set out Labour's commitment to the 'common ownership of the means of production and exchange' and was so important that it was printed on the back of every membership card. It was the Labour Party's commitment to socialism – and in effect, Blair wanted to abolish it. In the late 1950s the Labour leader Hugh Gaitskell had tried to abolish Clause 4 and failed, faced with opposition from party members and trade unions. The fierce debate about Blair's proposal to scrap it is now almost forgotten, but I had been elected to the Labour Party NEC (the first Black person to have achieved this) and I played a full part in that debate: writing articles, addressing rallies and speaking out at meetings of the NEC itself. It was this campaign that began to get me recognized as a national voice for the left in the Labour Party. In the end, Blair succeeded where Gaitskell had failed. His revision of Clause 4 was a decisive move to the right for the Labour Party.

The New Labour hold over party officials, and its grip on the party's organization, structures and staff, strengthened rapidly. People who had been left-wingers in the 1980s abandoned their beliefs and became born-again New Labour supporters. It was increasingly obvious that New Labour would become the dominant ideology in the party, so if you had career ambitions the sensible thing was to hitch yourself to its wagon.

The more prominent I became within the Labour Party, the more hostile the party leadership became towards me. Blair and his inner circle were keen to suppress left-wingers, and complained to colleagues about me 'inhaling Tory propaganda about us and exhaling it in a different form'. John Prescott was ostensibly a sturdy voice for trade unions and the left, but he had become a Blair loyalist and took to demanding that the Shadow Chief Whip, Donald Dewar, 'do something' about me, though I never worked out what that 'something' might be.

At the same time the Black community was facing enormous challenges. The tragic murder of Stephen Lawrence in April 1993 had caused shockwaves throughout the community, but there appeared to be no prospect of justice for his family. Stephen was an eighteen-year-old Black British teenager who had been waiting to catch a bus one evening in south-east London when he was attacked by a group of white men who shouted out racial slurs before fatally stabbing him. The men suspected of the crime were arrested, but all of them had the charges against them dropped. One of the key activists in the campaign was my good friend, Ros Howells. Ros was the one who first introduced me to Neville and Doreen Lawrence, long before their campaign for their son Stephen had much support outside south-east London or had been picked up by the national media, and before Labour came to power in 1997. Neville and Doreen had tried unsuccessfully to bring a private prosecution of the young men who had murdered their son, but even when an inquest ruled officially that Stephen had been killed 'in a completely unprovoked racist attack by five youths', the authorities did nothing. The Lawrence family was desperate, and to the Black community it appeared that wider society – and particularly the government – did not care. I was in touch with some of the local activists and I tried to help Stephen's family, in both practical and political ways. Stephen's father Neville Lawrence was a carpenter and decorator, so I recommended him to people I knew, to help the family bring in some income.

Blair and the Labour Party leadership seemed not to realize the magnitude of the Stephen Lawrence case for the Black community. They had not even reached out to Stephen's family. My colleague Bernie Grant and I couldn't let this stand, so we made a plan to move things forward. I asked the Shadow Home Secretary, Jack Straw, to meet Stephen's mother, Doreen. Jack agreed, but a few days before the meeting he told me that the Metropolitan Police had warned him not to meet Doreen. He went ahead with the meeting anyway, perhaps because he did not want to break his word to Bernie and me. On the appointed day we ushered Doreen into Jack's office in the House of Commons. He might have begun the meeting feeling a little sceptical because of the Met's warnings, but he was completely swept up by Doreen's passion and sincerity.

He promised her an official inquiry into Stephen's death if Labour won the next general election.

Election day 1997 was unforgettable. My own count in Hackney pronounced that I had won, so I rushed to the Royal Festival Hall at the Southbank Centre, where Labour Party members were waiting to hear the national result. As I hurried along the Southbank walkway in the dark, complete strangers shouted out their congratulations. Inside the hall we listened with rapt attention to the election results coming in from all over the country as the excitement mounted minute by minute. When it was announced that Labour had won a landslide victory with an astonishing majority of 179, I burst into tears. Those who saw me as an opponent of some New Labour schemes might have been surprised to see me crying with joy, but my love for the Labour movement has always outweighed factional concerns. In the early hours of the morning Tony Blair said, 'A new dawn has broken, has it not?' He was the youngest prime minister of the twentieth century, which in itself lent his government a certain dynamism. It really did feel like a new era.

The first thing Blair did was to appoint his Cabinet. I was pleased that, among the predictable appointments, he gave a job to my old friend Tony Banks. Tony was a stalwart of the London left, and his humour and charm meant he was the only one of us offered a Cabinet job by Blair; he was made Minister for Sport, a role that suited him perfectly. Other appointments were more controversial. Peter Mandelson, who had first been elected in 1992 and was Director of Communications for the 1997 campaign, was appointed to the Cabinet as Minister without Portfolio (in other words, a government minister with no specific responsibilities). Ordinary party members were suspicious of Mandelson because of his past financial dealings, including a loan that he had accepted in 1996 from his Cabinet colleague Geoffrey Robinson, whose business dealings Mandelson's department was investigating at the time; Robinson was later forced to resign over the scandal.

Mandelson's appointment to the Cabinet at this point was therefore contentious, since he was seen as one of the architects of New Labour, which even then was not as universally popular at the grass roots as it was in the Westminster bubble.

Not every promise made by politicians in opposition is carried out when they come to power; it is the kind of thing that fuels cynicism about politics. But Jack Straw, newly appointed as Home Secretary, fulfilled his promise to Doreen Lawrence and set up a landmark inquiry into her son's killing. It was led by Sir William Macpherson, a retired High Court judge and former soldier who was indisputably a member of the establishment, so the conclusions of his inquiry had a huge impact. Among other things, the inquiry concluded that the police investigation was 'marred by a combination of professional incompetence, institutional racism and a failure of leadership'. It was a seminal event in the politics of race; this was the first time that an official publication had used the term 'institutional racism', and that conclusion resonated. The inquiry led to major changes in the law, in policing, in the response to institutional racism and in the treatment of racist crimes, and ultimately led to two convictions in 2012 for Stephen Lawrence's murder.[1]

The results of the landslide election had also brought in a record number of women MPs: 101 to be exact. I reached out to all the new Labour women MPs with a handwritten note of welcome. Unfortunately, not one replied. Soon afterwards I passed one fellow Labour woman MP in a corridor, who mumbled nervously, 'Thank you for the letter' and rushed away. It was the only response I ever got to my welcoming notes.

After ten years as the only Black woman out of 650 MPs, I was also pleased that finally more minority ethnic MPs had been elected – two men of South Asian origin (Marsha Singh and Mohammad Sarwar) and another Black woman, Oona King. Considerably more respectable than me, Oona had been a contemporary of David Miliband and his brother, Ed, at Haverstock

Hill in Camden. I had met Oona before she became a Labour MP; she decided to run against me for the parliamentary candidacy in Hackney North in the run-up to the 1997 election. I do not know whether it was her own idea to get me deselected or whether the national party had encouraged her to try, but her campaign failed and I was comfortably re-selected. Oona was eventually selected for another London constituency, Bethnal Green and Bow. Despite this history between us, I was perfectly pleasant to her once she was elected to Parliament. There were only two of us, so we might as well get along.

At the beginning of the new Parliament, Chief Whip Nick Brown had to sort out new Select Committee assignments. Unbeknownst to me, the new Chancellor of the Exchequer, Gordon Brown, was adamant that I be taken off the Treasury Select Committee. Perhaps he thought me too independent-minded, and so after a decade of experience on the committee I was moved to Foreign Affairs. When I went to Nick to complain, he said ruefully, 'Diane, it was the best I could do.'

Meanwhile at some point it occurred to Blair and his inner circles that the New Labour project looked inordinately white. To counter this, he made a point of putting two Black women in the House of Lords, Valerie Amos and Patricia Scotland. Valerie had, among other things, been chief executive of the Equal Opportunities Commission from 1989 to 1994, advised the South African government on human rights and had been deputy chair of the Runnymede Trust, while Patricia was the first Black woman to be made a QC and served on the Commission for Racial Equality. In time, they both served as ministers in the Blair government, whereas I remained public enemy number one for New Labour. Early in the Blair years I was heckled in the chamber of the House of Commons from the government front bench by David Blunkett and two of his ministers. Unusual as it is for ministers to heckle their own backbenchers, that was how much New Labour disliked me.

There were many great achievements under Tony Blair's leadership, from increased public spending on health and education and the introduction of a national minimum wage, to the passing of the Human Rights Act 1998 and the Civil Partnership Act 2004. But there were also actions that worried some of us, even in the excitement of those early years. Single-parent benefits were abolished for new claimants not seeking work; means-tested tuition fees were introduced in the Teaching and Higher Education Act 1988; and university grants were scrapped in favour of student loans. I felt especially strongly about scrapping grants: without access to a grant and free tuition, a Black working-class teenager like me could never have dreamed of going to Cambridge, and I said as much during the debate in Parliament. Education had provided a ladder of opportunity for me, so the last thing I wanted to do was pull up the ladder behind me.

Talking to Black mothers in Hackney, I knew how worried they were about their children's experience in school, so one of the projects that I set up, not long after this, was London Schools and the Black Child (LSBC). The statistics revealed that Black children nationally were underachieving, particularly Black boys. The school system, even including teachers who considered themselves progressive, tended to see Black children as a problem and would write off their aspirations. I was often reminded of my own experiences as a schoolgirl, and the lack of support that I had received at crucial times from my teachers. In 1999 I held my first conference on Black children and education in Hackney Town Hall, titled 'Hackney Schools and the Black Child'. We planned for 200 people, but 450 squeezed in, with attendees coming from as far away as Birmingham. It was the first event of its kind, anywhere in the country. The conference centre buzzed with so many parents learning, listening and talking about their children's education. They shared their experiences in a way they had not been able to do previously, in a context that gave them confidence, and the energy was amazing.

By then, Ken Livingstone and I had put the Brent East selection behind us and we were good friends and colleagues, and I was able to expand the initiative with his support, holding other versions of this conference locally (including, for instance, London Schools and the Turkish Child), owing to the huge diversity in my constituency. Over the years the conferences developed consistent themes: tackling Black children's educational underachievement; the recruitment and retention of a teaching workforce that accurately reflected London; and equipping London educators with the skills to teach a diverse pupil group. We held workshops on mentoring, supporting Black fathers, and school exclusions. I felt fulfilled by this work because education had always been of supreme importance to me. I had worked my way through all the obstacles that the education system puts in front of working-class and Black children. Education had opened up a whole world of history and literature to me, but it also gave me the confidence to believe that, whatever others' social advantages, I was as good as anyone else I met. I wanted these possibilities for other children, and helping them mattered to me. I was also concerned about the 'school to prison pipeline'; as the former director-general of the Prison Service, Sir Martin Narey, said, 'On the day that you exclude a child from school, you might as well give them a date and time to turn up at prison.'

The millennium was met with much excitement and a little uncertainty. Our systems didn't crash and the world didn't come to an end, but politics was as tumultuous as ever and, in that year, certainly tragic. In 2000 my friend and colleague Bernie Grant unexpectedly passed away after a heart attack. I was shaken by this loss, for Bernie and I had battled for racial justice in the Labour Party together. We had smashed a glass ceiling by being elected to Parliament together in 1987, and as an MP he continued to be an indefatigable campaigner for Black people and their rights. His death was a shock; he had been so energetic and full of life.

As soon as I heard, Jeremy Corbyn and I went to his home to pay our respects and commiserate with his widow, Sharon. Paul Boateng was there too. We hadn't always seen eye to eye, but that day we slipped out of the house away from everybody else and into the back garden, held each other and cried. Eventually Paul said, 'You know, we are the only ones who know what Bernie went through.'

Bernie's death meant a by-election. Earlier that year a young Black lawyer called David Lammy had been elected to the London Assembly and, quite soon into his political career, I had my eye on him as a possible successor to Bernie, never expecting that Bernie would pass away so soon. David had come to Bernie's house to pay his respects, and he told me in halting tones that he had promised Bernie's widow, Sharon Grant, that he would not run, for there had been rumours that she herself was thinking of running and he didn't want to tread on her toes. I told him that was rubbish: Bernie was one of Britain's first Black MPs and it was important to many in the Black community that he was succeeded by another Black man. David listened to me, for the first and maybe the only time. He was successfully selected by the local party as Labour's candidate in the Tottenham by-election and went on to win the seat, becoming the youngest MP in Parliament, at twenty-seven years old.

One of Labour's pledges in our 1997 manifesto had been to set up a Greater London Authority and bring in an elected mayor. It was difficult to get out of such a clear manifesto commitment, but Blair realized with mounting horror that the person most likely to be selected by London Labour Party members as their candidate for mayor was Ken Livingstone. The former leader of the GLC, Ken was the most prominent left-winger in London and was an avowed enemy of New Labour. His circle included people like Redmond O'Neill, Jude Woodward, Barry Grey, Anni Marjoram, Jayne Fisher and John Ross, who were perhaps some of the most effective strategists in the London Labour Party. Ken was a shoo-in. Nowadays the Labour Party leadership would just have blocked him from the shortlist without explanation, but at the time there was a little more adherence to democratic norms inside the party. The leadership did their best to stymie Ken, by deciding that Labour's mayoral candidate should be selected using an electoral college system. This meant that instead of a simple 'one person, one vote' method, there was a complicated system by which London MPs, London Members of the European Parliament (MEPs) and the members of the Greater London Authority (GLA) all had weighted votes. In effect their votes were worth a multiple of an individual member's votes. The leadership could rely on those groups to vote as they were told, and it must have hoped that by artificially boosting their role in the vote Ken Livingstone could be defeated.

In the end there were two men competing to be Labour's candidate for Mayor of London in 2000: Ken Livingstone and the leadership's favoured candidate, Frank Dobson, MP. Frank was Health Minister, a jolly man whom it was hard to dislike. For all practical purposes, he was under the thumb of the New Labour leadership. I later learned that he did not want to run against Ken; he was worried that, if he stepped down from the Health job, it would go to an up-and-coming Blairite such as Alan Milburn, who was much keener on privatization than Frank was. He also suspected that, ultimately, he would lose against Ken, but in the end he did as Blair asked. In the internal Labour Party election, Ken predictably won big with ordinary members, getting 75,000 votes to Frank Dobson's 22,000, but because of the intricacies of the Labour electoral college system, Frank was declared the winner. When it came to running as Labour's candidate in the actual mayoral election, however, Frank stood no chance and he knew it. Ken left the Labour Party, ran as an independent candidate and swept to victory. The Labour left in London could not have been more excited. Just as New Labour was tightening its grip on the party procedures by changing the rules to make it harder to elect a left-winger, a true socialist was running one of the greatest cities in the world – and that was a prize worth having.

That same year I joined Ken's Cabinet as the advisor on women and equality, and he was happy to fund my education work through LSBC. Educational conferences were stolid affairs usually reserved for educationalists and academics, and the attendees were generally all white, but LSBC buzzed with excitement and attracted thousands of parents, young people, teachers, academics and activists. The conferences were well attended by Black people, particularly parents, who were coming together in order to discuss the obstacles and potential solutions to help Black children achieve their academic potential. My second conference on Black children and education was held in 2000 and, thanks to the new London mayor Ken Livingstone, was funded by the GLA. It took place in the grand and glossy corporate splendour of the Queen Elizabeth II Centre in Westminster, a far cry from Hackney Town Hall. With more than 2,000 attendees, the numbers were so great, and the people queuing to get in so enthusiastic, that the staff at the conference centre panicked. At one point they even barred the doors. Although it was billed as a London event, attendees had come from all over the country, and the conference was a smashing success.

Ken Livingstone funded these annual conferences for nearly eight years until he lost the mayoralty in 2008. With that funding, I was able to achieve a number of things, such as producing a written report on each conference and circulating it nationally, so that people across the country could see what we were discussing and doing. I brought in American educationalists to speak, and commissioned reports on such issues as the importance of recruiting and retaining Black teachers; and I worked with successive schools ministers to try, with varying degrees of success, to get the Education Department to take issues about Black children and underachievement more seriously. Among the people who spoke at and supported the LSBC conferences were activists and allies such as Professor Gus John (who in 1989 had been the first Black person to hold the role of Director of Education and Leisure Services), Darcus Howe, Rosemary Campbell-Stephens, Lee Jasper, Beryl Gilroy, Garth Crooks and the co-founder of the Windrush Foundation, Arthur Torrington. Thanks to my urging, a government scheme was launched in 2004 called 'Aimhigher', the first-ever government programme designed to support educational participation and achievement among students from minority groups, especially disabled children and African and Caribbean pupils.

I also held an annual 'London Schools and the Black Child' awards ceremony that honoured the best-achieving Black children in London. I still meet young Black professionals who remember receiving their award; the companies sponsoring the event often offered internships and programmes for the winners. Every year we held an amazing star-studded awards ceremony in the House of Commons during Black History Month, and the presenters and speakers were a whole host of Black British celebrities and leading Black professionals from the legal, literary and political worlds, as well as from other industries such as entertainment and science. Among these speakers were the barrister Courtenay Griffiths; writer and critic Bonnie Greer; award-winning children's writer Malorie Blackman; MPs like David Lammy and Chuka Umunna; actors Sophie Okonedo and Naomie Harris; footballer Sol Campbell; athlete Christine Ohuruogu; and scientist Maggie Aderin-Pocock. Although at least 2,000 people would attend this star-studded event annually, the mainstream media took no interest in us whatsoever. One year I tried to get the *Evening Standard* to cover it, thinking it might be interested because the conference attracted so many parents, as well as teachers and campaigners. The only question the reporter asked was: 'Were any of these young people gangsters?' Unfortunately the initiative foundered when Boris Johnson became mayor; LSBC and Black History Month were not causes that he and his team were minded to support, financially or rhetorically. One of his senior advisors was against any initiatives that focused on race and diversity and even said that Black History Month was 'a bit boring as it "does" slavery every year'.

In 2003, after all these years of working on the issue, I took the very difficult decision to send my son James to the City of London School, a private institution. It was an extraordinary move for someone on the left of politics, especially someone who had campaigned so hard on this issue, as I had. I discussed the matter with James first, and in the end I gave him the choice. For years I had campaigned around Black underachievement in schools and could not get any interest in the newspapers or broadcast media, but my choice of school for my son generated a feeding frenzy in the media. It seemed they had no interest in Black children in general, though they were only too interested in this one child. The story broke in the *Mail on Sunday*. That morning I got out of bed as usual to make breakfast for James and casually looked out of my bedroom window. To my horror, I saw a whole crowd of Fleet Street photographers on my doorstep. It was the first time the press pack had laid siege to me in my home in this way, and it frightened me. If I could have run away, I would have done, but any escape was impossible without going through that crowd of photographers with their flashbulbs. I had to stay perfectly calm and pretend nothing untoward was happening, because I did not want to upset my son.

To my surprise, one of the first people to phone me that morning, with the media in uproar, was my old NCCL colleague Harriet Harman. Over the years we had gradually gravitated to different wings of the Labour Party and we did not talk much. I was shocked that she rang to speak to me that morning, but Harriet knew what I was going through. There had been a similar uproar a few years back about her own decision to send her son to a selective grammar school. Harriet was reassuring and sympathetic, and insisted that I should not give up my campaigning for Black children. 'If you don't do it,' she said, 'nobody else will.'

Harriet was the type of feminist who would always reach out to another woman in difficulty. Unlike other people in the Westminster bubble, she understood that I had taken my decision in the full knowledge that it would be very damaging to me personally, precisely because all my education work had shown me how the state-school system was letting down Black boys. The media were uninterested in my experience on the matter, which I had gained through my work on LSBC, yet they had plenty of space to attack me on my choice of school for my son. They even derided the very idea that James could achieve academically. The underlying narrative was that everyone knew Black boys were destined to fail in school.

I received volumes of abuse in the media and online, and the worst moment came when my son was at home one evening, with the babysitter upstairs. He was listening to the radio station LBC and there was a phone-in with a lot of criticism of me. James felt obliged to ring in and speak up for me. It is inexplicable that LBC thought it acceptable to put a young child on air without checking that a responsible adult had agreed to it. I imagine that, for them, my family and I were just media fodder. I will always feel guilty and sad that my eleven-year-old son felt he had to wade in to defend his mother. Some of the anger directed at me was from people who genuinely and passionately opposed private education, but much of the abuse came from those who had no interest in schools or education; they were simply happy to have a fresh reason to attack me.

Aside from dealing with this turmoil, I had growing concerns about the state of civil liberties under the Blair government. It was a particular interest of mine, as an ex-Home Office civil servant and a former employee of the NCCL. The Home Office lay at the heart of every civil-liberty issue one could imagine, and I had learned from studying the departmental files that at heart the Home Office believed that a concern for civil liberties was the enemy of good administration. I reacted strongly against this thinking, through rallies and my campaigning on issues like stop-and-search. I realized early on that taking away the community's civil liberties was bad for everybody, but impacted particularly on minorities such as the Irish, Muslim and Black communities.

The Blair administration began well on civil liberties. Blair brought in the Human Rights Act 1998, which incorporated the European Convention on Human Rights into British law and came into force in the UK in October 2000. This was a major step forward in codifying British human rights. However, as time went on, New Labour began to introduce legislation that took a different direction and posed a threat to civil liberties and human rights: the Regulation of Investigatory Powers Act 2000, better known as the 'snoopers' charter'; and the Terrorism Act of 2000, which allowed for the detention of suspects without charge for up to seven days. Section 44 of the Act also permitted the police to stop and search any person or vehicle without 'reasonable suspicion' of terrorism.

While campaigning against these types of measures, I met Shami Chakrabarti for the first time. Shami was the head of my old organization, the NCCL (by then called Liberty). Small but ferocious, she led Liberty with considerable verve and faced down a series of Home Secretaries. In the case of the 'snoopers' charter', we did not win and it became law. But everything that I and campaigners like Liberty warned about this new legislation was proved correct when the statistics showed that only 0.6 per cent of Section 44 stop-and-searches under the new legislation led to an arrest. This proved what some of us had been saying all along: that it served no useful purpose except to make New Labour look tough on crime. Like most anti-terror legislation, it was used with some enthusiasm by the authorities to harass Black people and other minorities. Predictably the statistics showed that Black and Asian men were six times more likely to be stopped by police under the new legislation than anyone else. Opponents of Section 44 were completely vindicated when, in 2010, the European Court of Human Rights ruled that it was incompatible with respect for private life under Article 8 of the Human Rights Convention.

Matters were no more positive when it came to foreign affairs. Tony Blair's guiding principle seemed to be to stay as close to the United States as possible, regardless of whether there was a Democratic US president like Bill Clinton or a Republican president like George W. Bush. It never seemed to occur to Blair that the British government might have different interests from the United States, and that the British Labour Party might have different values from the US political establishment.

On 11 September 2001 the militant organization al-Qaeda used nineteen terrorists to hijack four commercial planes en route to California. They crashed the first two planes into the Twin Towers of the World Trade Center in New York City, while the third plane hit the Pentagon (headquarters of the United States military) in Arlington County, Virginia; the fourth plane, which was supposed to hit a federal government building in Washington DC, crashed into a field after its passengers intervened. These shocking attacks killed nearly 3,000 people and sparked a global war on terror that was to last for decades.[2]

Britain had always tended towards illiberal anti-terror legislation because of the republican struggle in Ireland, and 9/11 turbocharged it. It would have taken a very principled and courageous British prime minister to stand up to an America bent on revenge, and Tony Blair was not that prime minister.

In Parliament it became obvious that there was momentum towards war with Iraq. This would be an American-led attack, which the two allies hoped would get international support. The rationale put to the public by both Blair and Bush was that Iraq had weapons of mass destruction (WMD) and was harbouring al-Qaeda and its leader, Osama bin Laden. There was no evidence for this; in reality, Bush wanted the war to incite a regime change in Iraq, but talk of bogus 'weapons of mass destruction' was supposed to give Labour MPs an excuse to vote for what was essentially a pre-emptive war, which it was clear by then had no support from the European Union, the Security Council or NATO.

The British public was clearly also not persuaded of the need for war. To try and soften people up, Alastair Campbell issued a dossier to journalists on 3 February 2003 on Iraq's weapons programme, which came to be known as the 'dodgy dossier'. Campbell himself had no knowledge of war and weaponry; it was purely a public-relations device, an attempt to persuade the doubters. Reading it at the time, I realized there was very little substance to it. I was more impressed by the testimony of the UN chief weapons inspector, Scott Ritter, who that year spoke at several packed meetings in Parliament. Unlike Campbell, Ritter had been to Iraq many times and knew about weapons and war. Ritter said repeatedly, and very firmly, that if anyone claimed there were weapons of mass destruction in Iraq, they must explain and provide evidence of how and when they got there. There was certainly no 'how and when' in Campbell's dossier. If Blair had ever met Ritter, perhaps he might not have swallowed what he was being told by George W. Bush and his advisors.

The reality of an American attack on Iraq came nearer, but it was also clear that there was no international support for it, which made Britain's involvement even more instrumental. America was perfectly able to mount an attack on its own, but it needed at least one other ally in order for this attack not to be nakedly unilateral.

Much of what happens in Parliament is theatre – symbolic and significant theatre, one step away from reality. But the discussion and debate in the weeks and days leading up to the Iraq War were the most intense and emotional that I have ever witnessed. It was literally about matters of life and death. It was obvious from the beginning that Blair was determined to go to war, shoulder-to-shoulder with George W. Bush. Blair's relationship with the American state mattered more to him than opinion in his own party, and it also seemed to matter more than whether the war was even legal or not. In the 1970s the Labour prime minister Harold

Wilson had never publicly attacked the United States for waging the wildly unpopular Vietnam War, but Wilson was also careful not to go so far as sending British troops to fight alongside the Americans.

Blair had no such qualms. He did not care about progressive opinion. Perhaps the fact that progressive opinion in Britain was *opposed* to the Iraq War even made him more determined to go ahead. The WMD rationale began to fall apart even before the day of the major debate on going to war, and public opposition to the war grew in an unprecedented way. On 15 February 2003 the Stop the War Coalition mounted the biggest demonstration ever staged in London, with the BBC estimating the numbers at more than one million. Jeremy Corbyn made one of his finest speeches to the demonstration, in which he said, 'Thousands more deaths in Iraq will not make things right. It will set off a spiral of conflict, of hate, of misery, of desperation, that will fuel the wars, the conflict, the terrorism, the depression and the misery of future generations.'

This public opposition to the war put intense pressure on MPs. Many Labour MPs had their local party members insisting that they vote against the war, and even some Tory MPs were declaring they would vote against it. Blair must have been increasingly alarmed, frightened that he might actually lose; in the days running up to the big vote, he had individual MPs brought to his offices one by one to put pressure on them to vote the right way. He did not invite me, or other determined anti-war MPs; he must have judged us to be a lost cause. When these private meetings did not seem to be working, Blair enlisted his wife, Cherie, and the former US president Bill Clinton to ring Labour MPs personally and apply even more pressure. Blair was always a little disdainful of ordinary MPs and of Parliament, but he was so desperate that he took to physically coming to the House of Commons and touring the bars, tea rooms and other places where MPs gather informally, then buttonholing MPs to make the case for war.

Parliament became a pressure cooker. Everyone knew that the coming vote was not actually about the merits of the war; only a minority of MPs believed it had any merit. Instead it was becoming a vote on whether you supported Blair personally or not. And everyone knew that voting against the war meant that your career in the Labour Party was effectively over.

For days before the big vote the House was swept by rumours that various senior Labour MPs would resign rather than vote for war. In the end only the Leader of the House, Robin Cook, resigned. But he was a former Foreign Secretary, which gave his resignation particular significance. He tendered his resignation in a speech the day before the final debate in Parliament. Cook was a famously good orator, and the House of Commons was packed to listen to his measured but damning resignation speech. It was heard in complete silence, something that is relatively unusual in the House. At the end of the speech, all the Labour MPs got up to applaud him – a sight that I had never witnessed before or since. Many of the MPs who clapped for him went on to vote for the war the following day. Maybe applauding Robin eased their consciences a little.

On the day of the final debate the atmosphere in Parliament was electric. Blair gave his speech in support of war, threatening resignation if MPs did not vote for it. Some of the Cabinet ministers sitting next to him on the front bench were squirming, perhaps in the knowledge that they were about to do something against their consciences. Blair left the chamber, but only to go to his office in Westminster, from where he continued ringing Labour MPs personally, even while the debate was going on, trying to turn the screw one last time. Some of my colleagues from the Socialist Campaign Group spoke, including John McDonnell, who said that the proposed war was an act of international vigilantism and that the Bush war plan was both immoral and illegal.

In the end the grim threats and the excruciating pressure paid off: Blair got his vote for war; 139 of us rebelled – the biggest ever rebellion against Blair – but it was not enough. The next day British troops went to war alongside the Americans, but no WMDs were ever found. The war did indeed fuel the conflict and terrorism of future generations, just as some of us had foreseen. Although Blair had had some considerable political achievements, including being the only Labour leader to win three successive general elections, his reputation never recovered from the ill-fated and illegal Iraq War.

By 2007 Blair had finally stepped down, after years of wrangling with Gordon Brown, who believed that he had been anointed Blair's successor and who had grown tired of waiting. At that point the SCG MPs had to decide whether to put up a candidate to challenge Brown. Challenging Labour leadership elections was the SCG's *raison d'être* and the group had in fact been set up to support Tony Benn's historic bid for the deputy leadership in 1981. We settled on John McDonnell as our candidate, but were thwarted by the lack of enough nominations from other MPs to get him on the ballot paper; fellow SCG member Michael Meacher was initially a nominee, but when he stepped aside his supporters didn't all switch to supporting McDonnell, hence the lack of sufficient nominations. Gordon Brown became leader of the Labour Party and prime minister unopposed.

From the very beginning there was something anticlimactic about the Brown premiership. The expectation that he would be more progressive than Blair had been encouraged by Brown's outriders in Parliament when they were trying to stir up opposition to Blair, but once Brown became prime minister, it seemed like business as usual. Two months into his premiership Brown announced that he was going to raise the upper limit for the detention of terror suspects without charging them, in part as a response to attempted terror attacks in London and Glasgow. January 2008 saw the first reading of a bill in which he proposed to increase the limit from twenty-eight days to forty-two, despite both the Home Affairs Select Committee and the Joint Committee on Human

Rights stating there was no evidence that increased detention was necessary. I was against it from the start; it was a completely arbitrary figure, and there was no doubt in my mind that the people most likely to become ensnared in this new law would be Muslim or Black. Several other Labour MPs were worried about this proposal, and it seemed that a rebellion was on the horizon. Brown, increasingly concerned that the legislation might not pass, did something he had hardly done in the twenty years that we had been in Parliament together: speak to me. In the run-up to the vote, Brown called me to lobby me to vote in favour of his forty-two days' detention-without-trial legislation. It amazes me that, as an intelligent man, he thought he had a rational case for this punitive and illiberal piece of legislation. His main argument seemed to be that I did not understand the legislation, and that it was not what I thought it was. Why he imagined that telling me I was stupid was a compelling argument, I'll never know. Of course I voted against the legislation.

Speaking in the debate on 11 June 2008, I said, 'The first duty of Parliament is the safety of the realm. It is because I believe that the proposals on forty-two-day detention will make us less safe, not more safe, that I oppose them. What makes us free is what makes us safe, and what makes us safe is what will make us free.'

Later in that speech I made an oblique reference to our earlier conversation: 'People whom the Prime Minister has never spoken to in his life have been ushered into his presence twice in forty-eight hours. People have been offered roles in Cuba, and no doubt promises of the governorship of Bermuda have been bandied about. Any rebel backbencher with a cause is confident – if they vote the right way, of course the Prime Minister will make the statement, give the money or make the special visit. It is a test of Parliament that we are willing to stand up for the civil liberties of the marginalized, the suspect and the unpopular.' I concluded by asking, 'If we as a parliament cannot stand up on this issue, and if people from our different ethnic communities cannot come here and genuinely reflect their fears and concerns, what is parliament for?'

I spoke with few notes, and the Tory MP David Davis, who spoke next, said it was one of the finest speeches he had heard since being elected to the House of Commons. The speech won me *The Spectator*'s 'Parliamentarian Speech of the Year' award and a Liberty Human Rights Award. At the end of the debate thirty-six Labour MPs voted against the legislation, which was remarkable, considering the amount of pressure that had been put upon them. Brown got his legislation, but only by the twin tactics of applying thumbscrews to his backbenchers and striking a last-minute deal with the Ulster Unionists.

On 8 July 2008, in her maiden speech in the House of Lords, the former head of MI5, Eliza Manningham-Buller, agreed that the forty-two-day pre-charge detention was an assault on civil liberties. It was extraordinary that a former head of MI5 could see that, while Gordon Brown could not.

Top: Outside Yarl's Wood Immigration Removal Centre with my colleague, shadow attorney general, Shami Chakrabarti in 2018. I had long campaigned against the ill-treatment of women in immigration detention centres and had fought the government for months to be allowed this visit.

Bottom: Here, Stephanie Tonmi, a former detainee, is telling me about her experiences. There were fires, hunger strikes, sexual assaults and even deaths there.

7.   Defending Civil Liberties

Gordon Brown's time in office was not a success. The 2010 general election resulted in a hung parliament, and although Brown tried to form a coalition with the Liberal Democrats, it was the Conservatives – led by Brown's polar opposite, the suave if relatively inexperienced David Cameron – who eventually did so. When Brown stepped down, there was another Labour Party leadership election. The first group of candidates to declare were four young guns of the party establishment: Ed Balls, Andy Burnham, David Miliband and David's brother, Ed Miliband. They were all male (*Guardian* cartoonist Steve Bell's brilliant take on this was a picture I love, titled 'Diane and the Tokens', featuring me in Diana Ross-style get-up with my fellow candidates as a bare-chested male backing group) and, as former special advisors to government ministers, they were members of the Labour Party magic circle. Once again the SCG met to decide on our candidate and the group put forward two possibilities: John McDonnell and me. Just as in 2007, McDonnell could not get enough nominations, which left me.

Getting enough nominations was a nail-biting experience. Some Labour MPs began to worry that they were not offering a particularly varied choice: all the declared candidates were male and white, and there was not much to choose between them politically. Despite these misgivings, I still was not amassing enough nominations.

When the final day for submitting nominations dawned, David Miliband had a superabundance of pledges from Labour MPs. At the last minute he and a few of his supporters 'lent' me enough ballots to help get me over the line, but we still did not have enough. As the noon deadline loomed, I apprised Harriet Harman (then the acting leader of the party) of the situation. She paused and looked at me, as if at that moment she was remembering that we went back a long way. Then she told me that, in her capacity as acting leader, she would instruct the Labour Party officials to hold the deadline open until 1 p.m. I cannot imagine they were too pleased, but there was nobody to take their complaints to. The added sixty minutes involved a mad scramble to get the last few nominations. I went into the chamber of the House of Commons and strong-armed Dennis Skinner, a former miner, into putting in his nomination.

When the time came, Harriet called Ed Miliband, Ed Balls, David Miliband, Andy Burnham and me into the leader's office, to announce to all of us that we had the required number of nominations and would be on the shortlist to contest for the leadership of the party. As the boys filed out, she asked me to stay behind. She looked me in the eye and told me to remember that from now on, whatever happened, I was part of the leadership of the party. When my supporters and I realized that we really had got me onto the ballot for the leadership, we all cried a little. Perhaps David had made sure that I was on the ballot paper because he genuinely wanted members to have a diverse choice; or perhaps he calculated that, as a left-winger, I would take votes off his brother Ed, who politically more closely resembled their distinguished Marxist father, Ralph Miliband. Either way, it was a significant moment. Not only was I the first Black woman to stand for the leadership of a major political party in the UK, but we had also set a precedent for having political diversity on the ballot paper, which proved instrumental in ensuring that others were encouraged to lend nominations to Jeremy Corbyn in 2015.

I started the 2010 Labour leadership campaign at an enormous disadvantage. Where the other candidates had plenty of funding and had been building their campaign machines for some time, I only had a group of enthusiastic young students, and no money.

David Miliband was very much seen as New Labour's anointed successor, and everyone in Westminster and media circles assumed he would be the eventual winner. I enjoyed going up and down the country speaking to audiences of Labour Party members; because I was not expected to win, I had nothing to lose, and I was probably more experienced in speaking off the top of my head and from the heart than the others. Curiously, one argument used against me was that I did not have enough experience to be leader of the Labour Party. I had by now been an MP for twenty-three years, while Andy Burnham and David Miliband had been MPs for just nine years. At every hustings we would troop onstage together, with party members looking at me quizzically as I sat alongside my white male colleagues. They were clearly wondering what on earth I was doing there. However, over time I began to make an impact on the contest. First, I formulated a response to the baffled looks from party members. At every hustings I would begin by saying, 'I know what you're all thinking. You're thinking that I don't look like a Labour leader. I'm saying that in the twenty-first century this is what a Labour leader looks like.' Because I had successfully guessed their thoughts, audiences never failed to laugh. It also planted a seed in their minds that a leader of the Labour Party did not have to be a white man in a suit.

All my rivals had spent most of their adult lives as Labour Party special advisors. They spoke in political clichés with little passion, for they had never been accustomed to speaking to large audiences before. Speaking from the heart was the last thing they had any idea about – their job was to make sure whichever minister they were working for parroted the official line. My speeches, by contrast, were very personal. I drew directly from my family background and my experiences as a Black woman, using them to formulate and communicate the roots of my political thinking. I set out the principles I had lived by for my entire time as an MP, including my refusal to vote in favour of going to war with Iraq. The reference to this always cut through, because party members were still burning with indignation at Tony Blair having taken Britain to war.

When my rivals saw how well that went down, they began to make their own speeches a little less clichéd and a little more personal. My involvement shifted the whole contest to the left, which was hardest on David Miliband, who if anything was more right-wing than his mentor, Tony Blair. It was clear that ordinary party members were getting fed up with New Labour and Blairism. David's brother Ed, however, blossomed in a debate framed in a more left-wing way. When the balloting was over, Harriet Harman – still acting leader – called us into her office to inform us of the result, ahead of the public announcement. I arrived early, perhaps the least anxious of all of us, given that I was not expecting to win. Everyone still thought David would win, so it came as something of a shock when Harriet announced that Ed had ultimately trounced his brother to become the next leader of the Labour Party. Nobody looked more shocked than Ed himself. He might have been wondering what on earth he was going to tell their mother; David was her eldest son, and Ed had now completely disrupted his brother's career. David's jaw hung open in shock. All he could blurt out was, 'But I have written my speech!'

I was proud of my achievement in that leadership contest, given how much money and institutional support the others had. The leadership was chosen by an electoral college, which included MPs and trade unions, who all had weighted votes. I came last in the electoral college, but third among ordinary party members, beating Ed Balls and Andy Burnham.

Around this time I decided to run for Mayor of London. I had done better in the leadership race than anyone had expected, so running for London mayor seemed a reasonable next step. However, my mayoral campaign brought me down to earth with a bump. Trade unions and MPs who had supported me for leader refused to support me for London mayor. I was exactly the same person, so perhaps the worry was that I actually had a chance at winning the mayoralty. Ken Livingstone, whom I had known for more than thirty years, said that if I promised to make him head of Transport for London he would support me. I replied that I could make no promises, so he went to Sadiq Khan, who was also competing for the mayoralty, and offered the same deal. Sadiq said yes, but once he became mayor, he dropped his promise within days.

One by one, my erstwhile supporters fell away, and in the end I came third in the selection for London's mayoral candidate, behind Sadiq Khan and Tessa Jowell. I had been squeezed between the Blairites on the one hand, who had an undying disdain for me, and by the white male leftists on the other, who did not want to see a Black woman in a position of power.

Meanwhile in Parliament, Ed Miliband was trying to position himself as a break from the past, saying, 'The era of New Labour has passed. A new generation has taken over.' While this message had worked in the leadership contest with ordinary members, the party establishment and mainstream media never reconciled themselves to Ed having beaten his brother David, the long-standing Blairite heir apparent.

After a Labour leadership contest, the winner customarily offers Cabinet positions to the losers. David Miliband, Ed Balls and Andy Burnham were all appointed to Shadow Cabinet positions, but I had to make do with a junior position as Shadow Minister for Public Health. I wavered before accepting. It was tempting to go back to my many political campaigns, and to appearing on the political programme *This Week* every Thursday. However, I was genuinely interested in the health brief. My mother had been a nurse, and public health was very important in a community such as Hackney. I wanted to think about the relationship between poverty and health, fighting alcohol abuse and reviewing policy on drug use, all of which were issues affecting my constituents.

To persuade me further, Ed assured me that I would be number two in the health team. Perhaps he really believed that I would be, even though those on the health team simply scoffed when I mentioned it. Some of the voluntary-sector organizations and campaigners on these issues were uncomfortable dealing with me, as they had probably never dealt with a Black shadow minister before (though it's possible they had worked with Paul Boateng, who was a junior government Minister for Health in the late 1990s). The shadow minister whose team I was in found it even more stressful to deal with me, but unfortunately for him, I already had a high media profile. Unlike many back-bench Labour MPs, I had a good relationship with the producers of news programmes. Programme-makers knew that I was a reliable and strong performer, and I continued to appear regularly on national political programmes, as I had done throughout my time on the back benches. This made the head of my team, and Ed Miliband's inner circle, furious. The latter would often ask me to pull out of programmes, so that the producers would have to replace me with somebody chosen by the Labour press office.

Ed was rapidly losing the allure that had helped him win the leadership contest, and we clashed over the extent to which he allowed himself to be shifted to the right on policy. This was particularly true on immigration, where his messaging was becoming increasingly problematic. Ahead of the 2015 election, Labour tried to market red mugs bearing its five policy pledges, including one with the words 'Controls on immigration – I'm voting Labour'. I criticized these mugs both privately and publicly, saying, 'This shameful mug is an embarrassment – but the real problem is that immigration controls are one of our five pledges at all.' Ed could only say to me regretfully that if Labour did not take this anti-immigrant line, 'We would not be heard on anything else.'

In response to this and other differences of opinion, Ed sacked me. I was by far his most left-wing minister, and I imagine that people around him had been calling for me to be given the boot for some time. Being Ed, he tried to do it in a nice way, saying in a conciliatory manner, 'I do not want us to keep falling out.' Then he added, 'I hope you think I'm doing the right thing.'

I could only reply, 'Of course you are doing the right thing. You are the leader of the party!'

The rightward drift of the party under Ed's leadership did not help Labour at the polls, and the party lost in the 2015 general election. It was sad to go back to Parliament the following week; the sight of so many defeated former Labour MPs wheeling their belongings out of their offices was a reminder that there is no such thing as a safe seat. After Ed stepped down, Labour was faced with yet another leadership election. By this time Ed had scrapped the electoral college and had brought in 'one person, one vote'. While he had won with the support of the trade unions, his brother David had a narrow majority among members, so the party apparatchiks assumed that 'one person, one vote' would help the right. Andy Burnham was the favourite to win; also in the running were Liz Kendall, a Blairite candidate who had considerable support in the media, and Yvette Cooper, a more centre-left Labour Party establishment candidate.

Once again we in the SCG had to decide which candidate we would put forward. Sitting in Parliament's Room W1, where the decision was to be taken, there was no vote: we simply went around the table until we found a volunteer. One by one, people made excuses as to why they were not prepared to be the candidate: one MP said that he was too old; John McDonnell declined because he had been the SCG candidate once already; I said the same. Finally we reached Jeremy Corbyn. He seemed a little hesitant, but since no one else wanted to run, Jeremy said, 'Oh, all right.'

Thus began one of the most extraordinary periods in the Labour Party's history. Ed had changed much about the leadership election process, but not the need for any potential candidate to have a minimum number of MPs' votes to get on the ballot paper in the first place. This gave MPs a veto over who could stand as a candidate and was effectively meant to keep any hard-left contenders off the ballot paper. But Jeremy was seen as genuinely good and unthreatening, so he began to amass nominations fairly easily, with my nomination being the first. The left in Unite the Union, led by Len McCluskey, were aware that they had made a mess of the mayoral nomination, so they made sure the union's nomination went to Jeremy.

It was only at the very last minute that Jeremy received the requisite number of nominations and scrambled onto the ballot paper. My 2010 leadership campaign had laid a trail for Jeremy, for it had bolstered the idea that a leadership contest should have candidates from every wing of the party. At first people thought Jeremy was the usual no-hope SCG candidate running for the sake of it – perhaps he even thought so himself. To the astonishment of the media and the Labour Party establishment, his campaign took off like a rocket. The first public meeting of his leadership campaign was one organized jointly with my mayoral campaign. It was packed to overflowing and was the first sign of how popular a candidate he was going to be.

The election of Ed Miliband over his brother David in the 2010 leadership campaign showed that members wanted to move on from the New Labour years, though the party leadership and the Westminster bubble could not see it. What had been a murmuring from the membership in 2010 became a full-throated roar in the 2015 leadership election. Jeremy was helped by his long years of campaigning on behalf of numerous left-wing causes, from CND and the anti-apartheid movement to the Campaign for Labour Party Democracy. He had voted against the Tory Welfare Reform Bill when the other candidates had abstained, and was completely opposed to austerity while the other candidates backed it, even though Labour Party members were by now sick of the effects of this policy. Above all, Jeremy had been unbending in his opposition to the Iraq War when all the other candidates had voted for it, which was a big mark in his favour for ordinary members.

It helped Jeremy's campaign that Ed Miliband had brought in a registered supporters' scheme, which was a new type of affiliated member who would be able to vote in leadership elections and would only pay a £3 fee. The intention was to dilute the power of the trade unions. At the time Ed had called it 'letting people back into politics', but the unintended consequence of the scheme was that it enabled people from all the campaigns Jeremy had worked with down the years to join the party and vote for him. His campaign also used new media in a way never previously seen in a Labour Party leadership contest and drew in huge numbers of idealistic young people. Swept on by a tidal wave of enthusiasm, Jeremy emerged as the only genuinely progressive candidate. Thousands of party members felt that for the first time they had somebody to vote for. They were drawn by Jeremy's message that a better world was possible.

The leadership campaign was a triumph for Jeremy and his grass-roots supporters. Liz Kendall, the most avowedly Blairite candidate, who had a great deal of support in the mainstream media, managed just 19,000 votes. Yvette Cooper got 72,000 votes. Andy Burnham, the favourite to win among union leaders and MPs who considered themselves left-wing, received 80,000 votes. To the astonishment of the entire Westminster village, Jeremy crushed them all with an extraordinary 251,000 votes. I was thrilled and excited to see my oldest friend in politics elected leader of the party. Labour Party members had made their views clear, but this completely unpredicted result sent the party establishment into shock. As far as they were concerned, Jeremy was a usurper, and his winning the leadership election was a terrible mistake – a nightmare that would pass.

Jeremy had several problems as the new Labour leader. Like Ed Miliband, he had been elected in the teeth of hostility from Labour Party headquarters, which refused to be reconciled. It was the first time in living memory that a leader had been elected who was so out of step with the predominant political view of most of the permanent staff. The unremitting hostility shown to Jeremy by the Labour right and their media supporters was rooted in their fury at being made to look fools by him and by Labour Party members. As the architect of the NHS, Aneurin Bevan, had once said, 'The right-wing of the Labour Party would rather see it fall into perpetual decline than abide by its democratic decisions.' The relationship between the Leader of the Opposition (LOTO) team and Headquarters (HQ) staff went from dire to even worse.

With Jeremy as leader, I took my place in a Labour Party Shadow Cabinet for the first time, beginning as Shadow Secretary of State for International Development. Although it was not one of the top positions, the left in London had always been strongly internationalist, so I threw myself into the role. Together with my staff, I visited eight countries in a year, mostly to look at refugee camps and meet several organizations working on humanitarian issues. The Labour Party was not willing to pay for this work, so we had to raise money from charities. I went to Somaliland and Uganda to see how they were coping with the AIDS crisis and noticed that, although the large international aid agencies received most of the aid money, it was the small local organizations that did most of the work.

I visited the refugee camps near Calais in northern France; camps on the Mediterranean island of Lampedusa; camps on the border of Turkey and Syria and on the border of Turkey and Lebanon. These camps were uniformly grim and squalid and brought home to me the plight of refugees who had been driven to flee their homes by armed conflict, ethnic intolerance, religious fundamentalism and drought.

British politicians love to complain about a supposed 'tidal wave' of asylum seekers, but in fact Britain takes relatively few, compared to countries closer to the centres of war, ethnic tensions and climate disasters. At that time, for instance, 59 per cent of the population of Lebanon comprised refugees from neighbouring countries. Back in London, I tried to launch a policy to create more safe and legal routes for asylum seekers. I felt it was important to change the narrative around immigration and asylum; it had long been seen as negative and a problem, with a focus on keeping people out, however unfair the means were. I wanted to make family reunions easier, so that children could bring their parents to the UK and vice versa; I wanted to introduce humanitarian visas, too, which could allow asylum seekers to work with educational institutions. The difficulty in fighting for these changes in policy was the bureaucracy of Parliament: the time it takes to make a distinct cultural change in the way people think and talk about asylum is almost always longer than the ever-shifting make-up of Shadow Cabinets.

In 2016 prime minister David Cameron called a referendum on the UK's membership of the European Union (EU). Both the Conservatives and Labour were becoming increasingly horrified at the rise of the United Kingdom Independence Party (UKIP), with Cameron privately describing UKIP supporters as 'fruitcakes, loonies and closet racists'. I spoke out about UKIP publicly, writing articles and talking at rallies; to my way of thinking, pandering to UKIP was – far from being an electoral necessity – a political dead end for the Labour Party. Two years prior to the referendum, UKIP had received more votes (27.5 per cent) in the European elections than any other British party, with twenty-four MEPs elected. It had made strong gains in traditionally Labour-voting areas in the north of England and was eating into the Tories' natural vote-share.

Calling a referendum was intended to be a masterstroke that would consolidate Cameron's pro-European position and enable him to face down UKIP. Instead of disproving public concerns about immigration with facts and data, the government sought to echo and amplify these concerns, stoking the fire of anti-immigrant sentiment by calling the referendum in the first place. Cameron underestimated the strength of Britain's Euroscepticism, particularly outside of Westminster, and to his and most of the political establishment's horror, anti-European forces triumphed. Britain had voted to leave the EU.

It was illogical for Cameron to call a referendum before negotiating a deal; he clearly thought he could use the strength of a Yes vote to negotiate an even better deal for Britain. Instead, the campaign descended into competing dystopias, with George Osborne's 'Project Fear' pitted against Nigel Farage, Michael Gove and Boris Johnson's xenophobia, including the lurid claims about Turkey joining the EU. In truth, this country already had an extraordinarily good deal in retaining its own currency (and the ability to devalue it) within a customs union and single market.

With his position undermined completely by the referendum loss, Cameron stood down almost immediately, and the Labour Party was thrown into turmoil. Jeremy's enemies at the top of the Labour Party pounced, insisting it was his fault that the EU referendum had been lost and claiming that he had not campaigned hard enough. Perhaps it was true that, in his heart of hearts, Jeremy was always pro-Brexit, not because of the 'Little Englander' sentiments that many British right-wing politicians held, but more because his idol Tony Benn had been a dogged Eurosceptic all his life. Perhaps this was even reflected in the traditionally Labour-voting post-industrial areas of Britain that also voted to leave the EU. Jeremy put his sentiments aside and made speeches at ten major pro-EU rallies, spoke at events in twenty-one cities, made endless media appearances and wrote a series of op-eds in national newspapers; but his enemies never let facts get in the way of an attack. The right of the Labour Party had long believed that opposing immigration was the way to hold on to what they called the white working-class vote, and so many of them were scornful that Jeremy didn't have a hard enough line on immigration. It was amazing these people could believe that a man who had been a staunch anti-racist all his life would suddenly abandon his principles and turn against immigrants.

After the disappointment of the EU referendum, Jeremy's enemies in the Parliamentary Labour Party (PLP) decided to strike: in June 2016, thirty-three Labour frontbenchers resigned, including Keir Starmer, who had joined Jeremy's Shadow Cabinet in 2015 as Shadow Minister for Immigration. This mass resignation was quickly followed by a no-confidence vote in the PLP, which Jeremy lost. Emboldened, his detractors staged a leadership election, with Owen Smith (a relative outsider) as the party establishment's candidate. Having defeated Jeremy in the parliamentary confidence vote and with the media solidly behind them, they felt certain of victory.

However, ordinary members – asked to choose between Jeremy and Owen Smith – chose Jeremy by a wide margin and he received 62 per cent of their votes. One might think that the party establishment, seeing Jeremy's popularity with members, would get behind him, albeit reluctantly. Instead they redoubled their efforts to destroy him. The success of the New Labour project meant that some elements in the party no longer believed in it as a 'broad church'. It was their party and they wanted it back.

In the midst of this attempted coup, I was moved to the post of Shadow Secretary of State for Health. As a nurse's daughter, I was pleased to take up this brief. I was only there for just over three months, but I did my best to roll back policies such as prescription charges; and to unpick Tony Blair's expansion of the Private Finance Initiative (PFI), which supposedly used investment from the private sector to deliver public services and infrastructure such as building new hospitals, but the scheme mired institutions like the NHS in mountains of debt. I strongly opposed this neo-privatization of public services, despite opposition from the full-time Labour Party staffers who – as holdovers from the New Labour era – tried to block me, and while most MPs were taking a break that summer I worked almost every day in July and August, putting out press releases and media stories about public-health issues.

By October, Jeremy – having won the leadership election once again – was planning a Cabinet reshuffle. Keir Starmer was appointed as Shadow Secretary of State for Exiting the European

Union. Many people wondered why he, as someone clearly to the right of the most left-wing Labour leader since 1945, was willing to join Jeremy's Cabinet at all; perhaps it was due to his personal aspiration towards a seat of power. Keir seemed content to go with the flow and never showed much point of difference with Jeremy, except about Brexit – Keir was passionately pro-European.

Meanwhile, after the resignation of Andy Burnham, I was moved to the role of Shadow Home Secretary, the job in the Shadow Cabinet that I had always wanted. My dream was to be Britain's first Black Home Secretary. I had begun my working life in the Home Office as a graduate trainee, and policing, immigration, racial justice and human rights had been the issues closest to my heart all my adult life. I was determined to lead the campaign against racism and in favour of more progressive immigration policy and human rights at a senior level, since all these issues were under attack from the right. I was the first Black person to hold one of the four great offices of state even as a shadow, but there were people in my own party, including comrades on the left, who could not get their heads around the idea of a Black woman as Home Secretary. Some were ambivalent about policies to support women's rights, oppose racism and defend LGBTQ+ people against discrimination, as they had been to the policies of the GLC under Ken Livingstone in the 1980s. Others on the left, including members of Jeremy's Shadow Cabinet, felt strongly that socialism was essentially – and almost exclusively – about trade-union issues such as better pay and conditions. They did not want to talk about foreign policy generally and took issue with my sustained opposition to nuclear weapons, because they organized workers in the nuclear industry and were concerned that decommissioning nuclear plants might lead to a loss in jobs.

Jeremy's popularity among members of the public continued to grow, particularly with young people. At the 2017 Glastonbury music festival there were the unprecedented scenes of thousands of youngsters chanting his name. Nobody in living memory has seen that kind of acclaim for any British politician, before or since, although Jeremy continued to attract vitriol in the mainstream media.

By this time Theresa May had become prime minister and was agitating for the softest possible Brexit deal, which would have kept Britain in the single market. However, it was proving impossible to unite the Conservative Party over the issue of Europe. She simply could not get enough votes to drive through her preferred solution and felt that the only way to resolve matters was to call a general election. She assumed that she would win more seats in Parliament, which would make it easier to pass her preferred Brexit deal. When May called the election in 2017, I seriously considered stepping down as an MP. Being attacked in the media almost daily had taken its toll and I was tired of being a public punchbag for racist abuse, whether in print journalism or online. Close colleagues persuaded me to stay on, arguing that to stand down at a time of such turmoil in the PLP would be seen as a personal no-confidence vote in Jeremy. So out of loyalty to him, and against my better judgement, I fought the 2017 general election.

When the election was called, the party leadership looked to me as perhaps one of the only MPs left who was prepared to support Jeremy publicly. On the day of the announcement I went out on College Green, an open space opposite Parliament where most TV interviews were done, and gave seventeen media interviews on the coming campaign, one after the other.

At the beginning of the election campaign, nobody was hopeful, not even those on the left of the Labour Party. One of the two largest trade unions in Britain was Unite, a general union. Its general secretary, Len McCluskey, was quoted as saying that a victory for Labour in the coming election would be 'extraordinary', adding that winning 200 seats would be a success. McCluskey was not merely lowering expectations; this was the general view at the time.

Of all the people in Jeremy's close circle, I received the most abuse. It was laced with misogyny, racism and threats of violence. My staff stopped showing it to me and even tried reporting the worst threats to the police, but nothing was done. A report by Amnesty revealed that in the run-up to that election I was targeted with more abuse than all other women MPs put together;[1] Ofcom even had to formally reprimand LBC for allowing a caller to refer to me as a 'retard' twice on air.

In the process of doing a long series of consecutive radio interviews one morning I made a mistake with some figures on policing during an interview with LBC's Nick Ferrari. At first I thought everyone would realize it was a slip of the tongue. After all, I was not the only senior politician to stumble over figures in that campaign. The Chancellor, Philip Hammond, had said that the HS2 rail project would cost £32 billion, and he was £20 billion out; Damian Green could not remember how much pensioners would lose after the election from proposed benefit reforms; Andrew Mitchell could not remember what the minimum wage was; and the Tory manifesto had several numerical errors in it. While these mistakes garnered only cursory mentions in the media, my mistake over some figures unleashed a torrent of abusive comments. It began online, was picked up by the national media and lasted for the rest of the general-election campaign. A thirty-second slip-up allowed journalists to default to the most elemental stereotype about me: that I was completely unintelligent.

This added fuel to the fire of a Conservative campaign that was already specifically targeting both me and Jeremy. The Tories ran Facebook ads edited to make it look as if I was in favour of terrorism; I was name-dropped by Tory ministers in interviews that had nothing to do with me; and there were alarmist posters with my face on them in many constituencies. Whatever effect this might have had on the electorate, it certainly terrified Labour MPs, including those on the left who were ostensibly Corbyn supporters. Colleagues in Jeremy's Shadow Cabinet commissioned private polling, which said that, were I to step down, Labour could win the general election. So began a campaign to have me sacked. A few days before the general election, Karie Murphy, Jeremy's chief of staff, came to my home to tell me to step back from the campaign. I refused and went to bed that night secure in my position as Shadow Home Secretary. The next morning I woke up to hear on the radio that I had been forcibly stood down. The Labour Party cited health reasons, but I knew Jeremy's advisors were running scared and were unwilling to stand up for the only Black woman in the Shadow Cabinet.

The media predicted a bad result for Labour in 2017. The febrile atmosphere among some of the anti-Jeremy plotters meant that their judgement was often clouded and they made some startlingly bad decisions. Prior to publication of the 2017 Labour manifesto, the right of the party intended to leak what it considered the more outlandish parts of it, then have them widely attacked in the press and denounce the entire document. The BBC led with the plans to nationalize energy and scrap tuition fees. *The Guardian* came in with renationalization of the railways. Channel 4 added scrapping benefit cuts. The trouble for these plotters and their media supporters was that all these policies proved wildly popular, and the effect of reporting them in detail was to maximize the number of people who got to hear about them. The positive reception was reinforced by the official manifesto launch a few days later; prior to the leak, Labour had been polling at around 30 per cent, but four weeks later, on the eve of election day, it had climbed to 40 per cent.

The election resulted in a better outcome for Labour than anyone had expected. My team and I had spent weeks toiling in a very difficult campaign. When the polls closed at 10 p.m. on election day and television presenters announced the exit poll, my team and I caught our breath in a mix of shock and excitement. It was clear that this election was going to be much closer than anyone had guessed. For a few hours, until every vote had been counted, there even seemed the thrilling prospect that Labour would be the largest single party. In the face of the all-encompassing negativity and hostility, the final figures were astonishing. The general election had seen the highest turnout since 1997, the biggest swing to Labour since 1945 – a gain of thirty seats – and more than 12.8 million people voting Labour.

I got my best-ever result in my own constituency of Hackney North: in my very first general election in 1987 I was voted in with a majority of 7,500, and thirty years later I won with a majority of 35,139. It was one of the biggest majorities in the country and was a triumph, despite the relentless media onslaught.

Nationally Theresa May had lost her overall majority – a totally unexpected result. To remain prime minister she had to come to a 'confidence and supply' agreement with the Ulster Unionists (DUP) – a type of limited coalition between two parties in Parliament, meaning that the smaller party agrees to vote with the government on confidence votes, budgets and government spending. Despite falling short of a majority, Jeremy had negated all the predictions and had gained seats, and it felt like we had won. In fact until a deal had been done with the DUP, there was a small chance that Jeremy himself could have formed a coalition. It is important to note that we came very close to winning with policies that were anathema to most of the British press and the Labour right, but which were very popular with the public.

While Theresa May was scrambling to form her coalition, I went into the Home Office for one of my regular security briefings. I sat down with the then Home Secretary, Amber Rudd, and said a little cheekily to her that I was sorry to hear about her three recounts (though she smilingly put me right and said there had only been one). What amazed me about that visit was that the Home Office staff could not do enough for me. The Permanent Secretary even followed me into the lift on my way out to exchange pleasantries. Until May concluded her agreement with the DUP, the officials obviously thought there was a risk (as they saw it) that I would become Home Secretary and their boss.

Immediately after the election I spoke for the first time about my diabetes. I don't like to be seen as a victim, so I had said nothing during the campaign. My brother called me to tell me he was shocked by the now-infamous LBC interview – not for the same reasons as everyone else, but because from childhood I had been very good with figures, so he knew straight away it was my diabetes taking its toll. As the abuse of me in the mainstream media intensified over the course of the campaign, ordinary people in Hackney and beyond were very supportive and I received thousands of encouraging messages. At the worst of it, people would say to me, 'Can I give you a hug?' It was indeed touching and helped to keep my spirits up. My constituents perceived these attacks on me as unfair, which had led them to come out in record numbers and give me my biggest-ever majority. One young woman, Stephanie Ozuo, had done her best to marshal support for me on Twitter with the hashtag #AbbottAppreciation. Her campaign received backing from all over the world, and she also organized a celebratory fund-raising event for me in Hackney, which was attended by fellow Labour MPs, including Clive Lewis, Keith Vaz, Kate Osamor, Marsha de Cordova and Eleanor Smith, and it raised funds for one of my dearest causes: sickle-cell anaemia. Being reminded in this way of the affection that many people had for me began to heal the wounds from the campaign.

After the election I was reinstated as Shadow Home Secretary. Among the issues I raised in Parliament was the tragic fire that in June 2017 consumed the high-rise Grenfell Tower in North Kensington, which left seventy-two people dead. Grenfell Tower was not far from my childhood home in Paddington and I knew the area well. The sense of shock and grief ran deep, and I realized the local residents needed an advocate. I met and spoke to survivors of the tragedy, and agitated for an investigation into the extent that the negligence of the local authority had contributed to the fire, supporting new Labour MP Emma Dent Coad – a wonderful representative for her community – in dealing with the aftermath of such a horrific event.

Another great concern of mine were the conditions that women in immigration detention centres were being forced to live in. I was keen to visit Yarl's Wood, which perhaps represented the gravest of these cases. Opened in 2001, Yarl's Wood was one of Britain's largest detention centres, and in 2015 the Chief Inspector of Prisons had described it as 'a place of national concern', saying that 'women should only be held there as a last resort, as the conditions are worse than prison'. Yarl's Wood was in the middle of nowhere and was run by a private-sector organization, Serco. From the time it opened it had an ugly reputation: there were fires, hunger strikes, sexual assaults and even deaths there.

My office dealt with a steady flow of casework from Yarl's Wood and I was determined to visit and observe the conditions there, which was easier said than done. I sent a formal letter to Amber Rudd asking to visit, which met with no reply. This was unusual; the Home Secretary rarely failed to reply to her opposite number, even if the response did not say very much. I sent another letter and this time posted it online. In my personal meetings with the Home Secretary, and in Home Office questions, I repeatedly raised the matter of visiting Yarl's Wood. Finally, after more than a year of battling for access to this closely guarded site, Rudd gave in to my demands.

That visit, which I took with my friend and colleague, Shadow Attorney-General Shami Chakrabarti, was one of the most moving occasions of my life. We had been told beforehand that we would not be allowed to speak to any of the women inside, but as soon as we entered the detention centre it erupted with women screaming, shouting and bursting into tears. The guards tried to keep us in a boardroom, but the women were so anxious to talk to me that they sat down in front of me in the corridors. In the end the guards had to open a sports hall so that all the women who wanted to speak to me could do so. There were women inside who had been detained improperly for months on end, with no release date. They were living in utterly squalid conditions, and several were on hunger strike to protest at the violation of habeas corpus, the lack of proper medical attention or access to legal advice, the incarceration of sick and disabled people as well as torture and rape survivors and minors. Serco categorically denied that any hunger strikes were happening.

After witnessing the inhumanity these women were forced to live through, I was determined to fight in Parliament against their ill-treatment, and I continued to push for stricter rules for detaining immigrants and an end to indefinite immigration detention. In the long term I wanted to close both major immigration detention centres (Yarl's Wood and Brook House), since most people did not need to be there at all and it might have saved an estimated £20 million. That money could have been used for services in the community, such as supporting survivors of modern slavery, people-trafficking and domestic abuse. Progress was difficult; although I had Jeremy's support on the issue, many others in the Shadow Cabinet felt that these were difficult subjects to talk to Labour voters about, because they believed voters cared more about domestic issues.

It was harder for them to ignore the other great scandal of this era: Windrush. A generation of Commonwealth immigrants – including my parents – had come to the UK when there was freedom of movement between Britain and the Commonwealth, but became victims of increasingly harsh immigration law and policies, including Theresa May's 'hostile environment'. My parents' passports, like those of all Commonwealth migrants from that era, said that they were citizens of the United Kingdom and colonies; as citizens, they had no need for visas or any other paperwork. As the years went on, immigration legislation became increasingly harsh and was designed to make it more difficult for people of colour to enter Britain. Immigration legislation – which up until then had only been applied at the borders of Britain as people entered the country – was now being applied to Black and brown people who had legally resided in the UK for decades. A generation that had assumed they were British found they were denied access to the public services that they had helped to build, were detained, refused re-entry or removed from the country. This was particularly painful for men and women who had originally believed they were coming to the 'mother country'.

I had been aware of and campaigning on this issue since 2012 and continued to publicly denounce it in my role as Shadow Home Secretary. Once the scandal was picked up in the mainstream media, I held a public meeting in the House of Commons for members of the community who were affected. Despite only advertising it for two days, more than 500 attended, packing out four committee rooms, and we had to turn down hundreds more. The sheer number of people and their family members who had been affected – and how strongly they felt about the unfairness of it – became clearer.

In 2018 Amber Rudd had to resign as Home Secretary over the government's handling of the Windrush scandal. For a Tory Cabinet minister to step down over an issue about people of colour at a time when, because of the Brexit debate, a degree of xenophobia had become normalized, was remarkable. In my last speech in the House of Commons on the subject before Rudd stepped down, I reiterated the consequences of Windrush: 'Patriotic Commonwealth citizens treated like liars; benefits cut; healthcare denied; jobs lost; and people evicted from their housing. Whether they were deported, refused re-entry or detained, these people were separated from family and friends in breach of their human rights. This was a system where those who had come here, very often as young children, were required to show four pieces of original documentation for each year they were supposedly in this country.'

When the unfairness of Windrush was revealed, Theresa May

and her government seemed contrite. They commissioned Wendy Williams, an inspector of constabulary, together with an independent advisory group (including the likes of Jacqui McKenzie, a human-rights lawyer specializing in migration, asylum and refugee law), to produce a report entitled *Windrush Lessons Learned Review*, which was published in 2020. Among other things, Williams spoke about the Home Office's 'institutional ignorance and thoughtlessness towards the issue of race and the history of the Windrush generation' and made thirty recommendations designed to ensure that nothing like Windrush could ever happen again. The report prompted an official apology from Home Secretary Priti Patel, who stated in the House of Commons, 'There is nothing I can say today that will undo the suffering . . . On behalf of this and successive governments I am truly sorry.'

Years later, the Tories have not implemented most of the Williams report recommendations, and the compensation scheme has disbursed to only a minority of those entitled to it. Far from learning from the unfair and cruel way that the Windrush generation was treated, the Conservative government developed ever-harsher ways of dealing with migration and asylum, including a policy to give asylum seekers coming across the English Channel in rubber boats a one-way plane ticket to Rwanda.

While I was trying to raise issues like Windrush in Parliament, support for Jeremy Corbyn and the Labour Party was ebbing away. The 2019 general-election result turned out to be disastrous for Labour. It was a painful defeat, both personally and politically. Most party members had voted to remain in the EU, not least in Jeremy's own constituency of Islington North; however, there were strong supporters of Brexit in many historically Labour constituencies in the North and the Midlands, which accounted for many of the constituencies that swung from Labour to the Conservatives in 2019. In the mythology of the 2019 election, we were defeated by a Tory–Brexit insurgency in our own heartlands, when in truth the combined percentage vote for the Tories and

UKIP/the Brexit Party was little changed from 2017. Although we lost a small number of votes to them, we lost even more to the anti-Brexit Liberal Democrats. Politically, the error of too many colleagues (except Jeremy) was to put the issue of Brexit ahead of getting him into Number 10. Perhaps it is inevitable for parties to have some divisions going into an election, but they cannot make their disagreements the principal issue and expect to win. All the hopes and plans we had to make our country better for ordinary people were crushed.

Jeremy's leadership of the Labour Party was ultimately shipwrecked on the rocks of Brexit and the anti-Semitism allegations that hounded the party. Those close to the leadership were startled when the first allegations of anti-Semitism began to emerge, and nobody was more shocked than Jeremy himself. The London left had dedicated their political lives to the cause of anti-racism and had always taken anti-Semitism very seriously. Many prominent Marxists and left-wing thinkers and writers were Jewish, so in some ways we had taken for granted a close relationship to the Jewish community, since there had been so many Jewish figures associated with our own causes. We were horrified that the media and Labour Party colleagues were suggesting that we were anti-Semites, Holocaust deniers and worse. I found it a particularly difficult accusation to take in, given that Hackney had a vibrant and important Jewish community. It had been a place where upwardly mobile East End Jews moved to between the two World Wars, and even when some of them moved on to the suburbs, Hackney North was still one of the top five constituencies for the Jewish population. If I really did hate Jewish people, I think that after more than thirty years my Hackney neighbours and constituents would certainly have worked that out.

In response to concerns about anti-Semitism in the party, Jeremy commissioned an inquiry in 2016 led by Shami Chakrabarti, former head of the human-rights group Liberty. The inquiry found no evidence of systematic anti-Semitism within Labour, although there was an 'occasionally toxic atmosphere'. Twenty recommendations – including outlawing offensive terms and improving disciplinary procedures – were made. In October of the same year Parliament's all-party Home Affairs Select Committee produced a report which said that it 'found no reliable, empirical evidence that there is a higher prevalence of antisemitic attitudes within the Labour Party than any other party', though the leadership's lack of action 'risks lending force to allegations that elements of the Labour movement are institutionally antisemitic'.[2]

There was some weight, therefore, to the widespread concerns about the party's structural and operational issues in dealing with complaints about anti-Semitism, despite the overall findings of the Chakrabarti inquiry and the Home Affairs Select Committee's report. In the run-up to the 2019 election the issue reached fever pitch. As the *Morning Star* later noted: 'A July 2018 front page editorial jointly published by the *Jewish Chronicle*, *Jewish News* and *Jewish Telegraph* newspapers warned a Corbyn-led government would pose an "existential threat to Jewish life" in Britain. A month later Marie van der Zyl, president of the Board of Deputies of British Jews, told an Israeli TV news show that Corbyn had "declared war on the Jews" . . . *Telegraph* columnist Simon Heffer, appearing on LBC radio in 2019, said Corbyn "wanted to reopen Auschwitz".'[3] None of these allegations were in any way true, but they undoubtedly did immense damage to the Labour Party's standing. A Survation poll revealed that the public thought complaints of anti-Semitism had been made against one-third of the Labour Party, although in reality the figure was roughly 0.3 per cent.[4]

As for the question of where these allegations came from: the answer is undoubtedly complex. This was not the first time the Labour Party had come under fire for anti-Semitic comments; for instance, there were the infamous posters commissioned by Alastair Campbell in the lead-up to the 2005 election in which the

Tory leader Michael Howard and then Shadow Chancellor Oliver Letwin were depicted as flying pigs.[5] Jeremy was repeatedly criticized from the beginning of his leadership for his perceived links to Hamas and Hezbollah, groups that include 'Holocaust deniers, terrorists and some outright antisemites'.[6] Jewish Labour Party members were therefore understandably very upset by what they saw as anti-Semitism in plain sight.

However, there has also been a tendency to conflate criticism of the Israeli state with anti-Semitism, a tendency that is amplified by a media landscape that seeks to feed the culture wars that we now find ourselves in. A politics that supports justice for the Palestinian people and is critical of Zionism has in turn been interpreted as a form of anti-Semitism, and for this reason there was much upset when it came to considering the politics of Jeremy and his close allies. For many British Jews this hurt was compounded by, in their eyes, Jeremy's failure to really comprehend their pain and understand why this had become such a grave and poisonous issue.

There have undoubtedly been bad actors who have used anti-Zionism as a pretext to spread hatred of Jewish people, and they should of course be condemned. But to say that this anti-Semitic stance was the bedrock of the way Labour operated under Jeremy is a dangerous and false conflation.

Despite his thorough apologies, Jeremy's reputation could not survive these allegations of anti-Semitism, which took on a new energy under his leadership of the party, in an atmosphere that saw the most heated factionalism of recent years in British politics. The conspiracy against him by his enemies in the party, who fed these stories to the media, together with the terrible election result, meant that Jeremy had no choice but to step down as leader. It was a sad end to a leadership that began with such high hopes and a belief that a better world was possible.

In the leadership election that followed in April 2020, Sir Keir Starmer, a former Director of Public Prosecutions and head of the Crown Prosecution Service, was elected the new leader of the

Labour Party. I had first met him in 2015, when Jeremy was still leader and Starmer joined his Cabinet as Shadow Minister for Immigration. In 2016, when he became Secretary of State for Exiting the European Union, Starmer and I had a fair amount of contact as shadow ministers in the areas where our briefs overlapped: immigration and certain aspects of Brexit. It became clear to me and my team that Starmer's approach was not winning friends in Europe. A source close to Michel Barnier, the EU commissioner in charge of Brexit negotiations at the time, told us that he found Starmer to be rather like the Tories, in that he talked at great length and with huge confidence, while understanding very little about Europe. He seemed to believe that all Britain had to do was demand an end to freedom of movement and the EU would grant Britain an exemption, while allowing us to remain a member of the single market. This matched the Tory policy on the issue, and it was never going to happen. After one joint trip to Brussels, where Michel Barnier had made it abundantly clear that freedom of movement was completely non-negotiable, Starmer continued to assert that we must insist on it to the rest of the EU. The way he spoke struck me as reminiscent of the Brit abroad who talks loudly in English so that the silly foreigner can understand.

Barristers who had known Starmer earlier in his career said that he was very effective with a judge in chambers, but not so impressive in front of a jury. His new role as leader of the Labour Party was potentially challenging then, because the role of a party leader is to appeal to the nationwide jury that is the British people. His role at the CPS, and the knighthood he was awarded, had made him into something of an establishment figure, but Starmer knew that to win, he had to demonstrate to the left wing of the membership that he understood them and was aligned with them. He sold himself to largely pro-EU Labour Party members as 'Mr Remain', and his campaign team produced a video that, if you were not paying close attention, would have you believe that he had been involved in every major industrial dispute of the 1980s. It was even narrated by an ex-coal miner. Nobody thought that this Keir Starmer, once he became leader, would ban his front-bench ministers from supporting strikers by standing on their picket lines. I, however, having worked closely alongside him, was more sceptical of seeing his leadership as any kind of continuity of Corbynism. The left had suffered a very sharp defeat in 2019 – partly self-inflicted – and there is nearly always a terrible price to pay for that scale of reversal.

This defeat, and the anti-Semitism allegations that had hounded Jeremy out of the party, loomed large over Starmer's leadership. He called anti-Semitism 'a stain on our party', vowing to eradicate it and cooperating with the investigation by the Equality and Human Rights Commission (EHRC) into the issue. This investigation, which reported in 2020, rightly identified 'serious failings in leadership and an inadequate process for handling antisemitism complaints across the Labour Party' and 'multiple failures in the systems it uses to resolve them'. It concluded that there were unlawful acts of harassment and discrimination for which the Labour Party was responsible.

Jeremy responded on the morning of the publication of the investigation by saying that there was an anti-Semitism problem in the party, but it had been 'dramatically overstated for political reasons'. That same day Keir Starmer suspended him from the Labour Party. Although Jeremy was readmitted as a member after a month, Starmer refused to restore the whip to him, which meant that Jeremy could not be readmitted to the PLP and so would not be able to run as a Labour MP in the next general election. Removing the whip tends to be a temporary measure imposed until the substantive issue is resolved. In Jeremy's case, the process was back to front: the substantive issue had been resolved, but Jeremy was still not readmitted to the PLP, though he was widely acknowledged to have been an exemplary Labour MP for Islington North for almost forty years. Despite major unions getting involved in behind-the-scenes negotiations to have Jeremy readmitted to the PLP, Starmer could no longer see Jeremy as a 'friend and a colleague'. Permanently removing Jeremy from the PLP – and, in so doing, betraying one of the party's longest-serving stalwarts – was the centrepiece of his campaign to distance the Labour Party from the Corbyn years and to emphasize that, contrary to the tribute Starmer paid Jeremy immediately after winning the leadership, he marked a definite change from Corbyn.

In 2020 Starmer commissioned a further report from the top barrister Martin Forde, QC, into the party's handling of anti-Semitism. Forde's report confirmed that anti-Semitism was a problem in the party not that it was all a smear or a witch hunt; it also confirmed that anti-Semitism had been weaponized in the factional battle between the LOTO office and HQ staff. This factionalism was so entrenched that it became impossible to acknowledge both the reality of anti-Semitism in the party and the fact that both factions would have to come together to deal with it. The report also revealed a 'hierarchy of racism' in the party, which marginalized those from other minority ethnic backgrounds, such as Black and Asian people. This hierarchy has never meaningfully been addressed under Starmer's leadership, and in fact played a part in the way he handled an incident that occurred in 2023, concerning a letter that I had sent to *The Observer*, for which I swiftly apologized.

My letter was a response to a column written by a journalist called Tomiwa Owolade, which stated that Irish, Jewish and Traveller communities all suffer from racism. The letter was ill-judged, a first draft which strongly merited further thought and amendment, but which I did not give before sending. It was a clumsy attempt to say what was distinct about the racism experienced by people of colour – not an attempt to claim a hierarchy of racism; or to deny the horrors of the Holocaust; or to deny that anti-Semitism was still rampant all over the world, including in Britain. I have always argued for the unity of the fight against racism as a whole. It is quite clear, of course, that different ethnic groups who are subject to racism experience that racism in different ways. That arises for a whole series of historical and societal reasons. But there is an essential unity in opposing discrimination in all its forms, and all types of racist violence and threats from individuals and the state.

That includes the Jewish community as a whole, a community that has historically suffered savage discrimination. There should be no hierarchy of racism, although the discourse from both of Britain's major parties has created one, where anti-Semitism has become paramount and many other forms of racism have been overlooked or erased.

We should not try to invert the official pyramid. It should not exist at all.

The briefness of my letter, sent in haste, meant that the reasoning behind my opinions was left unexplained. Realizing within hours of its publication the upset I had caused and that the letter was indefensible, I immediately issued an apology. Nevertheless, a volcano erupted on the Monday after my letter was published in *The Observer*. The vitriol of the response in the press and the public debate surprised me, although perhaps I should have known by that point not to be surprised by any attacks against me in the media.

The next day Keir Starmer decreed that the letter was anti-Semitic and suspended me from the Labour Party. I was struck by this: it is unusual for a party leader to make any official statement before an investigation has occurred, particularly a leader who is a barrister by profession. There was no indication that due process would be followed, given that he had already made this declaration and, in so doing, had pre-empted the result of any investigation. Forde, in his report, specifically warned against this abuse of power by the leadership. The party launched an inquiry of sorts, which was never completed; it never spoke to me or any of my team about what I had meant by my remarks. It is telling too that the only community Starmer and others mentioned was the Jewish community; all others were ignored.

Other Labour MPs who had been suspended over similar incidents had had their suspensions lifted after apologizing, or had no further action taken against them; among them were Steve Reed (who in 2020 described Richard Desmond, a Jewish Conservative donor, as 'the puppet master for the entire Tory cabinet'; no further action was taken after he apologized); Barry Sheerman (who in August 2020 sent an anti-Semitic tweet saying there had been 'a run on silver shekels' when it was reported that two Jewish businessmen had missed out on peerages; no further action was taken after he apologized and deleted the tweets); and Naz Shah (suspended as John McDonnell's Parliamentary Private Secretary and investigated after it was discovered that she had shared a couple of anti-Semitic posts on Facebook prior to her election at the 2015 general election; no further action was taken after she apologized).

I received no such treatment. My allies in the party went to Starmer to advocate for me and plead my case, but he would not listen. I wasn't allowed to make a statement or explain myself through official party channels, and the fact that my own party was being so hostile and judgemental towards me made everything feel so much worse. This felt like a continuation of the aggression between two wings of the party during the Corbyn era. Mine was the biggest scalp they could win after Jeremy, and they relished doing so.

As Keir Starmer has settled further into his leadership of the Labour Party he has tried to put more and more distance between himself and the Corbyn years, in terms of both domestic and foreign policy. At the time of writing, we have entered a sad and terrible era of the decades-long conflict in the Middle East. On 7 October 2023 the Islamist militant group Hamas launched a series of deadly attacks from the Gaza strip onto nearby areas in Israel, killing more than a thousand people and taking hundreds hostage.

The Israeli government responded with a ruthless, relentless bombardment of Gaza, and a ground offensive that has seen many thousands of Palestinian civilians brutally killed in a form of collective punishment that is among the most severe I have witnessed during my time as an MP. Palestinian people have been cut off from water, electricity, medical supplies and fuel, and their bodies are piling up.

The devastating scenes emanating from this humanitarian crisis prompted citizens, politicians and human-rights groups around the world to call for an urgent ceasefire. Starmer, however, initially refused to do so, completely echoing the line of the Biden administration in its support for Israel. Every fractional adjustment in the US position has been echoed almost immediately by Starmer and his shadow ministers, in a policy overwhelmingly dominated by military and diplomatic support for Israel. It stands in stark contrast to global public opinion as expressed in a string of UN votes, and to British public opinion, which has been overwhelmingly in favour of a full ceasefire even from the earliest days in October, as numerous polls have shown.

Starmer's position was slow to change even after hundreds of thousands of British people (me included) took to the streets to demand that both the government and the opposition call for an end to the violence and bloodshed. Starmer only called for a 'ceasefire that lasts' in February 2024, after several months had passed and only after a joint statement by Canada, Australia and New Zealand that called for an immediate ceasefire. He remains constantly aware of the spectre of anti-Semitism that hangs over the party, and this makes it difficult for him to criticize the actions of the Israeli government, which by many accounts is committing severe and bloody war crimes and contravening international human-rights law. Starmer doesn't want a whisper of anti-Semitism against him and, in pursuit of this goal, has put himself at odds with public opinion and with the party membership in general. To some degree this is merely the continuation of Blair's 'shoulder to shoulder' position with the US in the Iraq War, but the death toll has been so enormous and the televised tactics so appalling that Starmer's unwillingness to break from the Tory/US line has horrified far greater numbers of people. This reached its nadir when, in an interview, Starmer offered his support for the Israeli tactic of cutting off food and water supplies to Gazans, which is widely understood to be a breach of international law and basic decency. Starving a whole people into submission is nothing less than morally repugnant, although Starmer claims that his words were taken out of the context of his response to the question of whether Israel had a right to defend itself.

Amidst this carnage, the attempt to silence critics of Israel with the charge of anti-Semitism has lost its force. Opposing genocide is not, and can never be, anti-Semitic. If anything, the assault on Gaza has clarified the issues related to charges of anti-Semitism in the Labour Party. We have seen repeatedly that allies of the current leadership are treated very differently when it comes to allegations of anti-Semitism, as compared to the left in the party and the critics of the current leadership. It is widely discussed in Labour circles and beyond that a purely factional approach is adopted on the charge of anti-Semitism by this leadership, and one of the cases most invoked to prove its factionalism is the way I have been treated, many months after my original letter to *The Observer*.

In some ways, the situation has eerie echoes of 2003 and the lead-up to the Iraq War. The politics of the Middle East is emotive in a way that almost no other foreign-policy issue is; it is so intertwined with society, with identity, with Britain's cultural memory. People remember how the Iraq War tore apart the Labour Party – and people remember that in 2003, even with the largest protest that Britain had ever seen, even when more than one million people marched through the streets of London to fight back against the threatened attack on Iraq, Blair still took us to war. It was a war that did irreparable damage to the country, and not least to

Blair's reputation. Starmer knows all this; yet, as Blair with Bush, it seems more important to this leadership to ally with America and with the Israeli state. It would be a mistake to repeat the errors of the past when we ought to have learned from them, but that seems to be the direction in which we are headed.

A lifelong anti-racist, here I am speaking to thousands of demonstrators in Parliament Square during a rally against racism, Islamophobia, antisemitism and fascism as part of United Nations Anti-Racism Day in 2022.

8. Lessons Learned

The turbulent politics of the last few decades, both in Britain and globally, have encompassed changes I could never have predicted. In 1987, when Bernie Grant, Paul Boateng, Keith Vaz and I were elected to Parliament, this in itself was a small revolution. We were commonly described as the first four Black MPs, though strictly speaking Keith was of South Asian descent and there had been a small number of non-white MPs elected to Parliament in the nineteenth and early twentieth centuries. Of the four of us who were elected in 1987, I am the only one who is still an MP. Like a lot of things in life, this longevity in office may be attributable to luck, but my years in the public eye have taught me a few lessons, whether these were absorbed instinctively or learned the hard way.

The first lesson I learned is that, to survive in politics, you need to know exactly why you want to pursue it as a profession. In the 1980s it was not uncommon to find MPs in all parties who were there to *be* somebody, rather than to achieve something. Were you to ask them what they believed in, they would have been stumped. Some had gone from student politics to Parliament without missing a beat, while others fancied the status that being a Member of Parliament would confer on them. Still others made their millions in the City and saw getting elected as the next step in their professional ascent, or even as the very summit of their ambition. A particular type of person might have owned land in their constituency for generations, and becoming an MP was therefore an extension of the 'lord of the manor' role. However, I believe that if you enter Parliament only for imagined status or wealth, you are unlikely to last. To stay the course, most MPs – whether they are Labour, Conservative, Lib Dem or Green – must be committed to something, if only to being a conscientious parliamentary representative for the place they have chosen to commit to. Such unshowy MPs form the backbone of Parliament.

It is no doubt tempting to fall prey to the seductive power that politics affords. Politicians serving in government are the ones who most need to keep in touch with ordinary people, but are least likely to. Too many government ministers know little (and perhaps care even less) about how their policies affect people living on the breadline, and are surrounded by those who make it harder for them to relate to ordinary citizens: junior ministers, political advisors, spin doctors, lobbyists, think-tank members and civil servants. These jobs ultimately depend on reflecting ministers' opinions back to them and telling them what they want to hear.

When I began as an MP, Parliament had the feel of a private gentlemen's club, and politics in general was less transparent. Admittedly there was a group of Labour MPs who were less likely to succumb to the lure of the Members' Smoking Room as they had come up through industrial trade unionism, working in a factory or down a mine. Dennis Skinner, a former miner who had spent twenty years below ground and then forty-nine years in Parliament representing the mining constituency of Bolsover, was the archetype. However, for the most part MPs of both major parties had a somewhat lordly attitude towards their constituents; few lived in their constituencies and there was little emphasis on constituency casework. The trappings of Parliament – the architecture, the attendants in black tailcoats deferring to MPs, the bewigged Speaker, the language – help to reinforce a sense of social exceptionalism, making it all too easy to succumb to delusions of superiority.

It's no surprise then that the Westminster bubble can be all-consuming, not just for politicians, but also for journalists who are there to report on what we do. Lobby correspondents – the journalists who specialize in Westminster matters, and who pop up in television news whenever there is a political story – can spend so much time drinking and socializing with senior politicians that there is not much investigation going on and their journalism loses its edge. Some lobby journalists even end up marrying members of the political class. This incestuous relationship with the media suits top politicians and their spin doctors, but does not aid public understanding of what is really going on in Westminster. Often the most incisive questions and the most dramatic exposés of corruption and wrongdoing by MPs come from journalists who are outsiders, such as regional journalists.

My time in Parliament has seen many parliamentary scandals unfold, from MPs abusing the parliamentary allowances system in 2009, to MPs sexually harassing staff. When I was a new MP the culture around me in Parliament bred complicity and collusion, and the prevailing ethos was 'what goes on in Parliament stays in Parliament'. Remaining in close and engaged contact with ordinary people, in particular your constituents, will help you to see your colleagues' behaviour for what it is. How can you speak up properly in Parliament for people if you do not know the reality of their lives?

When I became MP for Hackney North and Stoke Newington in 1987, the first thing I did was to move into Hackney and set up a weekly local advice session. This was usually held on a Friday in my office on Stoke Newington High Street. I took it for granted that I would do it on my own. It was first come, first served, and constituents were content to wait until I could see them. Some people were shocked that I not only lived in Hackney, but would make time to see constituents like this; in the early months one lady came in and, upon seeing me, said in an accusatory tone, 'What are you doing here? Ernie was always in Parliament.'

I also employed Black staff, despite the assumption that they would not be suitable as parliamentary assistants or policy advisors (presumably because they were thought not to have the right experience or ability). Even my colleague Bernie Grant warned me not to get a Black secretary. I ignored all this and hired able staff, whatever their colour. If I could not give Black applicants a break, who would? My staff – themselves often Black women – and I would feel embattled together, and if I had to deal with patronizing assumptions, so did they.

To this day I live in my constituency. I have always felt perfectly safe there, even though people sometimes intimate that Hackney is a difficult, even dangerous, place to live. You can learn things just by walking along the high street, or chatting to people on the bus, that you cannot learn while sitting in an office in Parliament. Seeing matters the way the public does helps to cut through the hype and spin and keeps matters in proportion. In the febrile atmosphere of Westminster, issues can blow up and seem overly important. Being on the receiving end of so much negative media myself, I am mindful of the fact that what upsets people in Westminster may not always be so relevant to those outside it. Politicians put great store by the mainstream media, particularly newspapers such as the *Guardian*, the *Daily Telegraph* and *The Times*, but those broadsheets tend to be aimed at the middle classes and have a lower circulation than the tabloid newspapers. The political class seem to spend their whole lives on Twitter (now known as X), without realizing it is not where most people of a certain age get their news. So when something blows up in the media, it is helpful to have ordinary people around you, to support you if necessary, but also to point out whether it really matters.

Some politicians are deluded enough to think that, because they study opinion polls or, worse, read the leader column in their favourite newspaper, they have an infallible insight into what ordinary people think. What the polls reveal obviously depends on the questions asked and how representative of the general public the sample being polled is. Polls can be a mere snapshot in a moment in time. Cruel and counterproductive policies on immigration are too often justified with the argument that polling shows Britons do not like migrants – but views on immigration, as on other social issues, are much more nuanced than the polls would suggest, as well as being politically on a feedback loop. Notably, those who are hostile to immigration in the abstract are more positive when engaging with individual migrants, though polling does not reflect this.

Furthermore, in the middle of a parliamentary term polling can be misleading as to a general-election result. Polling did not predict the Tory victory in the 2015 general election, and in 2017 no poll predicted how close the result would be. Polling is not a substitute for talking to constituents, as too many politicians think it can be. Over-dependence on polling and insufficient contact with ordinary people partially explains why some government ministers cling on to bad policies, in ways that can be mind boggling to the outside world. At best, these policies are poorly conceived and counterproductive, but at worst they can be harmful to millions of people. I doubt if some ministers would be so quick to cut welfare benefits if, instead of looking at polling that states how much the general public hates welfare claimants, they spent some time sitting with, and listening to, those trying to get by on benefits.

Staying in touch with ordinary citizens who aren't involved in the world of politics has been one of my major sources of sustenance as a politician, as it has enabled me to champion the causes that affect those people directly. One cause I have always felt particularly strongly about is defending civil liberties. As a former Home Office civil servant and the race-relations officer at the NCCL, I saw first-hand how abuses of civil liberties were fashioned. I studied the files and read the memos. I could see that too much legislation was drawn up to target certain demographics, and although this was never spoken aloud in parliamentary debates, it was nevertheless tacitly understood by all to be aimed at minorities. The unspoken attitude was that if, for instance, you were Irish, Black or Muslim, your civil liberties did not matter.

The role of Parliament down the centuries has been to defend the rights of the individual, and it has become clear that anti-civil-liberties measures that start out targeting some minority or the other end up undermining rights for everyone. I have never regretted fighting on issues of principle and have always been prepared to vote against legislation that harmed civil liberties, even if it upset the party leadership or harmed my career prospects. For instance, I was among a small group of MPs who argued vocally against the proposed Anti-Terrorism, Crime and Security Bill, which was part of the British government ramping up its anti-terror legislation after the horrific terrorist attacks carried out by al-Qaeda against the United States in September 2001. This Act proposed to increase police and security-service powers, including the indefinite detention of foreign national terror suspects without trial, largely in HMP Belmarsh. If someone is suspected of a crime or a terrorist act they should be charged and tried in a court of law, not simply held in prison indefinitely. I argued for time limits and increased scrutiny of the process, and I thought it wrong that just because someone was accused of being a terrorist they should not get a fair trial.

It turned out that the Law Lords agreed with me when they ruled that holding suspects indefinitely without charge or trial was incompatible with the European Convention on Human Rights. Yet instead of being chastened by yet another piece of botched and illiberal anti-terrorist legislation being struck down by the courts, ministers decided to get round this. In 2005 they introduced a new Prevention of Terrorism Bill, which invented the concept of 'control orders' that would allow the government to restrict the activities of suspected terrorists. Everybody knew it was the powers in the Anti-Terrorism, Crime and Security Bill dressed up in a different guise, but although forty-nine MPs – including me – rebelled, the bill got through the House of Commons, ping-ponged between the Commons and the Lords and eventually passed.

Later that year the 7/7 bomb attacks in London, in which fifty-two people were killed and hundreds injured, brought terrorism to the front and centre of the UK's political debate. The rise in

Islamophobia was predictable: mere days after the attacks, Boris Johnson wrote in *The Spectator* that 'Islam is the problem' and suggested that Islamophobia was a 'natural reaction'.

A few days after 7/7 I was in a London taxi when the cab driver began, 'These bombings, these bombings . . .' As I steeled myself for an Islamophobic rant, he went on thoughtfully, 'They don't understand; they think we can be frightened by a few bombs, but we're Londoners, we're Londoners.'

Whereas ordinary Londoners tried to be stoic in the face of the 7/7 bombings, not so the government. It came forward with ill-thought-out and draconian legislation that constituted a frontal attack on civil liberties, attempting to increase to ninety days the length of time that men and women could be held in detention without trial. Even mild-mannered Labour MPs rebelled against this and the proposal was defeated by 322 votes to 291. It was New Labour's first defeat. In the end it compromised on twenty-eight days, which I voted for with the utmost reluctance.

Most ministers and their minions would suggest that legislation of this sort has been about targeting IRA bomb-throwers, Black criminal gangs or Islamic terrorists, in order to soothe the consciences of those MPs who might have doubts about it. The unspoken thought behind this is that the civil liberties of people who looked like them would not be impacted. However, I cannot bear the idea that someone might be harassed by the police or imprisoned because of legislation that I failed to vote against; it is as if I can see their face in my mind's eye.

My experiences in the early years of my career of being the only Black woman in a series of institutions have led me to feel that, unless I have the courage to speak on issues of racial justice, nobody else will. That is not to say this has not been an exhausting task. Although I know the issues at first hand, I certainly do not think that, as a Black professional, you should be *obliged* to talk about issues of race. Even I get fed up when, after more than thirty-five years in Parliament and serving on at least two significant House of

Commons committees, the only thing people think I can talk about is race. What Black lawyers, Black doctors and all Black professionals want is to be respected as professionals.

The pressure to speak out on issues of race can be overwhelming, and there were times in my professional life when I did not have that courage. However, my concerns about racial justice and my deep belief in the paramount importance of fighting for it are part of what has sustained me as a politician for such a long time. Early on, I put my energy and passion into after-hours activism, including my work as a Westminster City councillor, and this campaigning work informed my work as an MP in a crucial way. It would have been far easier for me, and for my career, to stay quiet on issues connected with race, particularly in the early years. But when there were so few of us Black MPs in Parliament, I felt a responsibility to speak up whenever necessary. I regularly organized and attended events on issues such as stop-and-search, police brutality against Black people, deaths in custody and institutional racism in the police force, often holding meetings in Parliament, because I felt it was important to open up Westminster to ordinary people.

'The personal is political', as the saying goes, so I would not draw a dividing line between the topics that concern me as a politician and those that concern me as a woman – from race, to women's equality, to social justice. However, it can be difficult to have a personal life as a woman in politics, because the conditions placed on any MP do not make it straightforward to maintain relationships. There have been advantages to the job, of course – for instance, being able to travel and network far and wide and, in the course of that, meeting lots of interesting people both in Britain and overseas. However, the drawbacks have complicated the prospect of a long-term partnership.

First, there is the pressure of time: in the late 1980s when I was first an MP, Parliament often sat until ten o'clock at night and sometimes even later. When I was free, I was often exhausted. I had to stop myself from going on about politics – the subject that took up all my waking hours, but was not always so enthralling to someone else. These were not the best circumstances in which to engage with and focus on another person.

There are also sometimes psychological issues for a potential partner who considers being with someone in the public eye. This was a smaller consideration when I was newly elected; although there were some stars at Cabinet level, by and large being an MP and a public figure felt less oppressive then – it was a time that allowed more respect for everyone's privacy, even that of MPs, and the average back-bench MP was relatively anonymous outside their constituency. Now we have a hungry celebrity culture. I did not go into politics to be a celebrity, and I would still rather not be regarded as one. Modern celebrity is rarely about celebrating skills, abilities or achievements; it is more about stripping you of your privacy, with an assumption that the tiniest detail about you and your family's life should be media fodder. Gone are the days when you could sit quietly in a pub having a drink with a friend. Smartphones make it possible for someone you don't know to take an unflattering picture of you entirely without your permission and, via social media, circulate this to thousands of people before you have even finished your drink. As an MP, I would rather be judged on my speeches than on how I look while drinking. It took me some time after the advent of the smartphone to realize that once you were in public, there was no such thing as leaving your MP persona behind and simply spending time with your friends. You were always at the mercy of some random smartphone-user.

This lack of privacy and the unsought public attention can be difficult for even the most easy-going of men, so it is difficult for relationships to blossom. Almost all the women MPs I know who enjoy stable and happy relationships got together with their partners before having become MPs – some of them a long time before – so their partners had time to gradually get used to their burgeoning profile. They might have been a councillor or had a successful and reputable career before ever becoming an MP. Or it may be that, in the partner's mind, the woman standing up in the chamber of the House of Commons or doing the television interviews is still the girl they met so many years ago. Some of the happiest marriages exist where the partner is content to remain in the background, even running her office for her.

I had some casual relationships in my early years as an MP, and I even married in 1991. Just as that did not last, neither did my later relationships, though I remain the eternal optimist and still think Prince Charming may be around the corner. And although I had difficulties in building and preserving a romantic relationship, I have drawn strength from my most stalwart female friends. My test of a good friend is whether I think they would be close to me even if I were not an MP. Friendships forged in the political arena can blow up from the pressure, and I have had people I thought were friends let me down. Most of those I count as close friends either knew me before I became a parliamentarian or live abroad, which puts my celebrity at a distance. They do not see me as an MP, or a public figure, or somebody off the television; to them, I'm just Di. Perhaps I'm drawn to them because they tend to be involved in writing, the arts and the media, which have always been my main interests outside politics. Most of my closest friends are independent-minded Black women, partly because we have common experiences in dealing with a sometimes-hostile world and inching up our respective professional ladders. They are the people I rely on to support me through the anxieties of single motherhood; to distract me from the world of politics and appreciate the sillier aspects of the Westminster bubble; to avoid the besetting sin of pomposity; and to keep my sense of proportion, lift me up and make me laugh.

Good friends can be invaluable to help you make the right decision, whether about politics or about men. They may inwardly raise their eyebrows at your choices, but they wait patiently for the fire to burn out and for you to come to your senses. When a relationship, a marriage or a job collapses, good friends are there to support one another and refrain from uttering those annoying words, 'I told you so.' They have celebrated with me in the good times, such as when I gave birth to my beautiful son; one even threw a splendid christening party, packed with relatives, friends and free-flowing champagne. And they have been there in the dark times, such as when I have been hounded by the press. There can be no more unnerving sight than waking up to see a crowd of press photographers outside your door. At times like these, I would seriously consider giving up politics altogether, but my friends have always been there to make sure that I kept going.

My career has also taught me to be resilient, and not to let the media get me down. Unfavourable media coverage is an issue for all politicians, particularly women; yet however bruising some of my experiences with the media have been, I am mindful that so many women, including those in my own constituency of Hackney, have infinitely worse lives. They might be unemployed and struggling to feed their children, or homeless and living in terrible conditions. Too many women suffer violence at the hands of a partner. I have learned not to be defeated by hostile media treatment, by using it to contextualize the suffering of women whom my staff and I try to help every day.

Negative media coverage has been an issue for me ever since I was elected in 1987. Initially I had no idea how difficult this was going to be; I even had the advantage of a little more media experience than some MPs, thanks to my jobs at *Thames News* and TV-am. Within months of my being elected, however, the attitude of the mainstream media towards me was reminiscent of the eighteenth-century writer Dr Samuel Johnson's comment: 'A woman's preaching is like a dog's walking on his hind legs. It is not done well; but you are surprised to find it done at all.' For British journalists, I was the dog on its hind legs.

As the only Black woman out of 650 Members of Parliament, I

was a novelty; there had never been anyone in Parliament who looked like me. However, the media quickly moved on from its patronizing approach. There was very little broadcast coverage of me, as was of course to be expected with a new young opposition backbencher. The print media – notably the political correspondents – settled into a pattern of negativity. This may partly have been because they did not know me; politicians and political journalists tend to move in the same circles, engaging with one another in the Westminster bubble and meeting socially and, needless to say, I was not on that circuit. In the mainstream media, coverage of Black people often conformed to one of several stereotypes, depicting them as servants, criminals, entertainers or victims of some kind. British political correspondents did not know quite what to make of a Black woman who was not an entertainer and was emphatically not a victim.

It was easier for them to fall back on making me out to be brainless. Many political correspondents were unaware that I was a university graduate, and even fewer knew that I had attended a top Russell Group university. They had a fixed view that, as a Black woman, I was not up to the job and could not be taken seriously, and the only political stories they were prepared to write were ones framing me as stupid. Later, even after I had served for more than two decades in Parliament and had been re-elected at several general elections, I was still being portrayed in the press as someone who could do nothing but make 'gaffes' (when by then it was fairly common knowledge that I was an educated and intelligent person). These 'gaffes' were often so trivial as to be unmemorable, and involved words or actions that would probably have gone unremarked had a white male MP been involved. All these stories played into the narrative that I was ignorant.

Another disparaging stereotype applied to me was that I was one of London's 'loony left' – particularly by the Labour Party leadership, which helped to reinforce the unbalanced negative view taken even by left or liberal journalists. When it came to writing about mainstream left politicians or trade unionists, they would be respectful and check facts, but no such rules applied when they were writing about the 'loony left'. There was a set of issues associated with us loonies – among them anti-racism, women's rights and gay rights – that, decades later, have come to be seen as mainstream, to the point where aggrieved right-wing commentators like to complain about a new 'woke' orthodoxy. But in 1987 political commentators could not have dreamed of a world where, in the Tory Cabinet, none of the great offices of state were filled by white men. Nor would they have believed that gay marriage could be legal. They thought speaking up about such issues – especially racial justice – was derisible.

For most of my political career I have borne the brunt of the antagonistic attitude that I was both a loony and stupid. Everything I said was unpicked to prove these points. I once tweeted something about the British Empire being built on 'divide and rule', thinking this to be a simple statement of fact. The media went crazy: journalists who appeared never even to have read any books on the British Empire fell over themselves to accuse me of racism. Long-standing ally Darcus Howe came to my defence in an appearance on *Newsnight*, and Meg Hillier (Labour MP since 2005 for the neighbouring constituency of Hackney South and Shoreditch), when she was repeatedly pushed on BBC Radio 4's *World at One* to call me racist, instead agreed with me that what I had said was merely factual. It remains a feature of the media attention given to Black and brown politicians that journalists swoop on anything we say in order to accuse us of racism, even when the basis for this is extremely tendentious; although they derive pleasure from accusing non-white politicians of racism, they are somehow less punctilious about spotting the racism of other politicians.

One might have thought the Labour Party would be proud of the country's 'first' four Black and Asian MPs, but instead it seemed to consider us an embarrassment. I got no support from the party in managing an antagonistic media and newspapers that routinely published untrue stories about me, and I often felt completely alone when facing frequent waves of hostile publicity and invented news stories. If the national Labour Party had been prepared to offer even a little backing, then the media might not so easily have regarded me as prey. The New Labour administration was even worse: for them I was a non-person.

I cannot pretend it was not upsetting. The real things I was doing – such as engaging with women entrepreneurs, campaigning on civil liberties and years of work on the education of Black children – garnered almost no coverage at all, but the newspapers always had space for a 'gaffe' story about me. At one point I considered stepping down from Parliament because of the continuously hostile press. Keith Vaz, who had been a friend since long before I became an MP, said firmly, 'You cannot step down, Diane. You have forgotten how hard it was to get here.'

There was a slight respite when, from 2003 to 2010, I appeared weekly on the late-night BBC political discussion programme *This Week* with the journalist Andrew Neil and former Conservative MP Michael Portillo. Originally I was to appear on it for only three weeks, but the synergy between me and my co-hosts was obvious straight away. I went on to appear on the programme every week for seven years, stepping down only when I ran for leadership of the Labour Party, as BBC managers thought that made me too partisan (though I wasn't sure why they hadn't realized I was partisan all along). The hostility towards me in the mainstream media was dialled down during this time, for it would have been difficult to keep insisting on my stupidity when the television audience saw me holding my own every week with Andrew and Michael. Furthermore, *This Week* had a regular slot in which different journalists acted as commentators, and so with many of them anxious to get into broadcast television, they probably thought that being too abusive about me might not get them that much-desired slot. In truth, I had no say whatsoever as to which journalists were invited each week, although the would-be guest journalists were not to know that.

Once I came off *This Week*, the coverage resumed its overwhelming negativity and, combined with the rise of online platforms and social media – notwithstanding their ability to open up political debate – the barrage of abuse that I receive has increased a hundredfold. When social media first took off, I loved it; as someone who is often too busy to keep in touch with my friends as much as I would like to, I found it an effective way of connecting with friends and family, especially if they were overseas. I admired the way it could be used to disseminate and gather information: if you're active in your community or in politics, it's a great way to find out what people are talking about. In some cases you can get a better understanding of the issues that are exciting and engaging them from half an hour on social media than from hours in a coffee shop. Furthermore, we live in a world where fewer people go to public meetings, so communicating online has been an invaluable way to reach those who have never heard my speeches, read my articles or even heard of me.

However, events have taken a darker turn since the advent of this technology. As news has pivoted online, so news and social-media sites have realized that my name makes for good clickbait and that articles or posts demonizing me receive lots of views, so they often stoke hatred with inaccurate or misleading reporting. No one ever checks these stories and thinks to verify them with fact. One bizarre story that began online saw someone tweet that he had spotted me in a photograph wearing two left shoes, and this was re-tweeted thousands of times until the mainstream media picked it up and repeated it with enthusiasm. It was a long way from my days at *Thames News*, when a lawyer was in the newsroom all day and every day, checking that our stories were true and were not actionable.

Social-media platforms create space for racists, bullies and obsessives to share their thoughts with their targets and with each other, and make it a great deal easier to deluge people, particularly politicians, with abuse. When I first became an MP, in order to send abuse you had to take the trouble to write a letter, find an envelope, buy a stamp and leave your house in order to post it in a letter-box. It might have given would-be abusers pause that writing a letter – especially one that threatened violence – could make you easier to trace. Now you merely have to press a button on your computer keyboard, and it takes seconds to bombard your victim with vitriol. The volume of abuse that I continue to receive on social-media platforms is debilitating and corrosive, and the sheer level of hatred that writers reveal can be very difficult to navigate. Negative media, whether in the newspapers or online, is not negative by chance: it is expressly intended to undermine and demoralize, by sabotaging what you stand for.

From its hopeful beginnings, social media has increasingly become a vehicle for the abuse of women in the public space. When the Scottish leader Nicola Sturgeon stepped down unexpectedly in 2022, she said, 'The nature and form of modern political discourse means there is much greater intensity – dare I say it, brutality – to life as a politician than in years ago.' She also commented that 'Social media provides a vehicle for the most awful abuse of women, misogyny, sexism and threats of violence for women who put their heads above the parapet.'[1]

A 2021 study from the Economic Intelligence Unit said more than one-third of women worldwide have experienced online abuse, rising to almost half for younger women. This becomes a vicious cycle: when women are abused online, that affects how we are written about in the newspapers and broadcast media, which in turn ramps up the nastiness online and can also affect how people in our own organizations talk about us. I was taken aback to read some of the comments made on WhatsApp about me by top officials in the Labour Party: 'Literally makes me sick', 'truly repulsive' and 'a very angry woman'. I was an ally of Jeremy Corbyn in a very difficult time for the Labour Party, but the male MPs who were also close to him were not spoken about in anywhere near such a hostile tone. Those saying these things were people who, to the best of my knowledge, I had never met.

For online commentators, a recurrent theme was that I could not be a member of Jeremy's Shadow Cabinet based on my abilities – it must be, they opined, because of our past relationship. Most of the stories about our relationship were completely invented; for instance, it was often repeated that Jeremy had brought his friends home to view me naked. In a survey produced and published by Amnesty International on how much abuse women MPs faced on social media in the run-up to the 2017 snap election, it was discovered that Black and Asian women MPs received 35 per cent more abusive tweets than white women MPs. During this six-week period I received almost half (45.14 per cent) of all abusive tweets, ten times more than any other female MP – and those figures were almost certainly an underestimate. Twitter refused to release to the researchers tweets from accounts that had been disabled or tweets that had been deleted. Had they done so, the tally of abusive tweets sent to me would have been even higher. Typical tweets that I receive are: 'This fat retarded Black bitch thinks that you should be forced to feed a bunch of violent foreign invaders. I strongly disagree' and 'Piss off you are disgusting useless fat bitch. You are a parasite alien looking to silence native people for your own power.'[2] I have had thousands of death and rape threats. People tweet that I should be hanged 'if they could find a tree big enough to take the fat bitch's weight'. The word 'nigger' is used repeatedly.

Online abuse can have real-life consequences. After *The Sun* and the *Daily Mail* once printed a false story that I had said all Brexit supporters were racists, people posted thousands of abusive comments on Twitter and Facebook in the days that followed and continuously rang my office to make monkey noises, shout abuse and threaten violence. The handful of racist letters that I received weekly when I became an MP escalated over time to hundreds every couple of days, including letters covered in swastikas, monkeys and chimpanzees. Though I am fortunate to have paid staff members to screen everything, they cannot be shielded from the difficulty of the role. One staff member said, 'If you had told me before I got into Parliament that I would read the word "nigger" so much, I would not have believed you.' Another who worked for me in that period said she could not seriously consider a career in politics because of the abuse she had witnessed.

Concern about MPs' safety issues has spiked, with the proliferation of social media and the associated threats of violence that are regularly posted on these sites. Although my staff report such threats to the police, it is difficult for them to do anything because the threats come from anonymous trolls. I believe from experience that, although you should be able to tweet and post anonymously, the platform concerned should keep a record of your real name and address. I suspect that fewer people would make death threats online if they knew they could be tracked down so easily. There are of course associated issues around data protection and, as a defender of civil liberties, I take them seriously; but it would be possible to legislate so that social-media companies could not share the data except in relation to crime. Anonymity on social media has been completely abused, and only if people knew they could be tracked down would there be any kind of check on it.

However, more recently virulent abuse has not been the sole purview of anonymous trolls. In the spring of 2024 I received a telephone call from a senior *Guardian* journalist I had known for years, in which he warned me that *The Guardian* was about to publish a news story about me and they were anxious for me to see it first. He shared with me some quotes *The Guardian* had uncovered, from a millionaire businessman named Frank Hester. Hester was at that point unknown to me, although I soon learned that he was the chief executive of the Phoenix Partnership, a clinical software company that has won millions of pounds worth of NHS and prison contracts. More importantly, he was the single largest donor to the Conservative Party. Hester had said of me, 'It's like trying not to be racist but you see Diane Abbott on the TV and . . . you just want to hate all Black women because she is there, and I don't hate all Black women but I think she should be shot . . . Diane Abbott needs to be shot.'

At first I could not take in his words. Although I had years ago stopped looking at the continuous stream of racist abuse that I receive on social media, it was a different thing entirely to see comments like these publicly plastered all over the mainstream media. Worst of all was Hester's wish that I should be shot. It was a clear incitement to violence and, after the murders of my two fellow MPs Jo Cox and David Amess in the past decade, it was frightening to be confronted with the real likelihood of a physical attack. Jo Cox had been shot three times and stabbed to death in her Batley and Spen constituency in 2016, outside a library where she was about to hold her advice session. The killer, Thomas Mair, had links to the far right. Then in 2021 David Amess, MP for Southend, was fatally stabbed while conducting his regular advice surgery in a church hall. The killer was an Islamic State supporter. Different political parties, different parts of the country, different motivations – but these killings brought home to all MPs the heightened risks associated with our jobs. Other attacks, though less targeted towards specific MPs, have been just as horrifying: in 2017 an alleged terrorist drove a car into pedestrians near Parliament, injuring fifty people and killing four, then crashed his car into Parliament's perimeter fence, jumped out and stabbed a police officer to death. I would no longer think of conducting a surgery alone in an office on the high street, where anyone can wander in off the street; and now, with Hester's comments, I felt this danger more keenly than ever. As a woman living alone in my Hackney constituency, I often find myself walking or using public transport in the area, since I do not drive; but knowing that someone had fuelled this kind of violence against me left me numb and in shock. Despite reassurances from friends, I could not shake off the feeling that I had a target on my back.

The Labour Party leadership, meanwhile, found itself in a dilemma; having suspended me over the comments I had made in *The Observer* the previous spring, with still no conclusion to the investigation in sight, Starmer and his advisors wanted to continue treating me as a non-person and avoid supporting me personally, even as they condemned Hester for his vile words. Initially the only senior PLP official to speak out was Wes Streeting, speaking on the floor of the House of Commons in the budget debate that day. He emphatically called Hester's words 'utterly revolting, racist and inciteful language' and said they had 'no place in our politics and public'. Anneliese Dodds, the chairwoman of the PLP, went on Sky News with the Labour Party's agreed line on Hester, which was that Sunak should give his donation back; but when asked whether she or anyone in the Shadow Cabinet had reached out to me, all Dodds could do was squirm. It took twenty-four hours before anyone in the Labour leadership contacted me.

The response from the Conservative Party was even more comical. They spent the entire day after the story was published insisting that Hester's remarks were not racist – a patently ridiculous position that was contravened by members of their own party, including Kemi Badenoch and Kwasi Kwarteng; by the end of the day, Rishi Sunak's spokesperson conceded (albeit reluctantly) that the remarks were racist and wrong, although the Conservatives pointedly refused to give back Hester's £10 million donation. Hester himself continued to insist that his remarks were not racist at all and in fact had nothing to do with my race or my sex.

As for my own response, I refused to do any interviews at first because it was important to me to speak for the first time about Hester in the chamber of the House of Commons during Prime Minister's Questions. I could not imagine that I would not be called, so it was to my and many other people's amazement that Lindsay Hoyle, the Speaker of the House, refused to call me, even when I stood up forty-six times during PMQs. In more than three decades in Parliament I had never witnessed a situation where someone was mentioned five times in the session – in particular by the leader of each main political party – and was not called to speak. Asked the following day on a breakfast news programme why I had not been called, former Cabinet minister Ed Balls – who was not exactly a friend of mine – smiled and said, 'Sunak did not want her called. Starmer did not want her called. She was not called.'

On the other side of the oceans, my case was causing particular uproar in Jamaica. I have long been well known there because of my Jamaican heritage, and Jamaicans were angry on my behalf, not only because of what Hester said, but because his friend and colleague Lord Marland claimed on LBC Radio that Hester could not be racist because he 'does a lot of business in Jamaica', including, most recently, securing a multimillion-pound contract to digitize Jamaica's health records. Jamaica strongly dislikes being used as a cover for blatant racism, and so began a ferocious local campaign to strip Hester of the contract.

At home and abroad it was heartening to see the surge of popular concern for me after what Hester had said, which completely outpaced the leadership of both political parties. By the end of the week I had received 1,200 supportive emails, and many of the writers made a point of saying that, although they did not share my politics, they were shocked at the way I was being abused. There were rallies in Wembley and Edmonton, and biggest of all in Hackney. More than a thousand people of all colours, and from all over the city, crammed in front of Hackney Town Hall that Friday evening, holding banners and handmade placards with slogans such as 'We stand with Diane', 'Hands off our MP' and 'Don't disrespect Black women'. I was stunned by the numbers at the rally, and by the breadth of the communities represented. Most people in public life only get heartfelt testimonials after they die, so it was particularly touching to be able to feel such a swell of love and support while I am still alive. In national politics it is easy to perceive oneself as an outsider and although Hester's comments did affect me, the response to them also made me realize that I was definitely not forgotten, and in fact that I remained important to many people up and down the country.

It's entirely understandable that some women, reading all this, might say that they don't want to go into public life or, in Sturgeon's words, 'put their head above the parapet'. It was, and still is, extremely difficult to keep going in the face of hostility in mainstream and social media; I often wonder how I have been able to do it. Typically we are being attacked by men who feel personally affronted by the progress that women have made in recent decades and want to reverse it. But women should not have to stay out of the public space because of the potential level of abuse; if we do that, then the bullies, racists and misogynists have won.

Although I have wavered at times, I have refused to let myself be driven out of politics. In the same way that the schoolgirl Diane Abbott did not let anything stop her achieving her aims, as an adult I will not allow a hostile media to prevent me standing up for my community and remaining firm in my convictions.

I used to think that if you and I held different political views, you were the enemy. Now I know it is not only your formal politics that matter, but your values and what kind of person you are. Even if you don't always make the biggest waves of change in your own lifetime, it is important to keep fighting for the causes you believe in. As the American feminist and political leader Angela Davis said to me in 1987, the year I was first elected, 'Be prepared to go the distance.'

Standing on the steps of Hackney Town Hall in May 2024 addressing a rally calling for me to be allowed to stand as the Labour candidate for Hackney North and Stoke Newington. The Labour leadership had been briefing that I would be barred from standing.

9.   What's Next?

Not long ago, on a visit to my old college, Newnham, where I was giving a talk about my experiences as a student, a shy young undergraduate approached and asked to meet me. Over coffee she explained that she was very interested in politics, had been involved in several campaigns and saw herself as being on the left of the political spectrum – but there was no mainstream political party that she identified with or wanted to join. She had clearly lost hope in the Labour Party being an agent of progressive change. I thought it sad that a highly educated young woman should think that Labour and the Conservative Party had moved so close together in terms of policy and rhetoric that she was uncertain which to join. When I was her age, despite my many reservations about the Labour Party, it would never have occurred to me to join any other political party. Despite all the ups and downs of my career, I will always belong to the Labour Party at heart.

Since its inception, the Labour Party has been the major vehicle for achieving progressive change at the level of national politics. I have been a member of the party and have served it at every level for almost my entire adult life, and although I have been forced by the leadership to sit as an independent MP, I can't imagine leaving it. Yet as a Labour MP for more than thirty years, I have seen how the party has moved away from its founding purpose. Some of this reflects changes in the demographics of society, but some of it concerns me, as the child of immigrants representing an inner-city constituency with pockets of poverty as terrible as anywhere in the UK. Labour began its life as the Labour Representation Committee in 1900; it was set up by the Trades Unions Congress out of frustration at the candidates being nominated by the Liberal Party and was intended to be the voice of working people. It officially became the Labour Party in 1906. The make-up of the world of work has changed since then; some of it is positive, such as the huge increase of women in the workforce, whereas other changes have tended to estrange the party from its roots – and not necessarily for the better.

The number of people who are both Labour MPs and members of the industrial working class has collapsed in little more than a generation. At the 1951 general election, 295 Labour MPs were elected, with 108 of those being former manual workers, including thirty-five miners. By the 2017 general election there was a dramatic drop in the number of Labour MPs who were former manual workers, at just four; and two years later there was not a single Labour MP who had ever been a manual worker. The shrinking of the organized industrial working class has weakened the left in the party, even as issues of poverty, unfairness and inequality remain as serious as they have ever been. In the first three years of Keir Starmer's leadership, we have lost about 30 per cent of the party's membership. This is a circular process: the more the centre-right grows in the Labour Party, the more left-wingers leave. Yet the more left-wingers leave, the stronger the centre-right becomes. Many of the Labour Party members who have left were among the most engaged and enthusiastic, yet they feel the party cannot offer them a truly progressive path any longer. I still believe that a Labour government is the last and best chance for working men and women, but it is important for us to offer hope, especially to young people. The party still uses 'workerist' rhetoric such as 'comrade', but chasing after middle-class votes means that it increasingly seems as if the party has forgotten the interests and concerns of ordinary working people.

Under Starmer's leadership there has seemed to be a rapidly decreasing difference between Labour and Tory policies, even though the Labour Party – quite rightly – attacks the Conservative

Party ferociously in the House of Commons. Boroughs like Hackney cannot survive solely on anti-Tory rhetoric; we desperately need investment in areas such as housing, health and welfare, yet investment of this kind does not appear to be forthcoming from Labour's leadership. The dire economic consequences resulting from the Russian invasion of Ukraine, depleted gas supplies in Europe, wage stagnation and increases in inflation leading to the cost-of-living crisis mean that it will be very difficult for Labour to make practical policy changes that result in spending more money.

Working people have been bled dry over more than a decade of austerity under the Tories, yet the Labour leadership is emphatic there will be no new money for the services that poor people depend on, arguing that any new spending on the public sector must come out of growth. This may work in the medium term, but how can it help those who are homeless, those who are struggling to survive on current levels of benefit or pay, those who have lost hope in the here and now? The Tories have remained resolutely against pay rises in the public sector, and yet so is Labour, the party that supposedly advocates for and on behalf of the working people. The Labour leadership even went so far as to say that Shadow Cabinet ministers could not go on picket lines, whereas under past Labour governments Cabinet ministers were free to support strikes, whether in their own constituency or those that involved their own union. The wave of public-sector strikes beginning in 2022 spoke of the rage and discontent that the general population feels towards the state of Britain, and the Labour Party as it stands is not being brave or radical enough in its outlook.

Labour had one of its worst results ever in 2019 under Jeremy Corbyn's leadership, which, according to Starmer's team, proves that the party can no longer afford luxury left-wing policies such as investment in health, schools and housing. They have cited huge opinion-poll leads as proof of how popular their sharp turn to the right is, conveniently ignoring the contribution made by the worst collapse of the Conservative Party in my lifetime. With three

Conservative prime ministers in one year, and disaster on the international bond markets, it is difficult to imagine a Labour opposition that could not do a better job than the Conservatives. Even if Labour *did* struggle to invest majorly in the public sector immediately after being elected, it could at least challenge Tory reasoning. Yet whichever issue you look at, the convergence between Labour and the Tories remains deeply disappointing.

On education, Keir Starmer has failed to live up to his promise to abolish tuition fees during his leadership campaign. He has also remained notably quiet on the issue of racism in the British schooling system, which is a pernicious subject and a crucial area of development, as I know from my work with LSBC. Achievement gaps among Afro-Caribbean children, particularly boys, have narrowed since I began the initiative, but there is still much more work to be done to fight the impact of racial inequality on education. Society cannot afford to fail its children, and too many Black children are not reaching their educational potential. The shocking Child Q incident of 2022, in which a fifteen-year-old Black girl was strip-searched by police after being called in by teachers who claimed they could smell cannabis on her, is an indication of how far we have yet to go. This young girl went from being top of the class to a shell of her former bubbly self; after being targeted unfairly by the police (who found no evidence of any criminal behaviour), she began self-harming and needed therapy to recover. In the wake of this disturbing flashpoint in the ongoing issue of the education of Black children I held a special LSBC conference to discuss the securitization of education, where teachers and the police increasingly work more closely together, and not necessarily to the benefit of children. We need to look again at this issue, at the disproportionate numbers of Black children who are excluded and at the low numbers of teachers from minority ethnic backgrounds, so that we can reform education for the benefit of all children.

On welfare, the Tories have been adamant about benefit cuts, such as the two-child limit for Universal Credit. Labour refuses to look again at these policies, even though cuts like this pander to right-wing rhetoric about benefit scroungers. Welfare is not charity; every family, especially the poorest in our society, deserves support. In the UK 38 per cent of those who claim Universal Credit – the social-security payment that is means-tested – are employed, but earn so little they are still entitled to benefit. Representing Hackney and living there, I know the desperation that can lie behind the front doors of the streets and council estates that gentrification has not reached. It is often women and their children who are struggling the most with that poverty. It is women who must make the money stretch, whether it comes as benefits or a meagre salary, or both. It is women who must battle with terrible housing conditions when housing management does not care. Some of the worst culprits are housing associations: most were set up in the nineteenth century as charities, although now they are run as businesses, with highly paid managers who have little or no concern for their tenants. The Conservatives clearly haven't prioritized affordable and safe housing for the thousands of people in Britain who need it, so Labour must do that in order to help those who are struggling.

On health, the Tories want a bigger role for the private sector in our NHS, and so does the Labour Party. Labour spokespeople talk about private involvement in our health service as if it is free money; but, far from the private sector's provision of healthcare services being at cost price, taxpayers' funding for the NHS would have to be top-sliced to provide private companies with their profits. In the long run, private involvement in the NHS does not save the taxpayer money. Even in the light of all these facts, Labour doesn't seem prepared to challenge Tory reasoning or make the difficult choices that would generate the funds to rebuild the services that many people in this country desperately need. Our policies seem determined by opinion polls, yet if Labour had merely relied on polls and media rhetoric, it would never have set up the National Health Service in the first place.

The Labour Party of the future must be able to inspire people and direct the national debate. If we cannot inspire people, they may not necessarily come out and vote for us, even though they may also not go out and vote Tory. Labour has been at its best when it has offered leadership, framed the debate and demonstrated that a better world is possible. It is easy to disparage socialism, but what is the point of a socialist party that is frightened to talk about what could be? The future of progressive politics must be about a willingness to challenge establishment thinking. No serious political change has been accomplished without that.

This will involve taking a long look at voting systems, since the first-past-the-post system has not been fit for purpose for years. It has denied proper representation to millions of voters, and it seems to have given the Conservative Party a lock on power, even though in many cases they have not had majority support. Since the Labour Party was set up in the early twentieth century, only three of Labour's nineteen leaders have won a general election; in the past forty years, Tony Blair has been the only winning Labour leader. I believe it's time to have a renewed debate about proportional representation (PR), so that Parliament can more accurately reflect the people it is meant to represent.

For most of my life I have been against PR; leftists have traditionally believed that the coalition with a centrist party that PR would almost certainly entail might hold back the policies of a radical Labour government. A preferable scenario might have been for the radical left to gain significant influence in the Labour Party, and in turn for the party to win general elections outright. Jeremy Corbyn led the most left-wing Shadow Cabinet for decades, which lasted four years and two general elections; that interlude tested to destruction the idea that the left will be allowed significant influence in the Labour Party any time soon. Furthermore, under many PR systems, the geographical link between people and their MPs is lost. In my constituency – as is true of constituencies all over Britain – there are people who do not engage much with politics, but who do know the name of their MP. For someone to be able to name their MP, as simple as that sounds, represents a form of engagement with the political process for men and women who do not necessarily spend too much time reading about politics in the newspapers or watching political coverage on television. Given that so much political activity has now moved online, this may be less true, particularly for younger voters, but local politics is a crucial part of the political landscape and can often be where grass-roots movements begin.

Another concern about PR is the potential emergence of small far-right parties, some of which could increase their hold on power. Far-right politics has been steadily spreading its poisonous roots across Europe, forming part of a coalition government in Finland and propping up another in Sweden in exchange for key policy concessions. Looking at Italy, for instance, the rise of neo-fascist parties such as the Brothers of Italy meant that their leader, Giorgia Meloni, was able to be elected Italian prime minister. The threat of right-wing supremacy is reinforced by the fact that far-right parties flourish in hard economic times, with opposition to immigration and the EU tending to be part of their policy plans. Yet precisely what makes PR potentially dangerous (in other words, that it facilitates small parties) is what makes it attractive too. In the UK it has the potential to shift national politics to the left.

The long-standing leftist objection to coalitions was reinforced by the result of the 2010 Tory/Lib Dem coalition. After positioning themselves as a possible coalition partner for the Labour Party during their campaign, the Lib Dems became mesmerized by the chauffeur-driven cars, the trappings of state power and the opportunities that serving in Parliament might offer them. In the 2010 general election they built their campaign around a pledge to abolish tuition fees, but once in power and part of a coalition with the Tories, the Lib Dems tripled tuition fees instead. They voted for and supported austerity, with all its crippling effects on ordinary people. In the end the main beneficiary of coalition seemed to be the former deputy prime minister Nick Clegg, who departed from British politics and now reportedly earns £2.7 million a year as Facebook's president of global affairs. The Lib Dems are therefore a deeply unattractive coalition partner for many leftists in the Labour Party, but in recent times other coalition partners for Labour have emerged.

One possibility might be the Greens: their vote-share has climbed steadily since the 2019 general election, and their policies have never been more relevant. The Green commitment to fighting climate change, conserving nature and protecting the environment is not only increasingly popular, particularly with young people, but is an urgent imperative for our species as a whole. Even many climate-change deniers have had to modify their tone, faced with unprecedented extreme weather conditions all over the world, droughts of an intensity that many communities have never seen before, hurricanes of unequalled power and wildfires that are extraordinary in size. Climate change has never been more central to the international debate, whether it concerns floods in South Asia or Canadian provinces up in flames. In recent years the Green Party has made steady electoral progress, locally and nationally, as one of the few political causes to attract both those who live in the country and young people in the inner city. In a coalition with the Greens, the Labour leadership would have to adopt at least some green policies, which would effectively shift the Labour Party to the left. It is hard to imagine anything else that could shift it so radically, given the trajectory of the party in the early 2020s.

Looking at the large gap between the popular mood and the official front-bench policies of both major national parties, there are grounds for hope. Despite the rightward shift in party politics, evidence from polls and surveys suggests that public opinion on some issues is moving steadily in the opposite direction. For instance, in 2011 polls showed that 40 per cent viewed migration as bad for Britain's economy, but by 2021 that figure had dropped to 20 per cent.[1] Polls also show that most of the electorate supports public ownership of utilities such as water. The early 2020s have seen an unprecedented number of public-sector strikes and, remarkably, many months after these began, and however inconvenient they have been to the public, support remains solid.

The political establishment has acted in a unified and vigorous way to stamp out phenomena such as Corbynism, which have burst onto the scene as a political consequence of this burgeoning solidarity. The tens of thousands of new members, particularly young people, who joined the Labour Party when Jeremy was leader were drawn to the idea of a new politics and the idea that a better world was possible. Now our leading politicians are set on a course of protecting big businesses, oligarchs, banks and landlords against the interests of the general population. With deteriorating economic circumstances, this could mean even more reactionary politics overall. While the impoverishment of the British population is already severe and set to increase,[2] commentators have noted that the traditional rightward drift of ageing cohorts is not taking place to as great a degree. Stagnating wages, the difficult of getting on the housing ladder and the struggle to repay student loans could all be factors that tend to keep a growing number on the progressive side of the political divide. This opens the possibility of renewed efforts to bring political representation into line with majority opinion – the revival or re-emergence at some point of a new Bennism or Corbynism. Given the rout of the left in 2019, there is much to overcome in the short term to achieve this. But there is hope. As a nation we must overcome the fear of radical progressive change, to recover from the setbacks we have faced in the last two decades and move forward.

Building on this radicalism will also necessitate a more feminist outlook, which will not just be about female representation in politics, but about empowerment. I want to see even more female politicians of colour elected worldwide, and a new radical politics that embraces feminism. When I was first elected in 1987, not only was I the first Black female MP in the British Parliament, but I was the only one in any European legislature. This was three years before the end of Margaret Thatcher's premiership, and there were only forty-one women MPs out of 650. Thatcher loomed large over the political landscape and, whether you liked her or loathed her, you couldn't deny that she held sway for so long within an extremely male-dominated field.

Extraordinarily, it was ten years before I was joined in Parliament by another Black female MP, Oona King, and more than twenty-five years before I was joined by another elected Black female politician in a European government. That parliament was the Italian legislature, and the new Black female member was Cécile Kyenge. Like me, she began as a councillor, and in 2013 was elected to the Italian Parliament and appointed Minister for Integration, thus becoming Italy's first Black Cabinet minister. She went on to become the only Black female MEP from 2014 to 2019. Seeing a Black woman in a senior position seemed to be as triggering for Italian racists as it was for their British counterparts. Kyenge had bananas thrown at her in public meetings, and a former vice-president of the Italian Senate, Roberto Calderoli, openly said, 'When I see pictures of Kyenge I cannot help but think of the features of an orangutang.' Other Italian politicians publicly called her a Black anti-Italian and a prostitute, and compared her to a Congolese monkey. The online vitriol was even worse. Despite this, Cécile continues to advocate for social justice and the rights of immigrants. The broader point here is about more than simply representation for the sake of representation; it's about changing the culture of European and global politics to recognize the essential voices of Black women, and it's about moving towards a more progressive political landscape by actively fighting the racism and sexism faced by these politicians, through changes in policy and culture.

America has been far ahead of Europe when it comes to Black representation in the national legislature. Barack Obama's election as US president in 2008 had such resonance, not only in the United States, but also in the UK, because it was the culmination of a long struggle to win civil rights for Black Americans. Watching Obama's victory speech in November 2008 were millions of people like me, thinking of the great civil-rights leader Martin Luther King and his historic 'I have a dream' speech, delivered during the March on Washington for Jobs and Freedom on 28 August 1963, in which he outlined his vision of one day living in a nation where people are judged not by the colour of their skin, but by the content of their character. Obama was born of the civil-rights movement and he was associated with the continuing struggle for racial equality. He was not the first Black politician in America – that position dated as far back as the late nineteenth century, with the election of Hiram Rhodes Revels. It took until 1968 for the first Black Congresswoman to be elected. Shirley Chisholm was, like me, of Caribbean descent, and she stepped down in 1983, a few years before I became a British MP. Through her example, I knew it was possible to walk the halls of power while remaining true to a platform of social justice.

More recently, a new wave of radical Democrat women of colour has been elected to the US Congress. They call themselves the 'Squad'; founding members include Alexandria Ocasio-Cortez (AOC), of Puerto Rican heritage, representing a New York congressional district; Ilhan Omar, of Somalian origin, representing a Minnesota district; Ayanna Pressley, an African American, representing a Massachusetts district; and Rashida Tlaib, of Palestinian origin, representing a Michigan district. Between them they have racked up several firsts: Omar and Tlaib were the first Muslim women to be elected to Congress, while Pressley and Omar were the first Black members of Congress from their home states. Although the US Congress seems to particularly prize seniority, the Squad are nearly twenty years younger than their fellow members of Congress and have eye-catching radical positions on issues such as immigration, healthcare, climate change, the United States' relationship with Israel, and racial justice. Unsurprisingly they have been abused by Donald Trump, who asked why they couldn't 'go back and help fix the totally broken and crime-infested places from which they came' (ignoring, of course, the fact that three of the 'Squad' were born in America and one came to America as a child refugee).

The rich history of Britain's radical thinkers and political organizers notwithstanding, this rise in America of a new generation of female politicians of colour, and the network of solidarity they have created, provides a clue as to how political change can be achieved here in Britain. It will involve a new ethnic politics where Caribbean, African and Muslim political activists come together with a common agenda. The post-war generation of Black British political activists was made up of migrants from every corner of its former colonies, and they took this sort of strategy as a given. We need to rediscover it in order to construct a new radical minority politics.

Undoubtedly this new vision must also have internationalism embedded into it. The countries of the EU are Britain's closest neighbours, and cutting ourselves off from them has represented the opposite of internationalism. In my view, Brexit has been the single most damaging social and economic move to have occurred during my time in Parliament. As a member of Jeremy Corbyn's Shadow Cabinet, I was one of the people closest to him who was most firmly opposed to Brexit; not only were there undoubtedly solid economic arguments against it, but I believe it was also rooted in crude chauvinism, with some of the pro-Brexit arguments profoundly 'Little Englander' in sentiment.

For many people the Brexit issue is a visceral, deeply emotional one. It is frequently associated with their sense of their own identity. Three years after Brexit officially took place, the leaders of both major political parties will not admit that Brexit was an act of economic self-harm, although we have seen the lowest growth rate among G7 countries.[3] These politicians insist on talking about 'making Brexit work', when the truth is that it cannot be made to work in the way British voters were told it would. Politicians and right-wing commentators insisted that Brexit would lead to prosperity, that Britain would save £350 million a week to spend on our NHS and that voters would 'get our country back'. Now the electorate is gradually having to face up to the fact that none of this has turned out to be true. Immigration and the rate of asylum claims in Britain have actually *increased* in the wake of Brexit, directly contravening the promises made to the British public by the Leave campaign.

Migration is the most difficult and emotive political issue of our time, and where a political movement stands on this issue shows, more than anything else, its position on protecting the defenceless, fighting for human rights and standing up to racism. As the writer Neal Ascherson put it, 'The way a government treats refugees is very instructive because it shows you how they would treat the rest of us if they thought they could get away with it.' Immigration is always a test of how far Labour governments are prepared to lead public opinion, rather than follow it. On this, Starmer is on record as insisting that there will be little difference between current Tory policy and the policies of a future Labour government. Labour will continue the Tory points-based immigration system, even though this is a policy designed mainly to meet the needs of big business, despite its inclusion of essential workers such as medical professionals. Labour's policies on migration weren't always so regressive. More than sixty years ago the then Labour leader, Hugh Gaitskell (who was not seen as particularly left-wing), described the first post-war immigration legislation in 1962 as 'brutal and cruel anti-colour legislation', and he led his fellow Labour MPs through Parliament's voting lobbies against it. It is hard to imagine a Labour leader speaking in those unequivocal terms today. Up until Gaitskell's death in 1963, Labour's position on immigration control was one of consistent opposition. But once he died, policy went into reverse. In 1968 it was a Labour government under prime minister Harold Wilson that steamrollered through a further Commonwealth Immigrants Act whose main purpose was to keep out Kenyan Asians.

The issue that has come to dominate political and public debate is the small-boats 'crisis': the increasing numbers of people crossing the Channel to Britain to seek asylum. One of the suggested solutions is to dump these refugees in Rwanda. Not only is this plan unworkable and almost certainly illegal, but it also will not stop the flow of asylum seekers and migrants. Labour may not support the Rwanda plan, but their insistence that they will implement current policies more efficiently without challenging the basis for them confirms in the popular imagination the scenario that Britain is being swamped by asylum seekers. Labour should be framing the debate and grounding its policies on migration in facts, chief among them that Britain is not being swamped by a disproportionate number of migrants and asylum seekers. Four out of five refugees stay in their region and are hosted by developing countries, as opposed to the EU. For instance, Turkey now hosts the highest number of refugees at 3.7 million. In 2022 Germany received a quarter of asylum applications in the EU, France got 16 per cent, Spain 12 per cent, Austria 11 per cent and Italy 9 per cent.[4] Britain's number of asylum applications per head is amongst the smallest in Europe, at thirteen applications for every 10,000 people, but the way that MPs across the political spectrum talk about it would suggest otherwise.[5]

There is a way to put a stop to asylum seekers crossing the Channel in the backs of lorries or in rubber dinghies: by allowing them to make their claims in a British consulate in France. Unfortunately, Labour is too terrified of the Tory press to suggest this. The party needs to challenge the myths peddled about migrants; to begin putting the facts in front of voters; to stress the importance of European cooperation. Such policies would not only be more humane, but would also stand some chance of working. There is even evidence that the general public is not against migration and increasingly wants to see fairer and more effective policies implemented.[6] Current policies seem to be based on the idea that the harsher this country makes conditions for migrants, the less likely they are to come here. These policies have not worked, will never work and will continue to cause unnecessary misery.

As the child of migrants, I understand the courage and determination of immigrants and asylum seekers in a way that many commentators do not seem to. My parents' generation of economic migrants were some of the bravest people I knew, and their contribution to our society has been immeasurable. Too much political discussion on migrants dehumanizes them. The debate about migrants is not about rubber dinghies; it is about people. The media and MPs like to talk about the migrant problem – but to me, migrants can never be a problem. They are my Uncle Mackie, the railway porter at Euston; my mother, the nurse; and my father, the factory worker. All of them were proud of their jobs and prouder still that they never missed a day of work. My first speech in Parliament was on immigration and I will never stop fighting for fairness on the issue. Justice for migrants is vital, not only because of what it means for individual migrants and their families, but also because of what it says about the sort of society we are. It may seem idealistic to think that migration policy can be based on that fact, but idealism and fearlessness are exactly what the Labour Party needs to show in order to have any hope of inspiring Britain towards a more progressive future.

Ultimately, progressive issues cannot be resolved by the nation state. War, famine, climate change and migration are all matters that require international cooperation, and the speed of global communication that is available to us now means we can have a more internationalized politics. I remain very aware of the things that connect us globally, both historically and in the present day. When my parents came to Britain from Jamaica in the early 1950s, Jamaica wasn't part of the Commonwealth. Reginald and Julia were proud citizens of the United Kingdom and Colonies, and with that emblazoned in gold on their passports, they enjoyed complete freedom of movement. In an era before the internet, or even before television was popularized, they were heading somewhere they had never seen. Embarking on the trip, sticking it out and making a life took a form of courage that should never be forgotten.

Citizenship of the UK was incredibly precious to people in colonies such as Jamaica. Whatever racism they experienced after their migration to Britain did not shake their belief that it was their country, and Elizabeth II was their queen. In return, Queen Elizabeth was serious in her commitment to the Commonwealth, travelling around those territories in the hope of holding them all together. There is a photograph from the early 1960s of the Queen dancing with Kwame Nkrumah, president of the newly independent Ghana. President Nkrumah has one hand around Queen Elizabeth's waist and is holding her other hand in his. Even in the 1960s there were many upper-class white women who would not have dreamed of having a Black man that close to them, but the Queen was calm and smiling. It was a demonstration of her determination to build the Commonwealth and prove to all that it was an association of equals.

In my travels across the Commonwealth I have observed that the issue of reparative justice for slavery has been gathering momentum, and it is something I will continue to fight for. When slavery was abolished, slave owners received trillions of pounds in compensation, but enslaved people received neither a formal apology nor financial restitution, despite repeated demands for successive British governments to recognize and apologize for their role in the transatlantic slave trade. Generations after slavery has formally ended, the descendants of African slaves are still suffering the consequences. As the UN Secretary-General António Guterres told the general assembly, 'We can draw a straight line from the centuries of colonial exploitation to the social and economic inequalities of today.' Reparations can take many forms, aside from financial compensation – environmental and land rights, education and employment, and legislation among them. The issue of reparative justice is one on which I worked closely with my late colleague Bernie Grant, who was chair of the Africa Reparations Movement (ARM UK). Continuing this legacy, in 2023 I co-chaired – with Dr Julius Garvey, son of the great activist Marcus Garvey – the inaugural Reparations Conference in the UK, which brought together campaigns and institutions to discuss the issue of reparations for Africans and people of African descent across the world. There is evidence that the British people are beginning to reckon with the nation's imperial memory and history, and we must build on that momentum to bring justice to the descendants of enslaved people, not only in Britain but across the world.

I am sometimes asked whether, if it were possible to live my life again, I would still choose politics as a career. For me, politics has never been just about having a career. By far the most important reason I chose this path is because it is empowering: it has given me the power to help people and change their lives for the better.

The practical barriers I have faced have been great, and the psychological obstacles sometimes even greater. The combined pressure of being Britain's first Black woman MP, the representative of a busy inner-city constituency and a single mother have meant that most of my adult life has been about juggling. In a way, this has always been about feeling the need to prove myself. I was the first in my family to gain a place at Cambridge in the 1970s; the first Black woman to stand for the leadership of a major British political party; the first Black woman to shadow one of the four great offices of state; the first Black woman to take PMQs – and many other firsts that I can't remember. I have achieved numerous things, and to others they may seem great achievements. But for a Black woman, it is never enough. We are constantly being held to a different standard. In every area of life we are told we are not, and have never been, enough. Above all we are never allowed to make mistakes, certainly not publicly. After so many years with a negative perception of yourself, and with that perception being reinforced by the way society views you, it makes it difficult to change.

When you are up-and-coming, no one feels threatened by you as a Black woman and, particularly if they regard themselves as 'liberal', they may even see you as an ornament to their organization. But there often comes a point when this benevolence ends, and you are seen as a threat. There is something about a Black woman in a senior position that can drive people into a rage – in my case, and in the response of certain Labour Party officials towards me, a completely incoherent rage. I do not know a Black woman in a professional role who has never encountered any kind of sexist or racially charged interaction in the course of her work. In these situations I have turned to friends to support me, even if it's only to validate that I'm not going mad when bristling at certain interactions I have had. Often it is about giving each other the love and encouragement that mean we don't have our confidence crushed and are able to carry on. Over the years, when I was psychologically knocked down, it was the support of friends that kept me going. This has been particularly important for me as the single mother of an only child. Only children can feel isolated even with two parents; how much more so when there is only your mother, who works ridiculous hours and, even when she is with you, is tired and distracted. But I was very proud when my son James graduated from the University of Cambridge in 2013 with a degree in law.

Going to Jamaica has been a source of comfort and support to me in the darkest times. I have always depended on my family there, visiting annually, not only for the beaches and the sunshine, but also because it is such a relief to breathe out and be enfolded in the arms of family after the stresses and strains of Westminster and the British media. When you spend your working life trying to prove yourself in a hostile environment, nothing gives greater pleasure than to be with people who love and care for you unconditionally, not because of your status, but because you are family. In Jamaica I have always received heart-warming recognition for my career, as 'an iconic pillar of the black community for over 40 years'.[7] To be a Black Member of Parliament in the UK, the mother of Empire, is considered an achievement, but to be the first Black woman is something they truly respect.

Existing at the front line of politics means that, in many ways, I have never really seen a world beyond it. It has never been dull, and no two days are the same. Because the causes I have campaigned for and championed are a part of me, rather than a script that I simply read from, I will not give up working on them, long after I may have ceased being an MP. Of other occupations I have tried – the civil service, lobbying, television journalism – politics is the world I have liked best. It is not that people in that world are nicer; as it happens, some of the most unpleasant individuals I know are professional politicians or political journalists. But if you venture outside the Westminster bubble, whether in Britain or travelling abroad, political activity enables you to meet a much wider range of people than you would in almost any other role. Moreover, you are not just meeting them as clients or customers. You are meeting them as people and seeing the world through their eyes.

Participating in party politics is not the only way to try and make a difference in the world around you, for there is no doubt that it can be a hostile environment. That I have managed to survive within this structure for so long without compromising my core values is a rare achievement, and I owe a great debt to the grass-roots community organizers who have stubbornly and persistently fought for change outside the traditional political apparatus. Anything that involves working with other people to effect social change is part of small politics. In the end, this kind of activism needs to involve the widest possible range of people to forge a more vibrant and effective politics and reflect the genuine concerns of ordinary citizens. Even if you do not see yourself standing up in Parliament and making speeches, you can definitely make a difference.

People wonder how a Black woman of Jamaican heritage, whose parents were brought up in rural Jamaica and both left school at fourteen, whose wider family had no history of political involvement and who had no contacts, became a British MP. I overcame these challenges through the resilience I inherited from my ancestors in Jamaica, and because I never stopped caring about the issues that brought me into activism. I see the reality of social injustice all around me, and caring passionately about achieving fairness and equality for marginalized people has enabled me to pick myself up and carry on. The legacy of the work I have done can be seen in the Black women and tireless activists around me, who will continue doing this work long after I am gone. If Britain, for all its flaws, could produce a woman like me, there is hope for us yet.

Acknowledgements

I would like to acknowledge family members scattered to the many corners of the Jamaican diaspora, including Britain, the United States of America, Canada and Jamaica itself. Over the years they have given me the unconditional love and support that have buoyed me up and helped me go forwards. Above all, I would like to thank my parents, Reginald Nathaniel Abbott and Julia Adassa Abbott. They made me the woman I am, and bequeathed me the courage that took them from rural Jamaica across the Atlantic, all the way to Britain and a new life.

I also want to acknowledge Ros Howells, a close friend, a role model and an important link with an earlier generation of Black activists, including very many remarkable women. She has been a supporter of my family and a long-standing supporter of me, both personally and politically.

I should also single out Adrienne Morgan and Mary Chadwick, two unassuming Hackney Labour Party members who were among the first to decide to back an unfancied Black female candidate in the race to become the parliamentary candidate for Hackney North and Stoke Newington Labour Party. They were as responsible as anyone for me first becoming the local party's candidate and then going on to become Britain's first Black female Member of Parliament.

I must also acknowledge Bernie Grant, Paul Boateng and Keith Vaz. Together, we were the first four people of colour to be elected to the British Parliament in 1987, and only we will ever know what it took to get there.

Down the years I have owed so much to friends and supporters. One of my long-standing friends is the left activist Anni Marjoram.

She used to say, before I was ever elected to Parliament, 'If you are working-class and you become an MP, remember that it is the job that your parents always wanted for you – clean, indoor work and no heavy lifting.' At moments when I have felt down, I always remember Anni's words.

But there are many other friends who have supported me over the years, including Jenni Francis, Joy Elias-Rilwan, Ade Solanke, Juliet Alexander, Shami Chakrabarti, Garth Crooks, Yvonne Wilks O'Grady, Gail Cohen, Marsha McDermott, Beverley Randall, Paulette Randall, Barry Gray, Atique Choudhury, Lucie Scott, Sulekha Hassan, Soraya Adejare and Jermain Jackman.

Some of the key members of my team over the years have been Deborah Vaughan, Carol Glenn, Ruby Morgan and Bell Ribeiro-Addy.

I need to thank Nimo Hussein, Michael Burke, Joshua Kelly and Victoria Osas, who made it possible for me to get on with the work of writing.

Thanks also to Margaret Busby, my agent Juliet Pickering and unfailingly patient editors, Alpana Sajip and Shyam Kumar.

Finally, I want to thank my son James, who taught me how to love and who remains the most important person in my life.

Notes

Chapter 3

1 novaramedia.com/2020/06/18/todays-anti-racist-movement-must-remember-britains-black-radical-history/

Chapter 4

1 en.wikipedia.org/wiki/Greater_London_Council#:~:text=The%20GLC%20was%20responsible%20for,city%20planning%20and%20leisure%20services
2 www.huffingtonpost.co.uk/entry/new-cross-fire-black-peoples-day-of-action_uk_5e582608c5b6450a30bc0ac3
3 www.georgepadmoreinstitute.org/collections/the-international-book-fairs-1970-2005#
4 www.screenonline.org.uk/people/id/502424/

Chapter 5

1 hansard.parliament.uk/Commons/1987-11-16/debates/3c372344-c6e4-4701-800b-78466232620b/ImmigrationBill?highlight=%22being%20the%20daughter%20of%20immigrants%20and%20representing%20a%20constituency%20in%20north-east%20london%22#contribution-c3056127-e96a-4dae-aa85-e5bbf6936d7f
2 studenttheses.uu.nl/bitstream/handle/20.500.12932/21663/Master_thesis_Mantay_final.pdf

Chapter 6

1 https://committees.parliament.uk/publications/7012/documents/72927/default/
2 en.wikipedia.org/wiki/September_11_attacks

Chapter 7

1 www.amnesty.org.uk/online-violence-women-mps
2 publications.parliament.uk/pa/cm201617/cmselect/cmhaff/136/13609.htm
3 www.morningstaronline.co.uk/article/f/unkillable-myths-corbyns-labour-party-and-anti-semitism
4 www.plutobooks.com/blog/bad-news-for-labour-channel-4-factcheck/
5 www.theguardian.com/politics/2005/feb/08/media.media1
6 www.theguardian.com/politics/2015/aug/13/jewish-chronicle-accuses-jeremy-corbyn-associating-holocaust-deniers

Chapter 8

1 www.thetimes.co.uk/article/sturgeon-abuse-deters-women-from-politics-xmzkzc78x
2 www.amnesty.org.uk/online-violence-women-mps

Chapter 9

1 migrationobservatory.ox.ac.uk/resources/briefings/uk-public-opinion-toward-immigration-overall-attitudes-and-level-of-concern/
2 www.jrf.org.uk/work/uk-poverty-2023-the-essential-guide-to-understanding-poverty-in-the-uk

3 www.reuters.com/world/uk/uk-set-have-weakest-growth-among-g7-2024-imf-forecasts-2023-10-10/

4 www.unhcr.org/uk/asylum-uk

5 researchbriefings.files.parliament.uk/documents/SN01403/SN01403.pdf

6 yougov.co.uk/politics/articles/39146-what-concerns-british-public-about-immigration-pol?

7 jamaica-gleaner.com/article/news/20221112/mp-diane-abbott-gets-platinum-award-weekly-gleaner-honours-stalwarts

Index

DA indicates Diane Abbott.
Page references in *italics* indicate images.